LEARN, TEACH...

SUCCEED...

With **REA's TExES™ Special Education EC–12 (161)**
test prep, you'll be in a class all your own.

TExES™ SPECIAL EDUCATION EC-12 (161)

TEXAS EXAMINATIONS OF EDUCATOR STANDARDS™

Jill L. Haney, M.A.

James E. Westcott, M.A.

Jamalyn Jaquess

Research & Education Association

Research & Education Association
61 Ethel Road West
Piscataway, New Jersey 08854
E-mail: info@rea.com

TExES™ Special Education EC–12 (161) With Online Practice Tests

Published 2016

Copyright © 2014 by Research & Education Association, Inc.

Printed in the United States of America

Library of Congress Control Number: 2013914723

ISBN-13: 978-0-7386-1141-9
ISBN-10: 0-7386-1141-7

The competencies presented in this book were created and implemented by the Texas Education Agency and Educational Testing Service (ETS®). Texas Examinations of Educator Standards and TExES are trademarks of the Texas Education Agency. All other trademarks cited in this publication are the property of their respective owners.

Cover image: Jamie Grill/Getty Images

Developed and produced by Focus Strategic Communications, Inc.

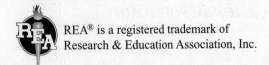 REA® is a registered trademark of
Research & Education Association, Inc.

Contents

Introduction

TExES SPECIAL EDUCATION EC-12 (161) DOMAIN REVIEWS

PART I • DOMAIN I

CONTENTS

CONTENTS

CONTENTS

About the Authors

Jill L. Haney

Jill L. Haney earned a bachelor of arts degree in English with honors and a master of arts degree in teaching from Trinity University in San Antonio, Texas.

A former middle school teacher, national reading consultant, and educational publishing executive, she is now an independent Special Education and reading consultant in San Antonio, Texas. Certified in Texas to teach Special Education EC-12, Elementary EC-6, and reading and language arts 6-12, Haney was the San Antonio ISD Teacher of the Year in 1999 and won the coveted Trinity Prize that same year.

Haney wrote all of the end-of-chapter and Practice Test questions as well as reviewing the entire book. She has coauthored several educational programs for students with special needs, including *PCI Reading Program, Environmental Print Series,* and the *Why Are You Calling Me LD?* teacher's guide. She has also served as executive editor for a wide array of educational products for students with special needs, including the *Essential Sight Words Reading Program.*

Haney taught seventh-grade reading and language arts in the San Antonio Independent School District for seven years. She served for 14 years in various product development and marketing positions in the educational publishing field. Haney has presented at numerous local, state, and national conferences, including the Texas Autism Conference, the Texas Council of Administrators of Special Education conferences, and both the state and national Council for Exceptional Children conferences.

Haney's dedication to students with special needs is both professional and personal. She has two children, including a son with autism who is nonverbal.

James E. Westcott

James E. Westcott is a former teacher, education content writer, and children's author. He wrote the domain and competency review chapters for this study guide. He holds a master's degree in Special Education from Nazareth College of Rochester, New York.

Westcott is a New York State-certified teacher in grades K–12. He has taught Special Education at both the elementary and secondary levels for 15 years outside of Rochester, New York. Westcott is especially proud of being chosen *Who's Who Among Special Education Teachers* in 2007.

Westcott has also helped write curricula and several assessments for educational publishing companies. His book, titled *Jack's Tales*, was written especially for boys ages 7–10 who are reluctant readers. It will be released in January 2014.

Jamalyn Jaquess

Jamalyn Jaquess is an elementary Specialized Support teacher in the Northeast Independent School District of San Antonio, Texas. She is certified in Special Education EC–12 and General Education EC–6. Her thoughtful review of this study guide provided extremely valuable input.

Jaquess became a Special Education teacher during what some might consider midlife, coming from a background in children's ministry. Her goal is to cultivate and foster the potential in each of her students, helping them to reach the purpose for which they were created.

About Research & Education Association

Founded in 1959, Research & Education Association (REA) is dedicated to publishing the finest and most effective educational materials—including study guides and test preps—for students of all ages.

Today, REA's wide-ranging catalog is a leading resource for students, teachers, and other professionals. Visit *www.rea.com* to see a complete listing of all our titles.

Acknowledgments

We would like to thank the people at Focus Strategic Communications, Inc., for their work on this study guide. We extend special gratitude to Focus's principals, Adrianna Edwards and Ron Edwards, for developing and producing the entire manual as well as putting together, overseeing, and supervising the writing, editorial, and production teams. We thank First Image for meticulously and patiently laying out and formatting the pages.

We would also like to thank Pam Weston, Publisher, for setting the quality standards for production integrity and managing the publication to completion; John Paul Cording, Vice President, Technology, for coordinating the design and development of the REA Study Center; Larry B. Kling, Vice President, Editorial, for his overall direction; Michael Reynolds, Managing Editor, for coordinating development of this edition; and Eve Grinnell, Graphic Designer, for preflighting.

INTRODUCTION

Passing the TExES
Special Education EC-12 (161) Test

Passing the TExES Special Education EC–12 (161) Test

Congratulations! By taking the TExES Special Education EC–12 (161) test, you're on your way to a rewarding career working with exceptional students. Our book and the online tools that come with it give you everything you need to succeed on this important exam, bringing you one step closer to being certified as a special education teacher in Texas.

Our *TExES Special Education EC-12* Book + Online test prep package provides these key features:

- Complete overview of the TExES Special Education EC–12 test

- Comprehensive review of all 4 domains and 12 competencies

- Two full-length practice tests, both in the book and online, with powerful diagnostic tools to help you personalize your prep

- Detailed answer explanations that not only identify correct answers but also explain why the other answer choices are incorrect

There are many different ways to prepare for the TExES Special Education EC–12 exam. What's best for you depends on how much time you have to study and how comfortable you are with the subject matter. Our Book + Online Prep has a plan that you can customize to fit both your lifestyle and study style.

How to Use This Book + Online Prep

About the Review

The review chapters in this book are designed to help you sharpen your command of pedagogical skills so you can pass the TExES Special Education EC–12 test. Each of the skills required for all 12 competencies is discussed at length to optimize your understanding. Keep in mind that the education courses you have taken thus far have taught you what you need to know to answer the questions on the test. You already possess the know-how to understand and make important decisions about professional situations involving Special Education students.

Our review is designed to help you relate the information you have acquired to Texas's specific competencies. Like the test itself, our review evenly covers the competencies within each domain. However, studying your class notes and textbooks together with our review will give you an excellent foundation for passing the exam.

This book is organized into four parts that correspond with the four domains on the test. The chapters in each part match up with the competencies within each domain.

About the REA Study Center

We know your time is valuable and you want an efficient study experience. At the online REA Study Center, you'll get feedback right from the start on what you know and what you don't know to help make the most of your study time.

Here's what you'll find at the REA Study Center:

■ **2 Full-Length Practice Tests** – These full-length tests cover everything you need to know for the TExES Special Education EC–12 test and are a great way to evaluate what you've learned.

Each practice test comes with:

■ **Automatic Scoring** – Find out you how you did on your test, instantly.

■ **Diagnostic Score Reports** – Get a specific score on each of the 12 competencies, so you can focus on the areas that challenge you the most.

■ **Detailed Answer Explanations** – See why the correct answer is right, and why the other answer choices are incorrect.

■ **Timed Testing** – Learn to manage your time as you practice, so you'll feel confident on test day.

All TExES tests, with the exception of Braille (183), are given only as **computer-administered (CAT) tests**, so we recommend you take the online versions of our practice tests to simulate test-day conditions.

■ An Overview of the Test

The TExES Special Education EC-12 test ensures that you have the essential knowledge and skills to teach the state-required curriculum, which is known as Texas Essential Knowledge and Skills, or TEKS.

This book helps you prepare for the area of specialization called Special Education K–12. Separate tests are required for certification in the areas such as American Sign Language (184), Braille (183), Deaf and Hard-of-Hearing (181), and Visually Impaired (182).

Whether you are a student, a graduate from a Texas state-approved teacher preparation program, or an educator who has received certification in another state, you should carefully read the requirements for working with Special Education students provided at the Texas Examinations of Educator Standards website *http://cms.texes-ets.org*.

What Is Tested on the TExES Special Education EC–12 Test?

Twelve competencies are covered on the TExES Special Education EC–12 exam. These competencies represent the knowledge that teams of teachers, administrators, subject-area specialists, and others have determined to be important for beginning teachers who work with Special Education students in the state's public schools.

Here is the approximate percentage of the total exam devoted to each domain.

Domains: Approximate Percentage of Exam		
Domain I	Understanding Individuals with Disabilities and Evaluating Their Needs	13%
Domain II	Promoting Student Learning and Development	33%
Domain III	Promoting Student Achievement in English Language Arts and Reading and in Mathematics	33%
Domain IV	Foundations and Professional Roles and Responsibilities	20%

What is the Format of the TExES Special Education EC–12 Test?

The 135 multiple-choice questions on the TExES Special Education EC–12 exam are designed to assess your knowledge of the competencies and the related skills required to become a special education teacher in Texas.

In general, the multiple-choice questions require critical thinking – mirroring the classroom imperative to promote exactly this among your future students. You are frequently expected to demonstrate more than an ability to recall factual information; you may be asked to evaluate the information, comparing it with knowledge you have, or are making a judgment about.

The multiple-choice questions are set up straightforwardly. Each question has four choices labeled A, B, C, and D. The test is scored based on the number of questions you answer correctly, and no points are deducted for wrong answers. Therefore, do not leave any item unanswered, since you will not be penalized for guessing.

You are given five hours to complete the test—which may seem like a lot—but be aware of the amount of time you are spending on each question so you allow yourself time to complete the whole test.

Keep a steady pace when answering questions. Taking our online practice tests with timed testing conditions will help you use your time efficiently. However, if you choose to take the printed versions of the tests in the book, be sure to time yourself.

When Should the TExES Be Taken?

Traditionally, teacher preparation programs determine when their candidates take the required tests for teacher certification. These programs will also clear you to take the examinations and make final recommendations for certification to the State Board for Educator Certification (SBEC). For those seeking certification right out of college, the TExES Special Education EC–12 exam is generally taken just before graduation.

The TExES Registration Bulletin offers more information about test dates and locations, as well as information on registration and testing accommodations—for those with special needs. The registration bulletin is available at *http://cms.texes-ets.org/registrationbulletin/*.

Registration bulletins are also available at the education departments of Texas colleges and universities. To address issues that cannot be solved at the teacher preparation program level, you can contact the offices of SBEC at (888) 863-5880 or (512) 469-8400. You can also find information about the test and registration on the SBEC website at *http://cms.texes-ets.org/*.

How Do I Register for the Test and Is There a Registration Fee?

The TExES exams are administered by Educational Testing Service (ETS), which has very specific rules for registering for the test. It is important that you read the registration information on ETS's website (*http://cms.texes-ets.org/texes*) and follow the instructions given there.

To register for an exam, you must create an account in the ETS online registration system. Registration will then be available to you online, 24/7, during the regular, late, and emergency registration periods. You must pay a registration fee to take the TExES, and you will also incur additional late fees if registering after the scheduled date.

When Will I Receive My Score Report?

On the score report release date, you will receive an email notifying you that your score report is available in your online account. Test scores are released on Tuesdays after 10 p.m. Eastern time within six weeks of the test date.

Can I Retake the Test?

If you don't do well on the TExES Special Education EC–12 test, don't panic! You can take the exam again, and in fact, many candidates do. However, you must wait 60 days to retake it.

Studying for the Test

When Should I Start Studying?

It is never too early to start studying for the TExES Special Education EC–12 exam. The earlier you begin, the more time you will have to sharpen your skills and focus your efforts. Do not procrastinate. Cramming is not an effective way to study, since it does not allow you enough time to learn the test material. Work out a study routine and stick to it. Reviewing your class notes and textbooks along with our book will provide you with an even better foundation for passing this exam.

Study Schedule

Although our study plan is designed to be used in the six weeks before your exam, it can be condensed to three weeks by combining each two-week period into one. Be sure to set aside enough time—at least two hours each day—to study. The more time you spend studying, the more prepared and relaxed you will feel on the day of the exam.

When you take the practice tests at the online REA Study Center, simulate the conditions of the test as closely as possible. Turn your television and radio off, and sit down at a quiet table free from distraction.

As you complete each test, review your score reports, study the diagnostic feedback, and review the explanations to the questions you answered incorrectly. However, do not review too much at any one time. Concentrate on one problem area at a time by reading the question and explanation, and by studying our review until you are confident that you have mastered the material. Give extra attention to the review chapters that cover your areas of difficulty, as this will build your skills in those areas.

Week	Activity
1	Take Practice Test 1 at the online REA Study Center. Your score report will identify topics where you need the most review.
2-4	Study the review, focusing on the topics you missed (or were unsure of) on Practice Test 1.
5	Take Practice Test 2 at the online REA Study Center. Review your score report and re-study any topics you missed.
6	Review your score reports from both practice tests, read the detailed answer explanations for the questions you got wrong and study those competencies. If you have extra time, take Practice Test 1 again and see how much your score has improved.
Note: If you are studying and don't have Internet access, you can take the printed versions of the tests in the book. These are the same practice tests offered online, but without the added benefits of timed testing conditions, automatic scoring, and diagnostic score reports.	

Test-Taking Tips

Taking an important standardized test like the TExES Special Education EC–12 test might make you nervous. Here are tried-and-true tips to help alleviate your test-taking anxieties.

Tip 1: Become comfortable with the format of the test. When you are practicing, stay calm and pace yourself. After simulating the test only once, you will boost your chances of doing well, and you will be able to sit down for the actual TExES Special Education EC–12 exam with much more confidence.

Tip 2: Familiarize yourself with the directions on the test. This will not only save time, but it will also help you avoid anxiety (and the mistakes anxiety causes).

Tip 3: Read all of the possible answers. Just because you think you have found the correct response, do not automatically assume that it is the best answer. Read through each choice to be sure that you are not making a mistake by jumping to conclusions.

Tip 4: Use the process of elimination. Go through each answer choice and eliminate as many as possible. If you can eliminate two answer choices, you will give yourself a better chance of getting the item correct since there will only be two choices left from which to make your guess. Do not leave an answer blank; it is better to guess than to not answer a question on the TExES Special Education EC–12 exam as there is no penalty for wrong answers.

Tip 5: Work at a steady pace and avoid focusing on any one question too long. Taking the timed tests at the online REA Study Center will help you learn to budget your time. Remember to time yourself when taking the practice tests in this printed book.

Tip 6: When taking computer-based tests like the TExES battery, be sure your answer registers before you go to the next item. Look at the screen to see that your mouse click causes the pointer to darken the proper oval. If your answer doesn't register, you won't get credit for that question.

Test Day

As test day draws near, here are a few things to keep in mind so that you'll be prepared for the TExES Special Education EC–12 test.

Before the Test

Check your registration information to find out what time to arrive at the testing center. Make sure you arrive early. This will allow you to collect your thoughts and relax before the test, and will also spare you the anguish that comes with being late. (If you arrive late, you might not be admitted to the test center.) Check your admission ticket 24 hours before the test in case there is a change. If there is a change, you will have to print out a new ticket.

Before you leave for the test center, make sure you have your admission ticket and two forms of identification, one of which must contain a recent and recognizable photograph, your name, and signature (e.g., a driver's license). All documents must be originals (no copies). You will not be admitted to the test center and you will forfeit your test fees if you do not have proper identification. (More information about proper forms of ID is listed on the official TEA website: *http://cms.texes-ets.org*.)

Dress comfortably, so you are not distracted by being too hot or too cold while taking the test. You may wear a watch to the test center. However, you may not wear one that makes noise, because it may disturb the other test-takers. Do not bring cell phones, smartphones, or other electronic, listening, recording, or photographic devices into the test center. Food and drink, dictionaries, textbooks, notebooks, calculators, briefcases, or packages are also not permitted. If you bring these devices into the test center, you will be dismissed from the test, your fee will be forfeited, and your test scores will be canceled.

During the Test

Procedures will be followed to maintain test security. Once you enter the test center, follow all of the rules and instructions given by the test supervisor. If you do not, you risk being dismissed from the test and having your scores canceled. The test administrator will provide pencils and scratch paper. You may not take your own scratch paper into the test center.

You will be provided with a Texas Instruments IIs scientific calculator. As we said, you may not use your own calculator.

After the Test

When you finish your test, hand in your materials and you will be dismissed. Then, go home and relax—you deserve it!

Good luck on the TExES Special Education EC–12 test!

TEXES
SPECIAL EDUCATION
EC-12 (161)

Domain Reviews

PART I: DOMAIN I

Understanding Individuals with Disabilities and Evaluating Their Needs

Understanding Individuals with Disabilities and Evaluating Their Needs

The two chapters in Part I: Domain I focus on understanding the characteristics and needs of students with disabilities, and understanding and providing formal and informal assessment and evaluation procedures to make instructional decisions. Before focusing on this, however, understanding—at least on a basic level—what it is actually like to be a first-year Special Education teacher is worthy of mentioning.

First-year teachers face a variety of challenges and have many responsibilities that are unique to teaching. Teaching in general is not for the faint of heart. It is undeniable that this is a tough profession.

Special Education teachers face challenges that stretch beyond what teachers face in any classroom and into different, sometimes complex, dimensions. Special Education is a discipline within this profession that educators-to-be should not choose this career path lightly. In addition to understanding and performing all of the duties that regular education teachers perform, a Special Education teacher must be able to understand and execute service-delivery options, specialized paperwork requirements, know CSE (Committee of Special Education) procedures and follow them in meetings with parents and colleagues, supervise support personnel, suffer role ambiguity, and work seamlessly with regular education and related service professionals. And we haven't gotten to the part yet about working with students who typically provide greater challenges to educate than students who do not have learning disabilities. So, let's dig in.

Teaching students with disabilities can be difficult in a standards- and assessment-based educational system. Teaching students with learning needs presents serious challenges within the context of this system. It can feel like a high-wire act while juggling several balls at the same time. Special Education teachers are confronted with unique challenges on a daily basis.

Making the best decisions for students with learning disabilities is often not easy:

- How should skill instruction be addressed?

- What skills are the most important given the time available to teach them?

- What serious problems are children bringing to school each and every day?

- How should one address what appear to be insurmountable achievement gaps in reading and writing, while attempting to bridge these gaps in diverse environments?

Because a Special Education teacher often faces minute-to-minute challenges, calibrated risks should be taken to address student needs. Support is needed but sometimes not available. But the challenges don't end there.

Even before addressing the aforementioned issues, teaching Special Education should start with understanding the characteristics of learning disabilities and those children who have them. Being an expert on how to teach students with learning disabilities is the essence of being a good Special Education teacher. Becoming an expert in this field also holds the potential for great rewards—rewards unique to teaching Special Education— that lie at the heart of becoming a Special Education teacher.

Domain I addresses Competencies 001 and 002.

Competency 001: The special education teacher understands and applies knowledge of the characteristics and needs of students with disabilities.

The beginning teacher:

A. Knows characteristics of individuals with different types of disabilities, including individuals with different levels of severity and multiple disabilities

across eligibility categories, and analyze[...]
on learning and experience.

B. Knows how the developmental, academic, [...]
acteristics of individuals with disabilities [...]
and applies knowledge of human develop[...]
implement appropriate curriculum.

C. Knows theoretical explanations for behavi[...]
varied characteristics of behavioral disorder[...]

D. Knows the different ways that students with [...]

E. Applies knowledge of human development and the effects of various types
of disabilities on developmental processes in order to identify the needs of
individuals with and without disabilities.

F. Understands the effects of cultural and environmental influences (e.g., linguistic characteristics, socioeconomic issues, abuse/neglect, substance
abuse) on the child and family.

G. Understands normal, delayed and disordered communication patterns, including nonsymbolic communication, and the impact of language development
on the academic and social skills of individuals with disabilities.

H. Knows aspects of medical conditions affecting individuals with disabilities,
including the effects of various medications on behavior and functioning and
the implications of medical complications for student support needs (e.g.,
seizure management, tube feeding, catheterization, cardiopulmonary resus-
citation [CPR]).

I. Understands ways in which physical disabilities and health impairments relate
to development and behavior, and knows the etiologies and effects of sensory
disabilities and other conditions affecting individuals with disabilities.

Competency 002: The special education teacher understands formal and informal
assessment and evaluation procedures and knows how to evaluate student competencies
to make instructional decisions.

The beginning teacher:

A. Applies knowledge of basic terminology used in assessment and evaluation,
the uses and limitations of various types of instruments and techniques and
methods for monitoring the progress of individuals with disabilities.

B. Understands ethical concerns related to assessment and evaluation, including legal provisions, regulations, and guidelines regarding unbiased evaluation and the use of psychometric instruments and instructional assessment measures with individuals with disabilities.

C. Identifies appropriate evaluation strategies for individual students with diverse characteristics and needs (e.g., related to culture, language, personal beliefs, nature, severity of disabilities).

D. Applies knowledge of procedures for screening, prereferral intervention, referral and determining eligibility, including criteria used to determine eligibility.

E. Knows how to gather background information regarding academic, medical, and family history, collaborate with parents/guardians and with other professionals to conduct assessments and evaluations, document ongoing student assessment and maintain accurate records.

F. Knows how to interpret and apply information from formal and informal assessment and evaluation instruments and procedures, including interpreting various types of scores (e.g., standard scores, percentile ranks, age/grade equivalents).

G. Knows how to communicate assessment and evaluation results appropriately to individuals with disabilities, parents/guardians, administrators, and other professionals.

H. Understands the reciprocal nature of assessment and instruction; applies skills for developing individualized assessment strategies to evaluate the results of instruction; and knows how to use assessment and evaluation results to design, monitor and modify instruction for individuals with disabilities.

I. Knows how to design and use ecological assessments, portfolio assessments, task analyses, and functional assessments (e.g., behavioral, social, communication) to accommodate the unique abilities and needs of individuals with disabilities.

J. Applies skills for using assessment and evaluation information from various sources (e.g., teachers, other professionals, parents/guardians, individuals with disabilities) to make instructional decisions, plan effective programs for individuals with disabilities, including those from culturally and/or linguistically diverse backgrounds, and identify supports needed for integration into various program placements.

Competency 001

Competency 001

The special education teacher understands and applies knowledge of the characteristics and needs of students with disabilities.

Chapter 1 will focus on Competency 001—the characteristics and needs of students with disabilities. Under the federal Individuals with Disabilities Education Act, 14 disability categories are used by the states to determine whether students aged 3 to 21 are eligible for special education and related services. Those categories are listed here and fully defined in the appendix on page 301.

1. Autism
2. Deaf-blindness
3. Deafness
4. Developmental delay
5. Emotional disturbance
6. Hearing impairment
7. Intellectual disability
8. Multiple disabilities

9. Orthopedic impairment

10. Other health impairment

11. Specific learning disability

12. Speech or language impairment

13. Traumatic brain injury

14. Visual impairment, including blindness

Characteristics of Learning Disabilities

Competency 001 addresses the fundamental reason for needing Special Education teachers and Special Education services in the public school system. It is essential that those seeking certification in special education and those who are current Special Education teachers pay attention to past and present research regarding learning disabilities.

The topic of learning disabilities and their causes and characteristics is an interesting and complex one. Learning disabilities manifest differently and are as unique as the children they affect. It is important to have a good understanding of how various learning disabilities act upon the basic cognitive functions in different ways.

Learning disabilities have a wide variety of characteristics, and their impact on learning is just as diverse. These impacts include the following:

- reading difficulties

- attention difficulties

- poor motor abilities

- psychological processing deficits

- inability to use cognitive strategies consistently

- oral language difficulties

- expressive language difficulties

- written language problems

- mathematical deficits

- social skill deficits

- perception deficits

Impact on Learning

Often, learning disabilities manifest as learning problems in more than one academic, social, or emotional area or may manifest in only one area of learning but in a very specific and severe manner. The areas that tend to cause the most difficulty in learning are as follows:

- reading

- written language

- mathematics

Impact on Reading

Some of the most common reading deficiencies are due to language learning disabilities. Word analysis, fluency, and reading comprehension are affected the most and at different levels according to the severity of the disability.

Word Analysis

Children with language learning disabilities may have difficulty associating sounds to letters. Analyzing letters, words, sentences, and different texts is a skill that provides the foundation for achievement in reading. At early ages, due to letter and word identification problems, children with language learning disabilities develop reading skills at a slower rate. This stagnation can be evident in every area of learning.

Fluency

Students with fluency issues read at a slower rate and often do not read with expression or intonation. Fluency difficulties are often a result of learning disabilities that affect processing. Below grade-level fluency rates for elementary children are very common for those with learning disabilities.

Reading Comprehension

Ultimately, the goal of reading anything is to achieve comprehension. Word analysis and fluency are the building blocks to comprehending written text. Unfortunately, without these building blocks for reading comprehension, learning diminishes.

Impacts on Written Language

Spelling, language processing, and written language are three major skill areas that are problematic for students with learning disabilities. Language learning disabilities that affect reading skills often affect writing skills as well. This is why these students usually struggle in both areas.

Spelling

Spelling words is often difficult because oral language processing requires sound discrimination to identify the sounds of individual letters and combinations of letters. This type of learning disability affects word analysis and fluency as well.

Language Processing

Language processing, either expressive (spoken) or receptive (internal processing), is a deficit area for many students with disabilities. Problems with identifying appropriate speech sounds, choosing and using appropriate words in speaking and writing, and identifying appropriate sentence structure and grammar usage are often affected. These deficits invariably cause problems in reading and written language development.

Written Language

Written language tasks or assignments, especially if they are longer, can be tedious and frustrating for students who have written language deficits. Written language deficits are often associated with language learning disabilities, which affect reading and language processing as well. Weak skills in grammar and sentence structure often affect written language.

Impacts on Mathematics

Deficits in reading seem to receive more attention than in mathematics. However, many students struggle in math due to learning disabilities. Difficulty understanding concepts such as place value, time, fractions, or decimals is common among students with learning difficulties. Remembering and ordering numbers and information is also a common problem, and reading to solve word problems is significant.

Special Education teachers will need to have a strong working foundation of knowledge on the types and characteristics of learning disabilities so that levels of appropriate service match with the varied needs of these students.

Intellectual Disabilities

According to the National Dissemination Center for Children with Disabilities, an intellectual disability is defined as "having significant limitations in mental functioning, communication, social skills, and independent living skills."[§] The center outlines the most common reasons for children with intellectual disabilities:

- **Problems During Pregnancy:** Children could be born with fetal alcohol syndrome or rubella, for example.

- **Problems at Birth:** Not enough oxygen during delivery can cause intellectual disabilities.

- **Genetic Conditions:** Down syndrome, Fragile X syndrome, and PKU are examples of genetic conditions that cause intellectual disabilities.

- **Accidents:** A child can suffer a traumatic brain injury (TBI) as a result of an accident.

Disorders

Behavioral Disorders

Students with learning disabilities have higher rates of behavioral problems. Behavioral/emotional disorders are characterized by the following:

- an inability to learn, which cannot be explained by intellectual, sensory, or health factors

- an inability to build satisfactory relationship with peers and teachers

- inappropriate types of behavior or feelings under normal situations or circumstances

- a general pervasive mood or unhappiness or depression

- a tendency to develop physical symptoms or fear associated with personal or school problems

[§]NICHCY Disability Fact Sheet 8, January 2011

Autism

Children with autism have lifelong difficulties in communication and social interaction, and have restrictive or repetitive interests and behaviors. Children with autism or related disorders may not interact and may avoid eye contact.

According to the Centers for Disease Control and Prevention, 1 out of 88 children are currently born with autism—an estimate much higher than a generation ago. Autism appears to be increasing, although it is not known how much of that increase is due to better reporting or changes in diagnosis. Autism is much more common among boys than girls.

Attention Disorders

Attention deficit hyperactivity disorders (ADHD) are the most commonly diagnosed behavioral disorders in children, affecting 3 to 6 percent of children. According to the American Psychiatric Association (1994), children with ADHD have "a persistent pattern of inattention and/or hyperactivity-impulsivity that is more frequent and severe than is typically observed in individuals at a comparable level of development." ADHD and learning disabilities often occur together. ADHD is much more common in boys than in girls, with boys from lower-income families being especially at high risk. Some studies have demonstrated increases in substance abuse, risk-taking, and criminal behaviors among adolescents and adults with ADHD.

Schizophrenia

Schizophrenia is a serious emotional disorder affecting between 0.5 and 1 percent of people. Hallucinations and delusions, disorganized speech, or catatonic behavior are common symptoms, which frequently manifest in young adults. The symptoms may also occur in younger children. There are a number of subtypes of schizophrenia.

Other Disorders

Cerebral palsy, epilepsy, and degenerative illnesses such as Parkinson's disease are other disorders that affect learning.

Causes of Learning Disabilities and Behavioral Disorders

Many factors interact in complex ways to determine how the brain develops and functions. These may be inherited or caused by other factors that impact brain development before, during, or after birth (such as drugs or poor nutrition before or after birth).

Environmental Factors to Consider

A few chemicals have been studied for their impacts on the brain. However, the vast majority of chemicals to which people are commonly exposed have never been examined. Among those that have been examined, evidence coming from a wide array of experiments in the lab point to possible impacts on people, especially children with developing brains.

Language Development and Social Skills

Children with developmental issues with verbal and nonverbal communication skills often have difficulty relating to others. The effects of any difficulty can begin to show, even at preschool, in terms of forming successful relationships among peers. Peer relationships play an important role in emotional, social, academic, and behavioral developments:

- It is in this context that new social skills are acquired and existing ones refined and elaborated.

- They provide emotional support and the models for behavior; they are the prototypes for subsequent relationships.

Children who do not have the support of their peers are at risk of developing low self-esteem. Strategies employed by schools can help make a difference for those children who experience difficulties in developing appropriate social interaction and communication skills.

Prevalence of Learning Disabilities

In 2009, the National Center for Learning Disabilities conducted a comprehensive study called The State of Learning Disabilities. Some of the key findings were that 2.5 million students, or 5 percent of the public school population, were identified as having

LD (learning disabilities). Sixty percent of the total population receiving Special Education services for having some kind of identified learning disability were male students.

Eighty percent of all reported learning disabilities fell under the category of dyslexia (the inability to read at developmental rates). The remaining 20 percent fell into the categories of dyscalculia (the inability to process numbers and math facts), dysgraphia (the inability to write legibly and form proper letter formation), auditory and visual processing disorder (the inability to process and discriminate different sounds and process images and visual-spatial patterns of objects or shapes), and nonverbal learning disabilities (the inability to process mathematical information and visual-spatial patterns of objects. Furthermore, 30 percent of students with a learning disability also had ADHD (attention deficit hyperactivity disorder).

Medical Conditions and Learning

Understanding the Other Health Impairment (OHI) learning disability category, as it is defined by the *Individuals with Disabilities Education Act* (IDEA), is helpful for special educators so that they may provide unique instructional services for any individuals with health conditions if ever called upon to do so.

The Definition of OHI in Part 300 of IDEA

According to Section 300.8 (c)(9) of IDEA, other health impairment means having limited strength, vitality, or alertness, including a heightened alertness to environmental stimuli, that results in limited alertness with respect to the educational environment, that—

(i) Is due to chronic or acute health problems such as asthma, attention deficit disorder or attention deficit hyperactivity disorder, diabetes, epilepsy, a heart condition, hemophilia, lead poisoning, leukemia, nephritis, rheumatic fever, sickle cell anemia, and Tourette syndrome; and

(ii) Adversely affects a child's educational performance.

IDEA includes the following conditions in its definition of OHI and its service requirements:

- ADD and AD/HD
- diabetes
- epilepsy

- heart conditions
- *blood won't clot* hemophilia
- lead poisoning
- leukemia
- nephritis
- rheumatic fever
- sickle cell anemia
- Tourette syndrome

It is important to note that although Special Education teachers will not provide direct services for children with certain medical conditions, these children will most likely receive related services as outlined by IDEA.

The following are two examples of related services provided under the OHI disability classification outlined by IDEA:

- **Medical Services** are provided for diagnostic and evaluative purposes only, and are defined as "…services provided by a licensed physician to determine a child's medically related disability that results in the child's need for Special Education and related services" (Sec. 300.34(c)(5)).

- **School Health Services and School Nurse Services** are defined by IDEA as "…health services that are designed to enable a child with a disability to receive FAPE as described in the child's IEP. School nurse services are services provided by a qualified school nurse. School health services are services that may be provided by either a qualified school nurse or other qualified person" (Sec. 300.34(c)(13)).

Review Questions

1. Which of the following behaviors observed over time in a three-year-old child would be a clear indicator that the child may have an autism spectrum disorder?

    (A) Uncoordinated movements when walking

    (B) Lack of joint attention

(C)   Refusal to write the letters of the alphabet

(D)   Hitting other children

The correct response is (**B**). Lack of joint attention is one of the earliest signs of an autism spectrum disorder because it is the basis of human communication. Very young children will follow their parent's pointing finger to share in looking at something, like an airplane in the sky. Children with autism often lack this joint attention to objects and will not point themselves. (A) could be a sign of motor delays in an older child but uncoordinated movements are common in young children as part of normal development. (C) could be a behavioral issue or a lack of comfort or confidence on the child's part. Again, very young children do not yet have the fine motor skills necessary for neat writing. (D) is a behavioral issue that may be a normal response for a child who has not yet learned to control his/her impulses, although it will have to be addressed as not appropriate.

2.   In which academic area do the majority of learning disabilities fall?

(A)   Mathematics

(B)   Writing

(C)   Reading   dyslixia.

(D)   Science

The correct response is (**C**). Statistics show that the predominant learning disability is in the area of reading, accounting for more than 80 percent of LD diagnoses. As a result, the U.S. Department of Education has urged states to implement Response to Intervention programs to target primary students who are falling behind in reading in hopes of reducing the number of LD diagnoses. (A) and (B) are also common learning disability categories, but they are not nearly as prevalent as reading. (D) is not considered an area of learning disability. If a student is struggling in science, it is generally related to a reading or mathematics difficulty.

3.   Which of the following situations would warrant recommending testing for a behavioral disorder?

(A)   A student is sent to the principal's office for acting out in class

(B)   A student does not look his teacher in the eye after writing on his desk

(C)   A student gets upset when corrected and cries

(D) A student gets angry every time anyone touches his/her belongings and stays angry for over an hour each time

The correct response is (**D**). When a student shows a pattern of overreacting to a situation and not being able to calm down for long periods of time, it is an indication of a potentially deeper issue. (A) would not warrant testing, as acting out in class is a common discipline issue. (B) is a common reaction in children who feel guilty. (C) is also a common reaction for some children who do not want to make mistakes.

4. Which of the following statements would likely be true of an individual with ADHD?

(A) The individual cannot communicate well

(B) The individual is often inattentive

(C) The individual has a difficult time making friends

(D) The individual always finishes her/his assignments

The correct response is (**B**). ADHD stands for Attention Deficit Hyperactivity Disorder, so it is characterized by frequent periods of inattention. (A) is not connected to ADHD, but more likely a sign of either a speech/language disorder or autism. Similarly, (C) is more likely associated with either shyness, social skills deficits, or autism. (D) is not the correct answer because individuals with ADHD often leave assignments unfinished when their attention wanders during class or homework time.

5. What would most likely be provided for a child with a documented OHI disability?

(A) School-health services

(B) After-school tutoring

(C) Extended school year program

(D) A full-time paraprofessional

The correct response is (**A**). OHI stands for Other Health Impairment and includes such diagnoses as epilepsy and heart conditions. Students with an OHI disability may not require any modifications or assistance in academic or social skills areas, but they may require health services if they experience a seizure or medical issue of some kind. (B), (C), and (D) would all be associated with disabilities that require academic intervention or close adult supervision.

Competency 002

Competency 002

The special education teacher understands formal and informal assessment and evaluation procedures and knows how to evaluate student competencies to make instructional decisions.

Chapter 2 will focus on Competency 002—assessment and evaluation procedures in order to make instructional decisions.

Educational assessments can be either formal (through standardized tests) or informal (through observation). They include collecting, recording, scoring, and interpreting information about a student's present levels of performance and academic areas of need.

Assessments for Special Education should be administered in all areas of suspected disability such as the following:

- cognitive functioning
- academic functioning
- speech and language
- fine motor

- gross motor

- auditory processing

- sensory processing

- visual processing

- social emotional behavior

- neuropsychological behavior

- memory

- attention

- development

Informal Assessment

Educators, both regular and Special Educators, are finding new ways to evaluate students' school performances using informal rather than formal (or standardized) assessment procedures. Collection of information by means of observation is often thought of as informal assessment, as is information gathered from interviews with parents or past teachers and by using teacher-constructed tests.

Formal Assessment

Norm-referenced or formal tests have standardized, formal procedures for administering, timing, and scoring. They have been "normed" or administered to a representative sample of similar age or grade level students so that final test results can be compared to students of similar characteristics. Test results indicate a person's relative performance in the group. These standardized tests must be administered as specified in this book to ensure valid and reliable results.

Formal vs. Informal Assessment

Formal and informal assessments fall into two assessment categories:

Formal Assessments	Informal/Natural Assessments
Norm-referenced tests	Observation
	Play-based
Criterion-referenced tests	Check lists and rating scales
	Parent interviews

Standardized and Informal Assessment Terminology

The following are terms relating to Special Education assessment:

Achievement Test: An achievement test is a standardized test designed to efficiently measure the amount of knowledge and/or skill a person has acquired, usually as a result of classroom instruction. Such testing produces a statistical profile used as a measurement to evaluate student learning in comparison with a standard or norm.

Alternative Assessment: Many educators prefer the description "assessment alternatives" to describe alternatives to traditional, standardized, norm- or criterion-referenced traditional paper-and-pencil testing. An alternative assessment might require students to answer an open-ended question, work out a solution to a problem, perform a demonstration of a skill, or in some way produce work rather than select an answer from choices on a sheet of paper.

Benchmark: A benchmark is an actual measurement of group performance against an established standard at defined points along the path toward the standard. Subsequent measurements of group performance use the benchmarks to measure progress toward achievement.

Formative Assessment: Formative assessment is assessment occurring during the process of a unit or a course.

Percentile—Standardized/Formal Assessment: This is a ranking scale ranging from a low of 1 to a high of 99, with 50 as the median score. A percentile rank indicates the percentage of a reference or norm group obtaining scores equal to or less than the test-taker's score. A percentile score does not refer to the percentage of questions answered correctly; it indicates the test-taker's standing relative to the norm group standard.

Rating Scale—Standardized/Formal Assessment: This is a scale based on descriptive words or phrases that indicate performance levels. Qualities of a performance are described (e.g., advanced, intermediate, novice) in order to designate a level of achievement. The scale may be used with rubrics or descriptions of each level of performance.

Scale Scores—Standardized/Formal Assessment: Scale scores are scores based on a scale ranging from 001 to 999. Scale scores are useful in comparing performance in one subject area across classes, schools, districts, and other large populations, especially in monitoring change over time.

Summative Assessment: Summative assessment is an evaluation at the conclusion of a unit or units of instruction or an activity or plan to determine or judge student skills and knowledge or effectiveness of a plan or activity.

Assessment Accommodations—Special Education Students

A beginning Special Education teacher will be required to know the difference between formal and informal assessments and have a good understanding on the multitude of uses for each form of assessment. Formal assessments provide precise information that determines disability classification, level of support, service level, types of support, and a student's cognitive strengths and areas of weakness. The majority of this information helps to create Individual Education Programs (IEPs) and is used to evaluate the programs and services of which an IEP consists.

Formal assessments are the chosen type of assessment for annual IEP updates and Committee of Special Education meetings. Formal or standardized achievement tests and psychological assessments determine disability qualification, progress in academic areas, and service levels; however, the majority of a Special Education teacher's attention is on making decisions that assist in accommodating Special Education students within the classroom or education environment.

An assessment accommodation is a change in the way a test is given. Accommodations generally come in five types:

- setting
- presentation
- timing

- response
- scheduling

An assessment accommodation is given so that the playing field is leveled, but not to give students advantages over other students who do not receive accommodations. Assessment accommodations allow students with disabilities to show what they know. Assessment accommodations are provided for students with disabilities receiving Special Education services and students on 504 plans.

Accommodations—Based on Need

The focus of implementing accommodations must be kept on instructional and assessment accommodations to level the playing field with students who do not have a disability.

Align Instruction with Assessment

Many accommodations that are given to Special Education students are given on an informal level, and these accommodations are often no different from accommodations given to nondisabled students. They just make sense. It is important, though, to align assessment accommodations with instruction. In essence, even though a student receives accommodations, being cognizant that the material being assessed matches precisely with what has been taught is essential. In addition, any assessment accommodation needs to be aligned just as well.

Table 1: Types of Assessment Accommodations

Setting	Presentation
<ul><li>Administer the test to a small group in a separate location.</li><li>Administer the test individually in a separate location.</li><li>Provide special lighting.</li><li>Provide adaptive or special furniture.</li><li>Provide special acoustics.</li><li>Administer the test in a location with minimal distractions.</li><li>Administer the test in a small group, study carrel, or individually.</li></ul>	<ul><li>Provide on audiotape.</li><li>Increase spacing between items or reduce items per page or line.</li><li>Increase size of answer bubbles.</li><li>Provide reading passages with one complete sentence per line.</li><li>Highlight keywords or phrases in directions.</li><li>Provide cues (e.g., arrows and stop signs) on answer form.</li><li>Secure papers to work area with tape/magnets.</li></ul>

(continued)

(*continued*)

Timing	Response
• Allow a flexible schedule. • Extend the time allotted to complete the test. • Allow frequent breaks during testing. • Provide frequent breaks on one subtest but not another.	• Allow marking of answers in booklet. • Tape-record responses for later verbatim translation. • Allow use of scribe. • Provide copying assistance between drafts

Source: *www.cehd.umn.edu*

To reiterate, the use of assessment accommodations is about helping students with disabilities to have an equal opportunity to demonstrate what they know. It is "leveling the playing field" by marginalizing the effects of their disability through thoughtful assessment accommodations.

Alternative and Functional Assessment for Students with Significant Intellectual Disabilities

According to Case and Almond (2004), alternate assessments are designed for testing students who are unable to take regular assessments, even when testing accommodations are provided. Case and Almond indicate that these assessments are given to a very small number of students with significant cognitive disabilities.

The National Center for Educational Outcomes describes the format for alternative assessments that most states have adopted. There are three prevalent formats:

1. **Portfolios:** These are a collection of student work (including, but not limited to, worksheets, student-produced products, videos, pictures, or data sheets) that limit a set number of benchmarks. Tasks are teacher designed.

2. **Rating Scales:** Teachers rate student performance on prescribed skills based on classroom observation.

3. **Item-Based Tests:** Students respond to prescribed test items in a one-on-one test-administration setting. Items include one or a combination of performance tasks, writing prompts, constructed-response items or multiple-choice items.

Another form of assessment for children with significant intellectual disabilities is functional assessment. The Center for Applied Neuropsychology uses Halpern and Fuhrer's

(1984) definition to define functional assessment as "the analysis and measurement of specific behaviors that occur in real environments and are relevant to life or vocational goals."

Functional assessment is used to determine the impact of a particular disability on behavior. In relation to individuals with significant intellectual disabilities, knowing how to use functional assessment to identify student individual strengths and weaknesses, as well as identify the demands of the environment in which students will be learning or performing tasks (Center for Applied Neuropsychology, 1994).

A clearer picture of a student's strengths should emerge after taking a functional-assessment approach. This helps in identifying which abilities and skills to include in the individualized education plan, which may help with transition and vocational planning. Individual weaknesses that result from an intellectual disability should emerge as well. These weaknesses usually impede a student's ability to attain certain goals or function independently in different learning environments. Furthermore, this information can be very useful in creating an individualized education plan that clearly identifies learning goals and objectives based on valid assessment information.

There are many assessments that are used to evaluate functional skills and abilities. Special Education teachers aren't trained to administer all of these assessments. However, professionals such as school psychologists, occupational therapists, speech/language pathologists, guidance counselors, and physical therapists can administer these assessments. Collaborating with these professionals will help you to understand the assessment information and how it is used to design, implement, and evaluate successful instruction for students with significant intellectual disabilities. This will be useful in creating a comprehensive learning framework in the form of an individualized education plan.

According to the Center for Applied Neuropsychology, domain areas that present deficient or serious obstacles for students with significant intellectual disabilities are as follows:

- **Issues with Executive Functioning:** Often the inability to identify and formulate goals, revise goals when needed, and develop practical approaches to solving problems in school and in daily life are symptoms of a deficiency in executive functioning. Issues with attention are also a significant symptom of a deficiency in executive functioning. Sustaining alertness and attention to a learning task or activity over a period of time is often measurably less from students with attention issues.

- **Issues with Learning and Memory:** Learning and memory includes the ability to recall oral and written instructions. It is also the ability to encode, store, and retrieve information from an information-providing environment, such as a classroom.

- **Issues with Language and Communication Skills:** Language skills are classified as expressive and receptive language. Expressive-language problems involve the inability to articulate phonetic sounds when speaking, omitting words in conversation, or using words in the wrong contexts. Sometimes students with expressive-language issues use far too many words to explain simple ideas, or they use far too few words to explain more complex ideas. The inability to process and comprehend language effectively falls under receptive-language issues. Receptive language involves how individuals process, store, and comprehends language.

- **Issues with Sensory/Perceptual/Spatial Abilities:** Basic awareness or the ability to perceive sensory information can affect cognitive and emotional functions. Students who have limited spatial skills often have difficulty with an accurate sense of direction, working with visual learning models, and tasks that involve drawing and building.

It is necessary for Special Education teachers working with this population of students to be able to ascertain as much assessment information as possible in these domain areas. They should then use this information to design and implement learning and instructional plans effectively and at a high level.

Assessment Ethics

The great majority of teachers follow strict codes when assessing students. Often, Special Educators are faced with daily decisions, whereas the answers aren't clear when the questions are concerning the assessment of Special Education students and adhering to ethical, legal, and even moral standards.

Whether you are a first-year Special Education teacher or one who has been teaching for many years, the following points for consideration apply:

- Create safe, effective, and culturally responsive assessments.

- Participate in the selection and use of effective and culturally responsive instructional materials, and align assessments to these instructional materials.

- Use culturally and linguistically appropriate assessment procedures that accurately measure what is intended to be measured, and take into account the culturally diverse learning needs.

- Report instances of unprofessional or unethical practice in relation to any assessment practices that don't take into account the specialized needs of students with disabilities where the results are misrepresentations of their abilities.

- Recommend Special Education services based on valid assessment results from a varied collection of informal and formal assessments, which help to provide a comprehensive picture of a student's needs.

Review Questions

1. Which of the following assessments is an example of a formal assessment?

    (A) Checklist of observable behaviors

    (B) Criterion-referenced test

    (C) Parent interview

    (D) Rubric

    The correct response is (**B**). A formal assessment, by definition, is a standardized test that has been tested with a large number of individuals of a given age range or group. This allows for comparisons to a norm or specific criteria. (A), (C), and (D) are all examples of informal assessments. They all require a measure of personal judgment to be completed.

2. What do test results of a norm-referenced test indicate?

    (A) A student's performance relative to a larger group of students of similar ages

    (B) How many questions a student answered correctly

    (C) Whether a student passed or failed a class

    (D) The likelihood a student will go to college

The correct response is (**A**). Norm-referenced tests are "normed" against the performance of a group of students who are similar in age or grade level. Scores are reported as percentages or scaled scores. (B) is incorrect because a scaled score or percentage is adjusted to reflect the norms of the group rather than a straight percentage of incorrect to correct answers. (C) is incorrect because norm-referenced tests by themselves do not indicated passing or failing a course. They indicate performance compared to a norm. (D) is incorrect because the factors that affect a student going to college are many and varied, including academic, family background, and socioeconomic factors.

3. An eighth-grade teacher administers a quiz halfway through a unit to see how much students remember about the topic. What kind of assessment is the quiz?

 (A) Summative

 (B) Diagnostic

 (C) Formative

 (D) Formal

The correct response is (**C**). Formative assessments are administered during the course of instruction to assist teachers in guiding instruction or knowing what concepts and skills need to be retaught. (A) is incorrect because summative assessments are administered at the conclusion of a unit to measure how much students have learned. (B) is incorrect because diagnostic tests are administered prior to instruction to show gaps in student's knowledge or as standardized tests to diagnose a disability. (D) is incorrect because a teacher-created quiz is an informal assessment.

4. Which of the following actions is an example of an assessment accommodation?

 (A) Highlighting keywords or phrases in the directions

 (B) Helping the student answer some of the questions

 (C) Excusing the student from the test

 (D) Writing the student's disability on the answer sheet

The correct response is (**A**). An assessment accommodation is a change in the way an assessment is given to help level the playing field for students with disabilities. For a student who has trouble reading, highlighting the keywords or phrases in the directions helps focus the student on what the test expects them to do without giving away any of the answers. (B) and (C) are incorrect because accommodations are not about changing the content of the test or providing answers. (D) is incorrect because disability designations are confidential information that would never be shared on an answer sheet.

5. What is one common use for formal assessment in Special Education?

(A) Determining a student's grade in a class

(B) Making daily decisions in the classroom

(C) Deciding whether an inclusion teacher's test is too hard for a student

(D) Determining a student's disability qualification

The correct response is (**D**). In Special Education, norm- and criterion-referenced tests are primarily used to establish a disability designation or to confirm a disability designation in a child already in Special Education. (A) and (B) are incorrect because the determination of grades and daily teaching decisions result from a variety of informal assessments, including observations, checklists, and quizzes. (C) is incorrect because judgments about the difficulty or appropriateness of a teacher's exam are made by committees or supervisors.

PART II: DOMAIN II

Promoting Student Learning and Development

PART II: DOMAIN II

Promoting Student Learning and Development

Educating our young people is of paramount importance. Teaching practices must align as much as possible to meet this endeavor. Teachers—not curriculums, not assessment tools, not programs, not delivery models—are the driving force. This may be easy to overlook for teachers who are just starting out, but sometimes even veteran teachers forget they are the key factor for our children's success within our educational system. Whether the state is large like Texas or small like Rhode Island or any size in between, teachers are the driving force. This is especially significant for Special Education teachers.

Special Education teachers are often the single most positive force in their students' lives. This is due to a variety of reasons, such as social conditions at home, learning disabilities, behavioral issues in school combined, or social issues at home. There are a myriad of challenges that many students with special needs face.

For example, in Texas there is a large population of students with English-language needs in addition to having learning disabilities. Each state, region, and area in the country—whether urban, suburban, rural, or combinations of these—has school districts that struggle with unique issues relating to educating special needs students.

Therefore, planning instruction that promotes the best possible chances for student learning is contingent on and affected by unique factors that either a first-year or veteran Special Education teacher is as likely to face.

In preparing for the TExES Special Education EC–12 Exam, prospective teachers are required to demonstrate knowledge and competency on exams that assess ability to understand learners so that instruction promotes the best possible chance for student learning, while not forgetting that teachers continue to be the driving force for student success.

Domain II addresses Competencies 003 to 007.

Competency 003: The special education teacher understands and applies knowledge of procedures for planning instruction for individuals with disabilities.

The beginning teacher:

A. Knows how to select, develop, and apply instructional content, materials, resources, and strategies that are responsive to cultural and other factors (e.g., language, religion, gender, personal beliefs, nature and severity of disability).

B. Knows curricula for developing cognitive, academic, social, language, affective, motor, functional, transition, and career life skills for individuals with disabilities.

C. Knows the role of the Texas Essential Knowledge and Skills (TEKS) curriculum in developing Individual Education Programs (IEPs) for students with disabilities and applies skills for sequencing, implementing, and evaluating individual learning objectives.

D. Applies procedures for developing and using Individual Education Program (IEP) objectives to plan instruction for individuals with disabilities.

E. Prepares, adapts and organizes materials to implement developmentally appropriate and age-appropriate lesson plans based on Individual Education Program (IEP) objectives for individuals with disabilities.

F. Applies knowledge of issues, resources and appropriate strategies for teaching students with disabilities in specialized settings (e.g., alternative schools, special centers, hospitals, residential facilities), including transitions to and from school- and community-based settings.

G. Knows how to collaborate with other professionals to interpret and use sensory, mobility, reflex and perceptual information to create appropriate learning plans (e.g., sensory stimulation, physical positioning, lifting).

H. Knows how to collaborate with other professionals to plan, adapt and implement effective instruction in the least restrictive setting for individuals with disabilities.

I. Knows how the general or special classroom and other learning environments (e.g., home, job site, cafeteria, transportation, community) impact student learning and behavior and applies strategies for planning educational environments that promote students' learning, active participation, communication, self-advocacy, increased independence and generalization of skills.

J. Identifies ways in which technology can assist in planning and managing instruction for individuals with disabilities.

K. Knows how to use local, state and federal resources to assist in programming for individuals with disabilities.

Competency 004: The special education teacher understands and applies knowledge of procedures for managing the teaching and learning environment, including procedures related to the use of assistive technology.

The beginning teacher:

A. Applies procedures for ensuring a safe, positive and supportive learning environment in which diversities are valued, and knows how to address common environmental and personal barriers that hinder accessibility for and acceptance of individuals with disabilities.

B. Knows how to use instructional time efficiently and effectively for individuals with disabilities.

C. Knows how to design, structure and manage daily routines, including transition time, for students in a variety of educational settings and applies procedures for monitoring behavior changes across activities and settings.

D. Applies knowledge of basic classroom management theories, methods and techniques for individuals with disabilities, research-based best practices for effective management of teaching and learning and management procedures that are appropriate to individual needs.

E. Identifies ways in which technology can assist in managing the teaching and learning environment to meet the needs of individual students.

F. Knows various types of assistive technologies, devices, services and resources and their role in facilitating students' educational achievement, communication, positioning, mobility and active participation in educational activities and routines.

G. Knows how to make informed decisions about types and levels of assistive technologies, devices and services for students with various needs, collect and analyze information about a student's environment and curriculum to identify and monitor assistive technology needs and support the use of assistive technologies, devices and services.

H. Applies procedures for participating in the selection and implementation of assistive technologies, devices and services for students with various needs.

I. Applies procedures for coordinating activities of related services personnel and directing the activities of paraprofessionals, aides, volunteers and peer tutors.

J. Under the direction of related services personnel, applies knowledge of appropriate body mechanics to ensure student and teacher safety in transfer, lifting, positioning, and seating.

Competency 005: The special education teacher knows how to promote students' educational performance in all content areas by facilitating their achievement in a variety of settings and situations.

The beginning teacher:

A. Analyzes cultural factors and perspectives that affect relationships among students, parents/guardians, schools and communities with regard to providing instruction for individuals with disabilities.

B. Knows how to serve as a resource person for families, general education teachers, administrators and other personnel in recognizing the characteristics of and meeting the needs of individuals with learning differences in the general education classroom.

C. Knows how to use assessment results to design, monitor and adapt instruction to enhance student learning and applies skills for selecting, adapting and using effective, research-based instructional strategies, practices and materials that are developmentally appropriate and age appropriate and that meet individual needs.

D. Knows instructional, compensatory, enrichment and remedial methods, techniques and curriculum materials and applies strategies for modifying instruction based on the differing learning styles and needs of students.

E. Applies knowledge of techniques for motivating students, including the effects of high teacher expectations on student motivation.

F. Knows life-skills and self-help curricula and strategies for providing students with life-skills instruction relevant to independent or assisted living and employment.

G. Knows how to select and use appropriate technologies to accomplish instructional objectives and applies skills for appropriately integrating technology into the instructional process.

H. Applies strategies for integrating affective, social and career/vocational skills with academic curricula, teaching students with disabilities to solve problems and use other cognitive strategies to meet their individual needs and facilitating maintenance and generalization of skills across learning environments.

I. Knows how to adapt lessons to maximize the physical abilities of individuals with specialized needs.

J. Knows how to integrate related services into all types of educational settings.

K. Knows how to provide community-referenced and community-based instruction as appropriate.

L. Knows how to design and implement instruction in independent living skills, vocational skills and career education for students with physical and health disabilities and how to promote the use of medical self-management procedures for students with specialized health care needs.

Competency 006: The special education teacher understands and applies knowledge of issues and procedures for teaching appropriate student behavior and social skills.

The beginning teacher:

A. Applies knowledge of how culturally and/or linguistically diverse backgrounds of students impact behavior management and social skills instruction.

B. Recognizes ways in which teacher attitudes and behaviors and personal cultural biases influence the behavior of students.

C. Applies knowledge of ethics, laws, rules and procedural safeguards related to planning and implementing behavior management and discipline for individuals with and without disabilities.

D. Knows theories relating to student problem behavior (e.g., noncompliance, self-stimulation, self-injury, withdrawal, aggression, defiance) and the theoretical basis of behavior management techniques (e.g., positive behavioral support, reinforcement, proactive strategies, reactive strategies that decrease negative behaviors).

E. Develops and/or selects social skills and behavioral curricula and strategies that promote socially appropriate behavior and prepares individuals to live cooperatively and productively in society.

F. Incorporates social skills instruction across settings and curricula and knows how to design, implement and evaluate instructional programs that enhance an individual's social participation in family, school and community activities.

G. Identifies realistic expectations for personal and social behavior in various settings and applies procedures for increasing an individual's self-awareness, self-control, self-management, self-reliance and self-confidence.

H. Knows strategies for modifying learning environments (e.g., schedule, physical and instructional arrangements) to promote appropriate behaviors.

I. Knows the impact of language on an individual's behavior and learning and knows how the communication skills of nonspeaking/nonverbal individuals affect their behavior.

J. Understands functional behavior assessments and evaluations and their role in developing behavior intervention plans.

K. Knows strategies for crisis prevention, intervention and postintervention; applies procedures for developing, implementing and evaluating individual behavior crisis-management plans in educational settings; and implements the least intensive intervention consistent with individual needs.

Competency 007: The special education teacher understands and applies knowledge of transition issues and procedures across the life span.

The beginning teacher:

A. Knows how to plan, facilitate and implement transition activities as documented in Individualized Family Services Plans (IFSPs) and Individual Education Programs (IEPs).

B. Knows how to plan for and link students' current and previous developmental and learning experiences, including teaching strategies, with those of subsequent settings.

C. Knows programs and services available at various levels and how to assist students and families in planning for transition.

D. Knows how to teach students skills for coping with and managing transitions.

E. Knows sources of unique services, networks and organizations for individuals with disabilities, including career, vocational and transition support.

F. Applies knowledge of procedures and supports needed to facilitate transitions across programs and placements.

G. Knows how to collaborate with the student, the family and others to design and implement transition plans that meet identified student needs and ensure successful transitions.

H. Applies skills for communicating with families about issues related to transition and strategies for helping their children make successful transitions.

Competency 003

Competency 003

The special education teacher understands and applies knowledge of procedures for planning instruction for individuals with disabilities.

Chapter 3 will focus on Competency 003—procedures for planning instruction for individuals with disabilities. The chapter is divided into sections that will apply to teaching Special Education in the regular education classroom and in the alternative environment.

Thoughtful and effective instructional planning is the cornerstone for student achievement. A beginning teacher in Special Education should have a clear understanding of how the latest research pertaining to effective pedagogy translates into effective instructional practices. In addition, a Special Educator should have an equally clear understanding of the latest research pertaining to planning highly effective instruction for Special Education learners.

Keep in mind that there are many similarities between effective planning for non-disabled students and disabled students. Often, highly effective practices in the regular education environment work just as well for Special Education students. The basis of research for highly effective pedagogy frequently overlaps. However, there are distinctions, and a Special Education teacher who is just beginning will need to have a clear understanding of these distinctions.

Distinctions are clearer when a Special Education teacher needs to determine the instructional techniques that are most effective for improving achievement for students with special learning needs. When planning instruction for Special Education students, one should consider factors such as the type of setting in which that instruction will take place, time allotment, available resources, and adherence to the curriculum (TEKS) when developing Individualized Education Programs (IEPs) or aligning IEP objectives to instruction. Instruction for special needs students will often take place in multiple educational settings such as special areas classes and physical education venues.

Planning Instruction for Special Needs Students

Utilizing student IEPs to assess student strengths and needs is a good place to start when planning instruction for Special Education students. Having a good understanding of the TEKS will help to develop IEPs that can be used effectively to plan instruction.

Read the Current Levels of Performance or the PLAAFP section of the IEP to begin to identify a student's strengths and needs. Other methods include the following:

- Analyze student needs and strengths in relation to instructional demands, the setting in which instruction will take place, the time allotment, and the resources that match instructional objectives.

- Determine which instructional techniques, materials, and activities address student IEP goals most effectively.

- Simultaneously build motivation through engaging instruction.

In addition, focus on both student needs and their strengths when determining the most effective instruction. Remember that success enhances student self-image and motivation.

Instructional Accommodations

Instructional accommodations are generally defined as changes that are made to help successful learning in most educational environments. Instructional accommodations are often confused with instructional modifications. Instructional modifications are changes made to the content that students are learning, so that the content becomes different somehow. It is important to remember that accommodations don't necessarily have to be identified on IEPs to be implemented, and that they are often used in the regular education environment for many students, not just for Special Education students. Accommodations can be as simple as a seating change for a student who may be distracted.

Effective Methods for Implementing Accommodations in the Regular Education Environment

There are a number of effective ways to implement accommodation in the regular education environment. Some of these methods are as follows:

- The accommodations should be as simple as possible. Try using accommodations that require the least amount of time and effort to have the desired, positive effect. When simpler accommodations do not produce the desired effect, try more complex or increasingly more complex methods of accommodations.

- It is easy to confuse instructional accommodations when the issue is behavioral in nature. For example, if a student isn't finishing work on time, determine whether that student requires extra guidance, additional time, or behavioral intervention because he or she is choosing to not complete the work requirements. Sometimes a student's behavior doesn't stem from disability. However, it takes time to determine this.

- Special Education teachers can also help to provide accommodations within the regular education setting by working with regular education teachers to plan accommodations. Some accommodations are quite simple and can be effective for more than one student. For example, you can accommodate students with attention problems by asking them to sit near the front of the room. Another accommodation to build on could be a reward system that encourages appropriate participation and focus during lesson times.

Targeted Instruction

In addition to determining effective instructional accommodations, instructional planning for Special Education students begins with being able to target essential skills for achieving all learning standards for each student. Becoming familiar with the Texas Essential Knowledge and Skills curriculum (TEKS) is a good start. Targeted instruction should be defined through IEP objectives. This type of instruction occurs typically in a small group setting and focuses on areas of weakness that are identified through achievement, cognitive assessments, and skill-based assessments.

A beginning Special Education teacher in Texas should understand how to connect the TEKS curriculum to IEP objectives. For example, students with reading comprehension issues with IEP goals for identifying and understanding content area vocabulary will most likely need targeted vocabulary instruction.

Small-group instruction—where the Special Education teacher connects the vocabulary to the content by teaching them in isolation—is a good example of planning and conducting targeted instruction. These students will then be able to engage more effectively with that text in a larger instructional group along their regular education peers.

Instructional Strategies/Techniques

Beginning Special Education teachers should have a good understanding of current and time-tested instructional techniques that increase achievement rates for students with learning disabilities. Incorporate the following techniques into instructional planning as much as possible:

- Use concrete materials and visual aids with instruction.

- Include real-life models and life-skill tasks to illustrate concepts and practice skills. Examples can include the following:

  - Measure ingredients in a recipe.

  - Determine the number of gallons of paint needed to paint a bedroom.

  - Read a map at a shopping mall and navigate to the store of choice.

- Use a multisensory approach to introduce or practice concepts. Visual, auditory, or kinesthetic approaches work very well.

- Repetition of key concepts and practice of key skills should be short but intense. Try practicing these in short bursts, and, if possible, several times a day. Practicing reading and math skills is particularly important. Incorporating movement can be very effective when combined with targeting skills in isolation, such as word identification or math-fact activities.

Strategies for Addressing Learning Needs in the Regular Education Environment

There are a number of strategies that you can use to address learning needs of students in a regular education environment. Some of these strategies include the following:

- Relate class to personal real-life skills and experiences.

- Limit expectations to two or three concepts per unit.

- Evaluate projects rather than doing traditional testing.

- Plan and teach with student strength's in mind.

- Use concise directions when teaching.

- Incorporate flexible learning groups.

- Preteach concepts, information, and key vocabulary using a variety of graphic organizers.

Strategies for Students with Writing Needs

There are a number of strategies that you can use to address students with writing needs. Some of these strategies include the following:

- Permit students to use a tape recorder to dictate writing.

- Permit students to use computers for outlining, word processing, spelling, and grammar check.

- Use guided notes for note taking.

- Use collaborative writing activities.

- Use flowcharts for writing ideas for prewriting.

- Use multimedia alternatives to traditional writing.

- Don't penalize for errors in mechanics and grammar, unless that is the objective being taught.

Strategies for Students with Reading Needs

There are a number of strategies that you can use to address students with reading needs. Some of these strategies include the following:

- Allow students to subvocalize quietly reading aloud.

- Teach self-questioning, previewing, searching for context clues, predicting, and summarizing comprehension strategies.

- Summarize key points when reading nonfiction.

- Identify nonfiction features such as main ideas, details, sequencing, cause/effect, and compare/contrast.

- When reading nonfiction, teach story elements.

- Allow highlighting of texts, passages, keywords, or concepts.

- Preview any vocabulary.

- Use prereading and post reading strategies.

Strategies for Students with Expressive Language Needs

There are several strategies that you can use to address students with expressive language needs. Some of these strategies include the following:

- Use visuals.

- Use built-in time for processing.

- Use cues for speaking in public.

- Phrase questions with choices embedded in them.

- Use choral reading or speaking.

- Use rhythm or music.

- Allow practice opportunities for speaking in small group settings to encourage success.

Strategies for Students with Retaining and Accessing Information Needs

There are a number of strategies that you can use to address students who need help with retaining and accessing information. Some of these strategies include the following:

- Teach concepts and information using a multisensory approach (tactile, visual, kinesthetic, auditory, and so on).

- Teach frequent repetition of key points.

- Teach instructional segment.

- Color-code to demonstrate key concepts and relationships.

- Use mnemonics as a memory tool.

- Sequence information into categories and lists.

- Organize information visually, showing connections between key ideas and concepts.

Strategies for Students with Organization Needs

There are a number of strategies that you can use to address students who need help with organization. Some of these strategies include the following:

- Teach how to use planners and calendars.

- Teach time management skills when working on long-term assignments or projects.

- Teach how to use different folders, notebooks, and planners and maintain these in an organized fashion.

- Teach how to keep storage spaces organized.

- Use daily assignment planner for homework, due dates on assignments, upcoming tests or quizzes, and for recording important events and dates.

Strategies for Students with Attending Issues

There are several strategies that you can use to address students who have attending issues. Some of these strategies include the following:

- Use preferential seating.

- Measure on task behavior and plan accordingly.

- Incorporate movement within a lesson.

- Teach self-monitoring strategies.

- Incorporate breaks.

- Provide reminder cues or prompts.

- Reduce assignment length or break down assignments into achievable segments.

Teaching in Alternative Settings

Alternative-education programs have been proliferating in this country, especially in the past 15 years. According to Kolchar-Bryant and Lacey (2005), 48 states indicated in 2004 that they would more than likely rely on alternative placements for students with significant learning and behavioral problems. During this time, half of all districts with alternative programs and schools reported that any of the following was a sufficient reason for transferring at-risk students from regular school (Alternative Education as a Quality Choice for Youth: Preparing Educators for Effective Programs, 2005):

- Alcohol or drug use: 52 percent

- Physical attacks or fights: 52 percent

- Chronic truancy: 51 percent

- Continual academic failure: 50 percent

- Possession or use of a weapon other than a firearm: 50 percent

- Disruptive verbal behavior: 45 percent

- Possession or use of a firearm: 44 percent.

Models for Alternative Schools

According to Raywid (1999), most alternative schools and programs cite educational philosophies based on ideas that promote educational personalization, small class sizes, positive relationship-building between teachers and students, and an overall focus on students no matter their background or current situation. Raywid (1999) defines three models for alternative schools and programs:

1. **Restructured Schools:** These relate closely to current charter or independent schools. While they are not designed for at-risk students, they often utilize ideas and programs that benefit students who struggle in mainstream public schools.

2. **Disciplinary Programs:** These schools and programs utilize a mix of highly intensive, daily behavior modification and close, personal student-teacher interaction. Typically, violent or highly disruptive students are sent to these schools and programs.

3. **Problem-Solving Schools and Programs:** Problem-solving schools and programs are positive and nonpunitive. These schools and programs provide

assistance for unsuccessful mainstream students by providing a network of academic, social, and emotional programs and instruction. Often, academic remediation and rehabilitation are the key tenets of these programs.

Qualifications for Teaching in Alternative Programs or Schools

Lehr (2003) conducted a study on state policies and legislation on teacher qualification requirements for alternative education programs and schools. The results indicated that half of states with alternative-education programs and schools did not have language about staffing qualifications that complies with state staffing standards. Only 18 states had legislation outlining Special Education services such as IEPs, entrance criteria, or provision of specialized services (Alternative Education as a Quality Choice for Youth: Preparing Educators for Effective Programs, 2005).

Currently, all teachers in any alternative setting must be highly qualified. This includes any juvenile centers, correctional institutions, and any other alternative placement under state law. According to the National Association of Special Education Teachers, this means that a teacher must hold a minimum of a bachelor's degree, and has demonstrated subject-matter competency in each of the academic subjects in which the teacher teaches.

Positive Behavioral Strategies for At-Risk Students in Alternative Programs and Schools

In 2002, the National Association of School Psychologists reported that research proves that positive discipline strategies are more effective than punitive strategies, especially for at-risk students. They cited the following:

- Opportunities to forge relationships with caring adults, coupled with engaging curriculum, prevent discipline problems.

- Discipline that is fair, corrective, and includes therapeutic relationship-building opportunities reduces the likelihood of further problems.

- Strategies that maintain appropriate social behavior make classrooms and schools safer.

- Positive solutions address student needs, environmental conditions, teacher interactions, and matching students with curriculum.

- Appropriately implemented, proactive behavior and learning support systems can lead to dramatic improvements that have long-term effects on the lifestyle, functional communication skills, and problem behavior in individuals with disabilities or who are at risk for negative adult outcomes.

Collaboration with Occupational and Physical Therapists

Collaborative consultation is a common model used to facilitate sensory, motor, and perceptual outcomes for students receiving services from occupational and physical therapists in public schools. A child's Special Education teacher and therapists work together to identify daily needs and then develop and implement strategies accordingly. As stated by the Wisconsin Department of Public Instruction, collaborative consultation lends itself to implementing educationally relevant functional activities and therapeutic learning plans so that students practice newly acquired and learned skills during natural occurring routines and environments. These routines are coordinated within the Special Education and regular education classrooms.

The Department indicates that this model allows students to practice multiple opportunities that involve motor, sensory, and perceptual skills in purposeful ways. The roles of a Special Education teacher within this model would involve some or all of the following responsibilities:

- provide information before and after a student's therapy

- help the therapist devise a therapy schedule

- participate in facilitating in-class therapy sessions

- plan and conduct activities that promote the student's motor, sensory, and perceptual skills while in the classroom setting

- provide feedback to the therapist as needed

- learn proper procedures for lifting students with physical impairments as well as proper techniques for positioning students appropriately during classroom activities and during instruction

- exchange information and expertise with therapists to help plan future therapy sessions, give and receive feedback, and foster a collaborative partnership with therapists

Most schools support the collaborative approach since research indicates it is more conducive to positive student outcomes than an expert consultation model. In an expert consultation model, the specialist independently evaluates needs, develops interventions, and provides all interventions. In this model, the Special Education teacher would receive recommendations. However, he or she does not work collaboratively with the specialist.

Review Questions

1. When preparing instruction for a student with special needs, where is the best place for a teacher to start?

    (A) The student's IEP goals and objectives

    (B) The student's grade level textbooks

    (C) The district's scope and sequence of skills

    (D) Activity books from a teacher supply store

    The correct response is (**A**). A team of educators, parents, diagnosticians, related service providers, and administrators met and agreed on the student's goals and objectives in the IEP. For any student with special needs, these goals and objectives must form the basis for all instructional planning. Since these goals are aligned as closely as possible with the grade-level TEKS, a teacher can be assured that they will meet the basic requirements of the district and state, so (C) is not the best answer. (B) and (D) are incorrect responses as publishers' lesson plans and activities should be used to carry out or supplement the instructional objectives of the IEP.

2. What is the best definition for an instructional accommodation?

    (A) Changes made to the content students are learning

    (B) Memorization technique

    (C) Changes made to the student's environment to improve learning

    (D) Teacher lesson plan

    The correct response is (**C**). Instructional accommodations are changes made to the environment to improve student learning. Accommodations never involve changes to the content, so (A) is incorrect. Likewise, (B) and (D) are incorrect since they have nothing to do with the kinds of changes an accommodation would entail.

CHAPTER 4

Competency 004

Competency 004

The special education teacher understands and applies knowledge of procedures for managing the teaching and learning environment, including procedures related to the use of assistive technology.

Chapter 4 will focus on Competency 004—procedures for managing the teaching and learning environment.

Without effective management of the learning environment, the soundest of instructional plans will not transpire. There is no magic bullet for classroom management, either. However, tried and true techniques are out there and used often by effective Special Education teachers.

Techniques for Managing the Teaching and Learning Environment

There are several techniques you can use to manage your teaching and learning environment. First, learn the names of your students quickly at the beginning of the year. This sends a clear message to your class that you care, which goes a long way.

As the year begins and you find particular students stealing your attention, find ways to meet these students' needs quickly. The reason for this need for attention usually has to do with the fact that these students are frustrated due to living with a learning disability. They may feel powerless. Think about the underlying reasons for their misbehavior, and actively seek solutions that don't steal all your time and attention. As a result, you will be able to meet the needs of every student you teach and care for.

Motivate your students to work hard to complete their in-class and out-of-class work through creative individual and class-wide incentive programs. Be creative. Special Education teachers generally have more opportunities for management and instructional creativity. Take advantage of this.

How you arrange your classroom's physical setting and how you use the space provided to you is something that you probably won't find offered in too many college courses. However, it is a very important topic. Many new teachers must share space in some form or another with regular elementary teachers as well as with secondary teachers.

The age and grade level which is taught will dictate how different activity centers and types of tables or student desks will be arranged. If you are lucky enough to have your own room, how you arrange your room depends on what you have at your disposal:

- Are there individual student desks or long tables?

- Will you have an overhead projector or whiteboard?

- What kind of teacher's desk or computer desks will you have?

- Will you have a teacher's desk?

- Will you have your own computer desks?

- Like many Special Education teachers, will you be a cart-pushing, traveling teacher?

- Will you teach in a specialized setting or a specialized school such as an alternative school?

- Will you teach students with physical handicaps?

- Will you need to work in, and adjust accordingly to, several different environments, environments that have been designed by other teachers and which may not be exactly conducive to meeting your students' (and therefore your) instructional needs?

These situations create challenges that a new Special Education teacher usually does not have the opportunities to consider before being hired. As a Special Education teacher in Texas (or in any state, for that matter), there is no way to know exactly what your future teaching environments will be like; however, there are some very important things to understand. Possession of this vital understanding is evaluated by the EC–12 test for beginning Special Education teachers in Texas.

Classroom Management and Space

When considering classroom management and space, consider the following questions:

- Where will you put your desk if you have a permanent one?

- What kinds of tables are available? Which tables are most effective in achieving your students' instructional IEP goals?

- What activity centers are important to you? Elementary-level Special Education teachers may have many. Secondary classrooms may have a reference area, a student organization area (for example, staplers, pens, pencils, paper), and a quiet study area. Think about establishing work areas with clear routes for traffic to and from other work and learning areas.

- What storage do you have? What storage do you need? At all costs, always try to avoid clutter. Smooth transitions are essential.

- Will you have space to display students' work or interesting visuals? What should you display?

Some Specific Strategies

- Arrange the classroom so that you can monitor quickly and easily and see all or as much as possible from any vantage point.

- Keep active areas separate from quiet work spaces.

- Keep two active areas distinctly separate to avoid distraction and interference.

- Again, have clear and safe traffic paths no matter how your room is arranged.

- Change according to instructional objectives. Change often if needed.

- Allow students to develop a degree of ownership of their learning space.

- If you have a desk, try positioning it on a side or in the back of the class.

The physical setting sends messages about authority and ownership, and it can foster effective interaction. Arrange your classroom in a way that accurately portrays your educational philosophy combined with knowledge of effective instructional strategies.

Coordinating Activities and Services as Case Manager

Special Education teachers also have the dual responsibility of acting as their students' case managers. As case managers, Special Education teachers are responsible for monitoring their students' individualized education plans and how the students are benefitting from the services. They are also responsible for ensuring that all timelines are being adhered to and that accommodations, modifications, and other services indicated on the plan are implemented in all school settings. Common duties and responsibilities of the Special Education case manager are as follows:

- Keep all confidential documents, such as IEPs and evaluations, in a secure location.

- Manage paraprofessionals by expressing expectations, holding regular meetings for review and feedback, and clarifying disciplinary practices and classroom routines.

- Communicate with administrators on any part of a student's plan that is not being followed.

- Communicate with general educators so that they have access to the IEPs of the students with whom they are working and conferring with them on proper implementation of services and accommodations.

- Confirm therapy schedules and goals and ensure that related service therapy is provided as indicated on the IEP.

Collaborating with Related Service Providers

According to Giangreco et al. (1990), it is essential for team members to have a shared understanding of which functions each person serves and how they are interrelated to support the student's program. Not only do Special Educators coordinate procedures that involve related services for their students, they also act as team members with related service providers who work to plan, implement, and evaluate a set of services for each of their students. Through this team approach, the Special Education teacher, together with the service providers, can identify gaps or overlaps in student programs and services and work to refine or modify services across settings.

Working with Paraprofessionals

According to Dr. Barry Ziff of the California State University Los Angeles Education Specialist Program, the role of the paraprofessional in the past decade has evolved from a clerical assistant to a far greater collaborative role with the teacher. Paraprofessionals perform important duties in the classroom, such as directing and managing students. He also states that it is the Special Education teacher who is expected to be the manager of any adults who work with Special Education students for whom they are legally responsible. Ziff also states that it is important to be flexible and understand that the paraprofessional's role is to provide support in the classroom. Paraprofessionals are not expected to develop lesson plans or be responsible for classroom management. They are also not personal assistants.

A notebook from the Special Education teacher that outlines responsibilities and provides helpful information for the paraprofessional is suggested to promote a sense of collegiality. A list of suggested items for the notebook are as follows:

- philosophical overview
- classroom-management strategies
- emergency procedures
- yearly, weekly, and daily calendar and schedule
- classroom rules
- paraprofessional's roles and responsibilities
- school personnel

- any setting information the teacher feels is important to convey

It is suggested that building positive relationships with all staff who work with a Special Education teacher is beneficial for the adults and for the students as well.

Assisting Students in Wheelchairs

A Special Education teacher of a student with a physical impairment that requires the need for the daily use of a wheelchair should follow the general guidelines offered by the student's physical or occupational therapist when helping the student transfer to and from her or his wheelchair. However, according to Giangreco et al. (2002), before attempting to transfer a student, be sure to learn how to go about doing this from the student's therapist rather than just following written guidelines.

Due to the inherent risks in transferring a student to and from a wheelchair (to both the student and to the person providing the assistance), using common sense and caution is necessary. When in doubt, err on the side of caution. An example is attempting to transfer a student alone when a two-person transfer makes more sense. This could result in injury to both the student and the assisting person. Following the guidelines of a physical therapist when lifting so that proper body position is maintained will eliminate any chance of injury.

Effective Use of Assistive Technology

Assistive technology is any form of technology, whether simple or complex, that assists in learning. Technology designed to help individuals with learning disabilities—cognitive impairment, reading and writing issues, or physical impairment such as visual or hearing—falls under the category of assistive technology.

Reading-Assistive Technology

Reading-assistive technology such as recorded books allow users to listen to text. These are available in a variety of formats, such as CDs and MP3 downloads. Digital word scanners, reading software, and reading apps with a variety of assistive features are other forms of reading-assistive technology available to Special Education teachers.

Writing-Assistive Technology

Some writing-assistive technology is designed to circumvent the physical task of writing, while others assist with planning, spelling, and the organization of writing tasks. Several examples of writing-assistive technology include the following:

- alternative keyboards

- graphic organizing software for brainstorming, outlining, draft writing, and editing

- speech-to-text software

General Assistive Technology Devices, Computer Apps, Software, and Hardware

The following are examples of general assistive technology devices, computer apps, software, and hardware to assist Special Education teachers:

- **Abbreviation Expanders:** This software immediately shows the full name for any abbreviations.

- **Alternative Keyboards:** These are modified keyboards that may have, for example, enlarged or highlighted keys. They may be keyboards that are larger or designed to work with specific physical disabilities by having their shape modified.

- **Audiobooks and Digital Publications:** For several years now, education publishers have included audiobooks of textbooks. Given the advent of new digital media, students now have various options for digital textbooks with a variety of embedded assistive options: speech to text, various highlighting features, grammar and conventions software, video, or research options.

- **Electronic Math Worksheets:** These are various digital worksheets that have embedded assistive features, such as formative assessment features.

- **Freeform Database Software:** These are various programs that allow students to manipulate data.

- **Graphic Organizers:** These can be the old-fashioned paper graphic organizers, or they can be digital.

- **Information/Data Managers:** This refers to cloud data managing or managing data on a school network.

- **Optical Character Recognition:** This software is used for communication or writing. It recognizes speech or graphic information and immediately encodes, interprets, stores, and displays the information. It is the driving force behind text-to-speech software.

- **Personal FM Listening Systems:** These are used for hearing-impaired or deaf students. FM systems are an audio amplification system used between the instructor and the student.

- **Portable Word Processors:** These are commonly referred to as Smartboards. They are small, portable keyboards with a text-memory capacity for storing written work.

- **Proofreading Programs:** Fortunately, these programs have become far more intuitive and are embedded in just about every educational learning media available.

- **Speech-Recognition Programs:** These are based on software that encodes spoken words as text.

- **Speech Synthesizers/Screen Readers:** This technology is used in various reading comprehension or learning media, and it can be very useful for students with reading disabilities.

- **Talking Calculators:** These calculators convert data to speech. They are especially useful for the visually-impaired community.

- **Talking Spell Checkers and Electronic Dictionaries:** These are especially useful for the visually-impaired community and for students with reading disabilities.

- **Variable-Speed Tape Recorders:** Most recorders are digital and have various embedded options.

- **Word-Prediction Programs:** These programs are standard with virtually any word-processing program available.

Keep in mind that assistive technology can be just about anything. It can be as complex as a computer or as simple as a pencil grip for writing. Some districts have people in charge of providing assistive technology. Take advantage of these related service professionals. They can be an extremely helpful and knowledgeable resource.

■ Review Questions

1. An ALE teacher sets up a class store with various items such as pencils, stickers, and posters. She explains to students that they can earn "class cash" to spend in the store by following classroom rules, completing their work, and being supportive of their classmates. What kind of behavioral strategy is this teacher employing?

   (A) Applied behavior analysis

   (B) Detention

   (C) Token economy

   (D) Replacement behavior

   The correct response is (**C**). A token economy is a form of behavior modification based around the consistent rewarding of positive or desired behaviors. When teachers see a positive behavior, they give a student a "token," some object that only has value in the classroom. That token can be turned in for a prize or something of value to the student. While token economies are common in applied behavior analysis settings, (A) is incorrect because applied behavior analysis is a much larger system of teaching through structured activities and rewarding targeted behaviors. In and of itself, ABA does not require a classroom store or a token economy to work. (B) is incorrect as detention is a form of negative reinforcement. (D) is incorrect because replacement behaviors are more appropriate responses that teachers and therapists help students acquire in place of undesirable behaviors.

2. Which of the following strategies is NOT an example of an assistive technology?

   (A) Recorded books

   (B) Spell-check program

   (C) Pencil grip

   (D) Seating chart

   The correct response is (**D**). Seating charts, a strategy where the teacher assigns students' seats, can be used as accommodations to encourage positive behavior. They are not examples of assistive technology, however. Assistive technology is a form of technology, simple or complex, that assists in learning. (A), (B), and (C) are all examples of assistive technologies and therefore incorrect answers.

Competency 005

Competency 005

The special education teacher knows how to promote students' educational performance in all content areas by facilitating their achievement in a variety of settings and situations.

Chapter 5 will focus on Competency 005—promoting student's educational performance in all content areas in a variety of settings and situations.

Academic Content Requirements

Special Education teachers in Texas and across the country must have a solid knowledge base of all content areas specific to their grade level, such as the general curricula (math, reading, English/language arts, science, social studies, and vocational studies). This knowledge base must be sufficient so that effective collaboration can occur with general educators such as co-teachers of academic subjects.

Individuals with exceptional learning needs require appropriate learning and performance accommodations and modifications in the academic content areas. This is just as important as providing accommodations or modifications for math, reading, and writing instruction. Competency 5 evaluates whether a beginning Special Education teacher has the basic understanding and skills to provide content area accommodations and instruction effectively.

■ Instruction: The Content Areas

Most content-area teachers are passionate about their subjects, especially at the higher grade levels. A common accommodation for students with learning disabilities at the secondary level is the dissemination of lecture notes, either before or after a lesson, and this is usually information that breaks down vocabulary-heavy and information-laden material. Secondary teachers usually have no problem providing this accommodation since they often are just as passionate about student success.

However, accommodations like this don't address the root of the problem: the inability to access information in nonfiction materials, mostly due to reading proficiency issues. The answer lies in providing differentiated instruction beginning at the elementary levels and extending to the secondary levels in combination with the appropriate accommodations for each grade level (for example, lecture notes, guided notes, or graphic organizers). Identification of proper reading, thinking, and writing strategies within content-area subjects; linking these to student IEPs; and then providing instruction is critical for the success of students with learning disabilities at any grade level. This is often the responsibility of the Special Education teacher.

Special Education teachers are often responsible for either providing accommodations that circumvent reading issues in content areas or providing reading materials that are alternatives to grade-level textbooks for their students in content areas. Special Education teachers should do both. They should also include a third responsibility: providing the proper intervention-reading strategies so that Special Education students can improve their content reading with the goal of eventually becoming independent.

Special Education teachers often find that it is quite common to be a participant in a classroom's instruction (especially at higher grade levels) as well as a participant in planning instruction (but not the chief deliverer of instruction). So, a Special Education teacher's role becomes more that of a coach for the regular education teacher or an instructional advisor rather than the head teacher. This is quite important.

Strategies to Assist Regular Education and Content-Area Teachers

The following are examples of strategies that you can use to assist regular education and content-area teachers:

- Help regular education teachers or content-area teachers recognize that students continue to develop their reading skills in middle and high school, and students with disabilities will need specific help to read grade-level texts of any kind.

- Students with reading issues will need multiple texts at varying reading levels as well as multiple accommodations that need to be incorporated at the instructional-planning and resource-gathering stages.

- Use assessment to inform planning and instruction.

- Learn to scaffold instruction.

Integrate writing to think and learn, and plan for the "big picture, with essential concepts in mind." Doing this enables regular education teachers to map the framework of a four- to eight-week unit.

By presenting reading-strategy instruction alongside instruction in content and learning standards in content areas, regular education teachers will not only be helping those students with reading needs, but the rest of their students as well. Reading strategies that utilize tools that help to comprehend, recall, and analyze content in informational books and textbooks are just good instructional practices that will raise the level of performance for everyone.

Content-Area Reading Strategies

The following are several examples of good content-area reading strategies:

- preteaching vocabulary
- using graphic organizers
- self-monitoring for comprehension
- using strategies before, during, and after reading
- using comprehension strategies, such as predicting, questioning, visualizing, and summarizing
- reading and thinking out loud
- picture, caption, and title walking before reading
- using prior knowledge

- instruction in common nonfiction structures:

  - main idea and details

  - author's purpose

  - cause and effect

  - sequence

  - description

Related Services in Content Areas

Coordinating goals with related service professionals who provide services that are congruent with the common learning objectives of students with special needs in content-area classes, is a common and very effective practice that Special Education teachers need to master. Speech/language pathologists, as well as reading-intervention specialists, are very good sources of assistance for any special education teacher and their students. Aligning IEP goals with the goals of these service providers only helps to foster strong collegial relationships, relationships that will only help to meet the needs of students with learning disabilities.

Speech language pathologists work with students who typically possess language, articulation, and information/language-processing disorders. Often, speech language pathologists will work collaboratively with Special Education teachers to integrate reading, writing, and language instruction in and out of the classroom. This is very helpful in all subject areas, including content areas. Utilize these professionals as much as possible.

Assessing Students for Career, Vocational, and Life Skills

Transition assessment and planning will be discussed at greater length in Chapter 7. However, it is appropriate to begin the discussion here. The transition from school to work and/or community-adult living can be difficult for all students, but especially so for many of those with learning disabilities. The tasks of choosing a job and preparing for work, deciding whether to attend college or a trade school, choosing where to live and with whom are areas of gray—for many students, not just those with disabilities.

Special Education teachers, often at the secondary level, assist students in making these decisions. At the middle-grade levels, this process begins with assessing and then matching students' abilities and interests to appropriate academic, vocational, and functional education. This information is useful at the higher secondary levels. Therefore, appropriate instruction in the areas of career readiness, independent living skills, college readiness, and vocational skills needed for the future should be integrated with instruction in the core-content areas.

One particular challenging area for Special Education teachers working with students with disabilities is assessing vocational skills and abilities, especially at the middle-grade levels. It requires considerable amounts of planning and thinking in order to assist and motivate students to begin thinking about their future, which is very difficult for most young people.

Transition Assessment

Transition assessments can accomplish the following:

- identify strengths, abilities, and deficits
- identify interests and vocational abilities
- identify appropriate instructional settings
- identify level of self-determination skills
- identify necessary accommodations, supports, and services

As members of the multidisciplinary IEP team, counselors at both the elementary and secondary levels often assist Special Education teachers with choosing, implementing, scoring, and using the information to provide appropriate instruction.

Independent Living Instruction

Based on transition assessment, independent living instruction is often the responsibility of the Special Education teacher, even in a public school setting. This often takes a heavier role in alternative settings for students who may have severe learning and independent-living issues.

Areas of Instructional Focus

Some basic areas of instructional focus include the following:

- grocery, clothing, and daily needs shopping

- travel training (for example, using public and/or personal transportation)

- basic banking (for example, basic math and money skills)

Vocational/Occupational Readiness Instruction

Some basic areas of instruction for vocational/occupational readiness include the following:

- food preparation, nutrition planning, cake decorating, child care, sewing skills

- plant care, landscaping, flower arranging, gardening, seasonal projects

- computer-assisted design, woodworking projects and skills, general computer skills

- word processing, desktop publishing, general computer skills

- office skills (for example, collating, filing, organizing information)

Vocational instruction may be difficult to incorporate into core academic subjects. At earlier grade levels, these skills often take the form of teaching appropriate social/emotional language, reading, writing, communication, organizational, and attention skills.

Understanding Community-Based Instruction

Special Education teachers in Texas who choose to teach in settings for students with significant cognitive disabilities should be familiar with the concept of community-based instruction (CBI). According to the Baltimore County Public Schools Guidelines for Community-Based Instruction (2005), community-based instruction is a critical component for students ages 5–21 with significant cognitive disabilities.

As students with significant cognitive disabilities become adults, they will live in the community and use the skills that they acquired during their school years. Community-based instruction means that students will live and work in the community, and they will participate, either with supports or independently, in many community settings. Therefore, instruction and skill practice for students with significant cognitive disabilities should occur in *natural environments* and during the school day when it is most natural.

It is also important to point out that community-based instruction is not what is considered to be a field trip. The emphasis is not on singular excursions into the community. Rather, it is on skills and behaviors that are instructed and assessed on an ongoing basis in the school setting and applied in the natural setting. The ultimate goal is generalization. Examples of community-based instruction activities include the following:

- purchasing items at a store when a student is practicing money in school

- ordering from a menu when a student is practicing functional reading skills

- practicing vocational skills at an actual job site

The following are some targeted learning domains addressed during CBI:

- **Community:** travel training such as bike and pedestrian safety, money and purchasing items at stores, and utilizing community resources such as the post office or library

- **Communication Skills:** public greetings, seeking help, and requesting information

- **Personal Management:** mobility, domestic skills such as grocery shopping, finding and using laundry services, and budgeting

- **Recreation:** obtaining and using a library card or participating in community activities

- **Vocational:** interacting with coworkers and completing job tasks

In addition to life-skill training in the natural community-based environment, academics can be addressed in the community in various ways as well. Community-based learning can provide authentic reading, writing, listening, and math experiences. Reading community signs, making purchases, counting change, and giving and receiving directions to places are good examples.

Review Questions

1. An eighth-grade social studies teacher complains that the Special Education students in his class fail every test. He explains that he assigns all of his students to read the chapters and complete the questions, and he even simulates a popular game show to review information before the test. What would be an appropriate strategy for his co-teacher to suggest?

   (A) Move the Special Education students to a resource class

   (B) Teach strategies for reading nonfiction, such as focusing on chapter headings and subheadings and using graphic organizers

   (C) Call the parents of all students who are failing to ask for more help with home-work

   (D) Have students copy key passages from the textbook in their notebooks

   The correct response is (**B**). In a content-area classroom, the most common reason for students performing poorly is also the most common learning disability: reading. By teaching reading strategies such as how to use headings and subheadings to navigate information in a textbook, the teacher is helping the students become better readers, and that will result in better performance. (A) is incorrect and illegal as Special Education laws require that students be served in the least restrictive environment. (C) is incorrect because, while parent involvement is a good goal, the suggestion does not help with the root of the problem: reading skills. (D) is incorrect because it does not help with the reading problem. It is also a method that will likely be seen as a punishment, not a study technique.

2. Tim is a student with physical disabilities with extremely limited mobility. He uses a wheelchair. He is in a ninth-grade algebra I class. The most appropriate strategy for the math teacher to use when teaching Tim's class would be

   (A) using an interactive whiteboard with student response clickers to assess students' understanding of the lesson as it progresses.

   (B) requiring students to come forward and work problems on the board in front of the class.

   (C) using math stations, with small groups rotating every 5 to 10 minutes.

   (D) doing a gallery walk with chart paper posted for writing responses.

The correct response is (**A**). Using an interactive whiteboard and student response clickers not only allows Tim to fully participate in class, but it does not call attention in any way to his disability. This technique also allows the teacher to use formative assessment to see how well the students are grasping the concepts being taught and what needs to be retaught. (B) is incorrect because it will take time for Tim to make it to the board, and he would be at a disadvantage to write on it due to being in a wheelchair. (C) is incorrect because it will be difficult for Tim to maneuver between stations, especially given the short amount of time expected at each station. (D) is incorrect because it would be difficult for Tim to maneuver through the classroom and awkward for him to try to write on posted chart paper.

Competency 006

6

Competency 006

The special education teacher understands and applies knowledge of issues and procedures for teaching appropriate student behavior and social skills.

Chapter 6 will focus on Competency 006—teaching appropriate student behavior and social skills.

It only takes one student to waste hours upon hours of careful instructional planning. As a new Special Education teacher, if you do find yourself in a situation in which one student is successfully ruining hours of carefully planned instruction, keep in mind that fixing this may be easier than it appears.

You must first identify why this particular student or these particular students are behaving in this fashion. Usually, even at the secondary levels, it is due to some very basic reasons. Often, all it takes is understanding these reasons and then executing some simple planning. It is essential that a beginning Special Education teacher have the knowledge and skills to assist students with problematic behavior.

Reasons for Problematic Social Behavior

There are a number of reasons for students to exhibit problematic social behavior, and these are discussed in the sections below.

Students Who Need Attention

Students who seek attention are typically loud, frequently do what they shouldn't be doing (for example, getting out of their seats when they should be working), and generally stir up issues that just do not need to exist in the classroom. These students seem to be the last ones ready for any kind of instruction. They lose materials at inopportune times, blurt out answers, ask silly or unnecessary questions, and often respond negatively to authority. But it is important to remember that this type of behavior is usually the result of students needing to prove that they truly exist.

Strategies for Students Who Need Attention

There are a number of strategies that you can use for students who seek attention, such as the following:

- Give these students responsibilities that the class may covet.

- Create leadership roles for these students.

- Simply find the underlying cause by developing rapport with these students. Pull them aside and discuss why they think they are acting the way they are.

- Don't ignore these students. The behavior will become worse if you do.

- Seek help from members of the multidisciplinary IEP team, such as counselors or the school psychologist.

- Be consistent with these students.

- Model the behavior you want to see. Don't let these students see you frustrated with them.

- When improvement occurs, reinforce this with praise as much as possible.

- Don't exclude or punish out of frustration with these students.

- Pair these students with other students who are role models and will be patient with these students.

Students Who Seek Power

For whatever reason, students who feel a lack of control in their lives seek power by exhibiting negative behaviors, often such a bullying. Bullying is essentially due to a lack of control. Bullies who seek control by hurting others, either verbally or physically, do this to feel a sense of power. This helps them to capture and sustain a sense of control in their lives that most likely is missing.

Strategies for Students Who Seek Power

There are a number of strategies that you can use for students who seek power, such as the following:

- Help students who bully and argue with teachers to recognize that this behavior is due to flaws they possess, and that it is not acceptable behavior.

- Don't be aggressive with bullies. Bullies are familiar with aggression. However, they aren't often familiar with people who are understanding and willing to help, who are willing to take the time to get to know them and show them they truly want to help.

- Address problems of insecurity openly with these students. They need to see that the problem is within them and not others.

- Reinforce appropriate choices and choices made through restraint by utilizing praise.

- Don't show any kind of dislike for these students.

- Provide discipline when necessary and let these students know that bullying is not tolerated in any way. Be firm but fair.

- Provide opportunities for personal success and accomplishments that instill a sense of pride and self-respect. Athletics often help to implant a sense of accomplishment and worth—an identity other than a "tough guy" or a "mean girl."

Dealing with Disrespect

Students who are constantly disrespectful to either adults or other students or both are sometimes the most difficult students to work with. They often illicit a very natural and common response in adults, which is wanting to correct the behavior with only punitive measures.

Why is this so? It's hard, even for adults, to not lose patience with students who constantly reveal disrespect to others—through looks, gestures, sneers, a lack of common courtesy or manners, and through an outright disdain for seemingly everyone, or by swearing or saying things that are considered ugly or ignorant, or by always complaining and being habitually negative.

Keep in mind that these students often have underlying reasons for this kind of behavior. Don't let these students take over a positive environment that you worked very hard to achieve. After all, this is what they truly want. They want everyone around them to be as unhappy as they are, so make every effort to not let this happen, even though it may be easy to become frustrated with these students. Remember *not* to do the following:

- react personally to these students

- reject them due to their behaviors or language

- become overly negative

- lose control and swear back if language is the issue

- react punitively and with open disdain for these students

- ignore them

Instead, try the following methods:

procrastinati

- Address their negative behavior directly, but in a discreet manner.

- Speak directly to the behavior by asking the student what could possibly be wrong, and why she or he seems always to be unhappy and negative. You may discover that there are serious problems either at home or in their personal lives. If this is the case, reach out to the school counselor or school psychologist.

- Give these students opportunities for success and personally gratifying achievement.

- Discover what they can do and if they have any abilities or skills that can be used to amplify any gratitude from doing something well. Advertise this.

- Catch them being positive and praise them for this.

- Discipline them if needed. Being clear and consistent is essential. Tell them certain negative behaviors, such as swearing or lewd behavior, is unacceptable and there will be consequences for this behavior. Again, firm but fair usually works.

Students Who Lack Self-Confidence

The majority of negative behaviors are due to students lacking self-confidence. There are many different reasons for this lack of self-confidence. So many negative behaviors are due to a fundamental lack of feeling worthy enough. Some students constantly cry when confronted, especially at the elementary levels. Some always feel the weight of the world pressing on them. Some are loners and blame everyone and everything but themselves for their shortcomings, lack of success, or unhappiness. Some feel as though everyone dislikes them, and that the teacher hates them or is always out to get them. Many constantly cry "unfair." Yes, some of these behaviors are chalked up to typical behaviors at certain ages of development. However, some behaviors are extreme and stand out, no matter the age of student.

Strategies for Students Who Lack Self-Confidence

Low self-confidence students require some strategy by the Special Education teacher. This is not to say that such students are found solely among Special Education students, because they certainly are not. However, if these students are also students with special needs, their behaviors can be amplified. In fact, these behaviors are often caused by the learning issues themselves. Students with behaviors that directly affect their academic achievement require intervention, especially if these students have learning issues that are in part due to these behaviors. Involve the school counselor/psychologist if you feel that your efforts aren't enough.

Students Who Procrastinate

Students who procrastinate do so for a number of reasons. They may simply lack interest, or they may lack confidence due to learning issues.

Strategies for Students Who Procrastinate

There are a number of strategies for students who procrastinate, such as the following:

- When nagging and prodding don't work, try exhibiting confidence that noncompliant students will finish assignments when given. Shorten the assignments, and try to create them at an interest level that engages these students.

- Show how waiting to complete tasks always hurts in the long run.

- Assign dates for partial and total completion of assignments.

- Talk about having a sense of urgency and the importance of sticking to their word.

- Remember that this behavior could very well be due to an inability to achieve due to learning issues.

Indifferent Learners

Students who seem to not care and who are not out to win any popularity awards with their teachers can be very difficult to teach, especially when they have significant learning gaps that the Special Education teacher is responsible for improving. These students appear to be completely apathetic. They actively seek to disconnect with any kind of learning, and they truly just do not seem to care. These students may not care about improving their ability to read, write, do math, or achieve on assignments, tests, or quizzes.

Sometimes they listen to teacher requests but do not follow through. Most of the time, they simply refuse to do anything that resembles work. This type of learner, as with most Special Education students, is completely fed up with failure or the hard work required to complete assignments that comes much more easily to students without learning needs. Try to remember this as you work with these students.

Strategies for Indifferent Learners

The following are examples of strategies that can be used to help indifferent learners:

- Constant kindness and patience may be a strain when working with students who refuse to work. Do the best you can to keep a positive attitude and show this as much as you can.

- Explore methods to get these students involved and interested in classroom activities.

- Remember that progress may not initiate immediately, but if what you are doing is meaningful and genuine, it will eventually pay off.

- Don't take these students' indifference personally.

- These students may have severe emotional problems. Involve the school counselor or psychologist if you feel that your efforts aren't enough.

Social-Skill Instruction

Positive social interactions can be a frequent challenge for students with learning disabilities and ADHD. According to the National Center for Technology Innovation and the Center for Implementing Technology in Education (2007), students with learning disabilities may interact frequently on an informal basis but lack experience and competence when engaging in formal social interactions. Students who don't have the appropriate social skills to interact in the classroom setting may find themselves isolated or ostracized. When students are excluded from the many social opportunities that are present in typical general education classrooms, they also miss out on academic learning opportunities.

Strategies for Teaching Social Skills

Students with disabilities may struggle with generalizing newly learned social skills to new settings and situations. The following are some examples of ways that Special Education teachers can assist students to generalize social skills:

- Teach new skills in the setting where they will most likely be used. If this is not possible, role-playing can be almost as effective.

- Social skills that are taught in school should be valued by the community as well as by family members.

- Use a variety of resources to teach social skills. Books, videos, games, and software are good examples of effective resources.

Choosing Effective Social-Skill Interventions and Programs

According to the National Association of School Psychologists (2002), social-skill programs that are effective are usually comprised of two elements: a process that uses a behavioral/social learning approach, and a universal set of language and steps that facilitates the learning of new behavior. Effective interventions can be implemented on a school-wide level, on a classroom level, or on an individual level. However, no matter the level, the emphasis is on teaching the desired skill and not on punishment for negative behaviors.

Research indicates that there are general guidelines for facilitating positive social behavior. Learning positive social interactions through normal activities can be very effective, and teachers can take advantage of this by identifying positive behavior and reinforcing it with praise. Another guideline is to attempt to evaluate any environmental obstacles that may interfere with a student's development of positive social behavior. These obstacles can take the form of less-defined routines in schedule and expectations for behavior during certain situations. Evaluating these and changing them accordingly may result in better behavior. Lastly, selected interventions, such as personalized training and instruction, is another guideline for targeting individuals that require more individualized instruction (National Association for School Psychologists, 2002).

Specifically, social skills training and instruction should

- focus on facilitating the desirable behavior as well as eliminating the undesirable behavior.

- emphasize learning and generalization through modeling, role-playing, and coaching.

- use mostly positive strategies, and utilize punitive strategies only when the positive strategies are unsuccessful.

- provide instruction, training, and practice opportunities in a wide variety of settings.

- draw on assessment strategies, including functional assessment.

Behavior Intervention Plans (BIPs) and Functional Behavior Assessments (FBAs)

A behavior intervention plan is a concrete plan designed for any child, but these plans work very well for students with special needs that have developed behaviors that further impede learning. Behavior plans take into account information gathered through conducting a Functional Behavior Assessment (FBA). Behavior Intervention Plans (BIP) convert observations into a plan to help manage a student's behavior. A beginning Special Education teacher in Texas will need to know why and how a BIP is constructed, and then have the knowledge and skills to use a BIP effectively to improve problematic student behavior.

A solid behavior intervention plan starts with information gathered from a functional behavioral assessment. Beginning Special Education teachers will need to know the purpose of an FBA, how it is constructed, what information it contains, and how to use this specialized tool. The Functional Behavioral Assessment is a problem-solving vehicle for student behavior severe enough that it consistently impedes learning. The purpose of the FBA is to identify specific negative behaviors and to help IEP teams select interventions to lessen and eliminate these behaviors. The IEP team will take into account all considerations for the negative behavior. For example, is the behavior due to learning issues? Is the behavior due to personal or home issues?

A Functional Behavioral Assessment looks beyond the behavior and tries to determine the reasons for the behavior. The real purpose of conducting an FBA is to identify significant, social, affective, cognitive, and/or environmental factors associated with specific behaviors. This understanding offers a view into the real reasons for student behavior.

The Overall Purpose of a Functional Behavioral Assessment (FBA)

The overall purpose of a Functional Behavioral Assessment is to determine the following:

- why the student engages in the behavior
- when the student is most likely to demonstrate the behavior
- the situations in which the behavior is least likely to occur

Components of a Functional Behavioral Assessment

A Functional Behavioral Assessment should minimally include the following components:

- identification of the problem behavior
- definition of the behavior in concrete terms

- identification of the factors that contribute to the behavior including affective, environmental, and cognitive factors

- formulation of a hypothesis regarding the general conditions under which a behavior usually occurs and probable consequences that serve to maintain it

Assessment Techniques

A variety of techniques are available to conduct a Functional Behavioral Assessment, including the following:

- Indirect Assessment: structured interviews, review of existing evaluation information

- Direct Assessment: standardized assessments or checklists or observing and recording situational factors surrounding the behavior

- Data Analysis: a comparison and analysis of data to determine whether or not there are patterns associated with the behavior

Behavior Intervention Plans (BIPs)

A Behavior Intervention Plan (BIP) should include the following:

- A BIP should include the baseline measure of the problem behavior, including the frequency, duration, intensity of the targeted behaviors. This information is taken from the functional behavioral assessment.

  - Such baseline data should include data taken across activities, settings, people, and times of the day.

  - The baseline data establishes performance criteria and is used to evaluate intervention criteria.

- Intervention strategies are necessary to alter antecedent events to prevent the occurrence of the behavior, teach alternative and adaptive behaviors to the student, and provide consequences for the targeted inappropriate behavior or behaviors and provide alternative acceptable behaviors to replace them.

A schedule is included so the effectiveness of the interventions, including the frequency, duration, and intensity of the targeted behaviors at scheduled intervals, is measured.

Review Questions

1. What is the most important thing to do when dealing with problem behaviors?

    (A) React immediately

    (B) Analyze the reasons for the behavior

    (C) Isolate the misbehaving student

    (D) Always call the assistant principal for help

    The correct response is (**B**). As a Special Education teacher, being able to step back and analyze why a student is acting out is essential to solving behavior issues. By identifying the cause or the underlying reason for the behavior, appropriate interventions can be planned. (A) is incorrect because sometimes immediate reactions can be emotional or negative. Remaining calm when dealing with behavior issues is essential. (C) is incorrect because isolating a student is only necessary if the student requires a quiet atmosphere to calm down. With most challenging behaviors, applying the preset consequence and moving forward with the class is the best approach. (D) is incorrect because a teacher should be able to deal with the majority of behaviors in the classroom. Administrative intervention should only be necessary for severe behaviors or challenging behaviors that the teacher has not been able to divert any other way.

2. BIP stands for

    (A) Behavior Improvement Program.

    (B) Bonded and Insured Paraprofessional.

    (C) Behavior Intervention Plan.

    (D) Behavior in Individuals Is Positive.

    The correct response is (**C**). BIP stands for Behavior Intervention Plan, and a BIP is required to be part of any Individual Education Program where a student is unable to follow the Student Code of Conduct because of the nature of his or her disability. (A), (B), and (D) are all incorrect choices.

Competency 007

Competency 007

The special education teacher understands and applies knowledge of transition issues and procedures across the life span.

Chapter 7 will focus on Competency 007— transition issues and procedures across the life span.

Whether teaching at the elementary, middle, or high-school level, as a Special Education teacher in Texas, you will need to have a good understanding of what the official transition process is and how it is implemented. As always, it starts with a well-planned, comprehensive method, which is then implemented systematically through the multidisciplinary IEP team over a period of designated time.

Transition Services—An Official Definition

The National Center for Learning Disabilities defines *transition services* as follows:

First, by redefining the term "Transition Services," the IDEA now states that activities focus on improving the academic and functional achievement of the child to facilitate movement from school to post-school activities. Additionally, the definition has been expanded to include a requirement that the transition services be based on the student's strengths, as well as their preferences and interests. The process is expected to be "results-oriented" as opposed to the earlier requirement for "outcome-oriented," signaling a clear intent to ensure that the process includes activities designed to produce success for the individual.

Why Is Transition Planning Important?

According to the 28th Annual Report to Congress on the Implementation of the *Individuals with Disabilities Education Act* (2006), over 30 percent of children with learning disabilities drop out of high school. The 1994 National Longitudinal Transition Study found that only 13 percent of students with learning disabilities (compared to 53 percent of students in the general population) have attended a four-year postsecondary school program within two years of leaving high school.

Concrete action steps must be taken to guide and prepare teens for college, a career, or for independent living. Without this guidance, students with learning disabilities often struggle in high school and beyond.

Official transition planning usually begins at age 14. IDEA '04 has established a clear starting point at 16 years of age. At this age, the IEP team must include official transition planning as a part of the student's IEP. However, IEP teams can still determine earlier ages to begin transition planning.

IDEA '04 includes a statement of required transition services, as follows:

- development of appropriate measurable postsecondary goals based upon age-appropriate transition assessments related to training, education, employment, and, where appropriate, independent living skills

- development of a statement of the transition services (including courses of study) needed to assist the child in reaching those goals

Why Does Transition Need Evaluation?

It is important to evaluate transition for the following reasons:

- work interests of student

- recreation and leisure

- home living

- community participation

- opportunities to learn new things after high school

The results of the evaluation are written in a report. The IEP team uses the report to figure out what the student needs now and what she or he will need later. The IEP has annual goals and short-term instructional objectives for each part of the student's education. The team has to write goals and objectives for transition and figure out what services the student will need to reach the goals. The student's transition plan must be updated every year.

School and Teacher Requirements

Many students need transition services for more than school or work. The school has to teach students to live independently. A student might need help in learning to use the bus system or to go to the doctor. Some students need help in learning how to handle money, join a gym, or make friends. Transition services should help with all of this and more.

Considering that the new planning requirements include goals, schools are required to report on progress. Secondary Special Education teachers are required to monitor transition progress and report to parents by including progress recorded in the IEP. Also, schools continue to be responsible for hiring outside agencies to assist in the postsecondary transition process.

The Special Education Teacher will work closely with the student and family in identifying an individual's needs and areas of interest, in collaborating with the family and other IEP team members, and in working to develop IEP goals for the student. The Special Education teacher will likely be responsible for planning what vocational assessments are needed and will collect information formally and anecdotally about the student's academic strengths, employability skills, interpersonal skills and other skills related to career awareness and aptitude.

Understanding Transition Procedures from Early-Childhood-Intervention Programs to Public School

Early-childhood-intervention programs (ECI) in Texas serve families by providing options for specialized educational and rehabilitative services for children with developmental or learning disabilities from birth to 36 months. Not unlike the individualized education program, the individual family service plan (IFSP) is the thread that pulls services and activities together.

It is important to know that school districts have the option to write an IFSP instead of an IEP for children ages three through five. They are mandated to explain the differences between an IEP and IFSP to parents if they choose to write an IFSP. Part B of the IDEA outlines how school districts must develop the IFSP.

It is valuable for Special Education teachers in Texas to understand that there are some differences between the IFSP and the IEP. Generally, the documents are the same, with the purpose of providing a legal vehicle for specialized services for children with disabilities. However, IFSP requirements are more comprehensive in areas in which functional ability levels are identified, as this is crucial at very young ages. In addition:

- The IFSP has a greater focus on a child's family routines, while the IEP focuses on the child's school routines.

- The IFSP requires quarterly reviews, while the IEP requires annual reviews.

- The IFSP requires that a service coordinator is designated.

- The IFSP requires the addition of family needs.

- According to the IFSP, the least restrictive environments are the home, community settings, or other nonschool environments. Often, the least restrictive environment in the public-school setting is the regular-education classroom. It is important that Special Education teachers understand the transition options afforded to children and families as children transition to different settings and services.

When children are between 27 and 33 months of age, an IFSP team will work with parents to develop transition options and potential services. Early-intervention service coordinators work with families to plan appropriate next steps based on these options and available services. Meanwhile, school districts and Special Education team members plan for students (who may be eligible for public school Special Education services) transitioning from early childhood intervention services.

Public schooling in Texas provides a program option called Preschool Programs for Children with Disabilities (PPCD), which begins for children as they turn three. School districts will have transition conferences for parents three to nine months before the child turns three. Special Education teachers attending transition conferences will need to have knowledge of the following:

- eligibility requirements for PPCD services

- evaluation procedures for determining eligibility for Special Education services

- parental or due-process rights during the transition process

As a whole, Special Education teachers in Texas, working with very young children and their families, will need to be able to plan, facilitate, and implement transition activities. Special Education teachers will also need to be able to assist and advise families during the coordinated transition process that takes place between early-childhood-intervention programs and public school. Understanding how the IFSP is used in this process and how it differs from IEPs is necessary as well.

Outside Agencies

Some of these outside agencies provide services to students, often starting at 16 years of age, but sometimes to student as young as 14 years old. Some of these services include career training, hearing/vision services, travel training, mobility training for the physically and visually impaired, assistance with registering with college disability offices to receive accommodations, and so on.

Outside Agencies—Services

There are a large number of transition services that outside agencies provide for students. Some examples are as follows:

- vocational evaluation and career counseling

- assistive technology

- training programs (Supported Employment, On-the-Job Training, Unpaid Work Experience)

- Postsecondary Education Rehabilitation Transition (PERT)

- access to job-searching tools and resources

- job placement and job retention

- follow-along services after job placement

- services for students with brain injury

- deaf and hard of hearing services

- improved independence and employability

- prevocational assessments

- independent living evaluation and training

- vocational counseling, evaluation, and training

- medical rehabilitation services

- driver education

- student internships

Overall, as in other states, the Texas Special Education teacher is required to assist with transition planning by acting as the facilitator and guide for students and their families.

Review Questions

1. Who is involved in the transition process for Special Education students in Texas?

   (A) Students, family, Special Education teachers, general education teachers, and administrators

   (B) Parents and the primary Special Education teacher only

   (C) Transition agency personnel

   (D) Students and Counselors only

The correct response is (**A**). Transition planning involves a number of people to ensure that the interests and needs of the student are met. First and foremost, the student is involved if at all possible as it is his or her postschool life that is being

CHAPTER
7

planned. Parents, family members, special and general education teachers, and administrators must all be involved just as they are with an ARD. (B) is incorrect because it leaves out a number of the required participants, including the student. (C) is incorrect because, while agency representatives may be involved if permission is obtained by the family or an adult student, they are not the sole participants. (D) is incorrect because transition planning involves a much wider team than just the student and counselor.

2.   In Texas, transition planning is expected to begin at age

   (A)   12.

   (B)   13.

   (C)   14.

   (D)   15.

The correct response is (**C**). While IDEA 2004 makes 16 the legal age when transition planning must begin, in Texas, the expectation is that it will begin by age 14 so that high school course choices can be considered. (A), (B), and (D) are all incorrect, as 14 is the agreed-upon age to begin transition planning in Texas.

PART III: DOMAIN III

Promoting Student Achievement in English Language Arts and Reading and Mathematics

Promoting Student Achievement in English Language Arts and Reading and Mathematics

English Language Arts and Reading Achievement

According to the National Assessment Education Progress Report by the National Center for Education Statistics (2005), 38 percent of fourth graders and 29 percent of eighth graders are reading below basic levels. Since 2005, these numbers have improved somewhat, but not enough. Despite intense efforts to improve literacy achievement for all students in our public schools, we still have a long way to go. This fact can be especially sobering for someone seeking certification in Special Education. However, these numbers should not whittle away at your fortitude. Remember that people who choose to teach Special Education usually have strong reasons for doing so; and, as we've said, they are usually not the faint of heart.

These numbers are a reminder that excellent Special Education teachers are needed now more than ever. The TExES evaluation process reflects the need for the very best in this field, because, by now, teachers seeking certification in Special Education are quite aware of the difficulties ahead of them, but they plow forward nonetheless, and those behind the certification exams are aware of this.

Mathematics Achievement

In relation to mathematics, research shows that a student who has teachers with the knowledge and skills needed to teach mathematics effectively is more likely to be able to close the achievement gaps that he or she experiences and be prepared as an individual for success in work and life. However, the number of certified math teachers who also have Special Education certifications isn't high enough.

Often, teaching math to Special Education students centers on teaching rote mathematics and basic life-skills math. This should not be the case. As a beginning Special Education teacher in the state of Texas, you will be required to understand up-to-date research on the best practices for teaching mathematics to students with learning disabilities.

This understanding and required skill set needs to be based on accommodations and interventions so that students with learning disabilities have access to the best possible mathematics instruction available—in other words, no different than students without learning disabilities.

Domain III addresses Competencies 008 and 009.

Competency 008: The special education teacher promotes students' performance in English language arts and reading.

The beginning teacher:

    A. Applies knowledge of developmental processes associated with communication systems (e.g., listening, speaking, writing), including emergent and preliteracy skills, and knows how to provide a variety of opportunities for students with disabilities to learn communication skills.

    B. Knows how to use a variety of assessment practices and procedures to plan and implement instruction in English language arts and reading that is responsive to the strengths and needs of individuals with disabilities.

    C. Knows the nature and stages of literacy development, and various contexts and methods for promoting students' literacy development.

    D. Applies knowledge of phonological and phonemic awareness and strategies for promoting the phonological and phonemic awareness of students with disabilities.

    E. Applies knowledge of the alphabetic principle and word analysis skills (e.g., decoding, structural analysis, sight-word vocabulary) and knows how to provide students with disabilities with systematic instruction that promotes their ability to apply the alphabetic principle and word analysis and decoding skills.

F. Applies knowledge of reading fluency and the relationship between reading fluency and reading comprehension and knows how to provide students with disabilities with systematic instruction that promotes their reading fluency.

G. Knows the importance of comprehension in reading and knows how to provide students with disabilities with instruction in the use of skills and strategies (e.g., critical/creative thinking) to promote their reading comprehension.

H. Knows how to provide students with disabilities with systematic instruction to develop skills in writing conventions and competence in written communication.

I. Knows the relationship between learning and effective study, critical-thinking and inquiry skills and knows how to use various methods and strategies to teach students with disabilities to apply study, critical-thinking and inquiry skills.

J. Knows skills for interpreting, analyzing, evaluating and providing visual images and messages and knows how to provide systematic instruction that helps students with disabilities learn to interpret, analyze, evaluate and create visual images and messages in various media and technologies.

Competency 009: The special education teacher promotes students' performance in mathematics.

The beginning teacher:

A. Knows how to use a variety of assessment methods to monitor the mathematical understanding of students with disabilities and adapt mathematics instruction to address individual strengths and needs.

B. Knows how to provide mathematics instruction that is based on principles of children's learning and development and that reflects recognition of common misconceptions and sources of error in mathematics.

C. Knows how individuals learn and develop mathematical skills, procedures and concepts.

D. Understands numbers, number systems and their structure, operations and algorithms and quantitative reasoning, and uses various instructional strategies and resources, including technology, to help students with disabilities understand and apply related content and skills.

E. Understands patterns, relations, functions and algebraic reasoning and analysis and uses various instructional strategies and resources, including technology, to help students with disabilities understand and apply related content and skills.

F. Understands geometry, spatial reasoning and measurement concepts and principles, and uses various instructional strategies and resources, including technology, to help students with disabilities understand and apply related content and skills.

G. Understands principles and applications of probability and statistics and uses various instructional strategies and resources, including technology, to help students with disabilities understand and apply related content and skills.

H. Applies knowledge of methods, strategies and resources for teaching students with disabilities to engage in mathematical reasoning and problem solving, apply mathematics in a variety of contexts and communicate mathematically.

Competency 008

Competency 008

The special education teacher promotes students' performance in English language arts and reading.

Chapter 8 will focus on Competency 008—promoting students' performance in English language arts and reading.

The TExES EC–12 assessment will evaluate the 008 competency by testing content that a beginning special education teacher should know about literacy achievement and intervention for those with learning disabilities that may inhibit progress in this area.

Research-Based Reading Intervention Practices

Modeling

Children of all ages observe behaviors displayed by adults and peers and engage in imitating that behavior. Therefore, it is important for parents and teachers to model appropriate reading behavior.

Repetition of Practice

When Special Education teachers provide several opportunities for students to engage in repeated practice of reading skills, students are more likely to acquire, maintain, and generalize skills. Special Education teachers should create opportunities to practice skills repeatedly. They must ensure that students are practicing correct reading behavior, such as the accurate reading of words. This accurate word-reading repetition is monitored closely, often in an one-on-one instructional situation or in very small groups, so that words are read correctly and fluency is repeated. If students grow tired of reading the same words and passages over and over again, it means that this technique is working. So, keep it up!

Phonemic Awareness

Often students, especially younger ones, have difficulty with decoding words because they have specific issues identifying individual sounds that make up spoken and written words. This is a deficiency in phonemic awareness. When students show signs of this type of reading and/or language problem, phonemic identification skills are the instructional target.

Strategies to Improve Phonemic Awareness

The following strategies are useful for improving students' phonemic awareness:

- sound-manipulation activities

- word-segmentation activities

- structural-analysis activities

- vowel- and consonant-repetition activities

- vowel-identification software and Internet reading sites

The Alphabetic Principle

Research strongly supports explicit teaching of phonemic awareness as a means of easing students need to acquire the alphabetic principle. Letter-sound relationships help students with reading needs to identify words with relative ease. When students can't decode words or make letter-sound connections, phonics needs to be explicitly taught. This is one of the most crucial responsibilities of the elementary Special Education teacher. Teaching phonic skills to younger students with learning disabilities will help them to bridge the reading gap at older ages.

Fluency

By building sight-word achievement through repetition and practice and then explicit instruction of phonemic awareness skills, combined with constant repetition, fluency will improve. This is the next skill set needed for overall literacy achievement for students with reading disabilities.

Strategies to Improve Fluency

The following strategies can be used to help improve students' fluency:

- traditional sight-word/word practice drills with flashcards

- traditional simple-sentence practice drills with flashcards

- oral practice through prompting with flashcards (for example, show the word and prompt students to say the word)

- repetition of controlled reading, orally and silently

Vocabulary and Comprehension

When students have difficulty understanding and deriving meaning from text, it is the responsibility of the Special Education teacher to provide instruction in comprehension. Students with reading disabilities almost always have difficulties understanding text, meanings of words or concepts, and are not able to acquire information from content reading in subjects such as science and social studies.

When addressing vocabulary instruction, the Special Education teacher needs to teach segments of words before, during, and after just about every reading text students use. Vocabulary and overall textual comprehension, whether the text is fiction or content-related, are interconnected.

The Special Education teacher will need to understand how to use specific materials and strategies to provide vocabulary and comprehension instruction as well as provide accommodations during instruction where information learning is the sole objective.

Strategies to Improve Vocabulary and Comprehension

The following strategies can be used to improve students' vocabulary and comprehension:

- Use semantic webs for a variety of vocabulary and textual comprehension instruction.

- Comprehension strategies such as utilizing background knowledge, questioning, summarizing, inferring, and rereading text, are at the foundational basis for teaching reading comprehension.

- Prereading, during reading, and postreading strategies should be taught separately in direct instruction and practiced across many different learning situations and environments.

- Direct instruction in decoding skills (for example, using context clues, structural analysis, and compensatory strategies such as word finding skills), and using resources such as digital dictionaries and word processing-identification software is essential.

New Special Education teachers may need to learn and be able to use different reading programs. There are many out there. The ones you choose will depend largely on what your first assignment is and the investments made for struggling readers. These programs come designed on solid research, so jump in and learn them. They will improve your professional knowledge and skills.

Writing Instruction for Students with Learning Disabilities

The majority of students with language-processing learning disabilities have writing difficulties as well as reading difficulties. For example, students with phonemic-awareness deficits often find it difficult to spell words correctly and to decode them when reading. Literacy development in language, reading, and writing are interconnected. It's seldom that children who have difficulty reading at grade level don't also have difficulty writing.

Beginning Special Education teachers in Texas are required to have a strong understanding of the different kinds of instructional strategies that have emerged from research and should be able to demonstrate how they're used in the classroom.

For struggling writers, even short writing tasks, are often insurmountable challenges. The effort that is required to write sentences that honor the laundry list of standard English conventions, are coherent in message while remembering what punctuation is needed and where, while sustaining attention to task, can be downright overwhelming. Overcoming these factors while providing sustained, effective writing instruction is challenging for both inexperienced and experienced Special Education teachers. Furthermore, writing has concise and measurable results. There is no hope to drift through writing assignments, feigning engagement. Unfortunately, this is why avoidance or refusal often occurs. As a result, children with language-learning disabilities struggle even greater as they get older because of avoidance at earlier grade levels.

Common Writing Problems for Students with Learning Disabilities

Compared to their nonlearning disabled peers, students with learning disabilities write with more mechanical errors—spelling, punctuation, and capitalization errors. Spelling errors are the most prevalent. Errors in grammar usually include subject/verb agreement. Fewer words are often used, and sentences are simpler with less variety. A general lack of cohesiveness is observed in comparison. Research shows that older students produce expository writing that displays frequent mechanical errors, irrelevancies, redundancies, and a lack of organization and coherence.

Effective Writing Instruction and Practices for Struggling Writers

Effective writing instruction that is adapted for students with learning disabilities should be based on explicit skill instruction. At the elementary levels, devoting instruction to punctuation, phonics, and word lists for spelling, and to handwriting for struggling writers helps to establish and strengthen a basic skill foundation, which helps to build confidence in the student. Reteaching skills through explicit instruction and multiple practices remains the most effective approach to improving the writing skills of learning-disabled students. Assistive technology that bypasses text transcription difficulties (for example, speech to text software, which allows students to focus on skill practice without the barrier of handwriting) is highly useful.

Today, there is an array of available assistive-writing software programs. Invest time and discover which programs fit the needs of your students. These assistive-writing programs can be very useful for boosting interest and sustaining motivation. You will find many programs for conventions practice as well as for improving compositional writing at the middle- and high-school levels. These programs help to craft argumentative, persuasive, informative, narrative, and expository pieces and provide assistance with planning, organizing, revising, and editing. Integrating such technology—combined with effective, research-based instructional practices that focus on explicit instruction and then sustained basic skill practice—continue to prove the most effective methodological approach to writing instruction for students with learning disabilities.

Teaching Study Skills

Sandra Kerka ("Teaching Study Skills ...," 2007) defines study skills as learning strategies that facilitate the processing of information. Study skills help to organize and process information and in remembering what is learned. Research indicates that study skills are most effective when students use them to devise their own methods of organizing their studying. According to Kerka, there is a wide range of behaviors that students can perform before, during, and after learning to help retain information presented in the classroom, as outlined below:

- **Preparing to Learn:** personal discipline, self-management, organizational skills, and self-monitoring

- **Retaining Learned Material:** note-taking, outlining, listening, and text learning

- **Applying Learned Material:** test-taking skills, and oral or written demonstration of what has been learned

Kerka (2007) states that research clearly shows that it is important for teachers to provide explicit instruction in learning strategies and study skills to students with learning and behavioral disorders. She sums up the research this way: "Teaching skills in planning, organizing, and managing time will help students to learn more efficiently and independently. Schedules, to-do lists, and learning contracts are examples of strategies that special education teachers can use to help students take control of their time and develop self-discipline."

Teaching Visual Literacy Skills to Support Reading

According to Flaum (2012), visual literacy is the ability of students to use, analyze, and think critically about visual images and their meaning. Research supports the importance for integrating visual literacy in classrooms, especially for children with learning needs or second-language learners who experience difficulty with traditional print media.

Visual strategies that support reading comprehension of print media—such as creating comic strips, drawings, collages, illustrations, or paintings—are engaging and offer unique methods for students to demonstrate their understanding of text. Technology, such as utilizing drawing and photo software, helps students to engage with text and represent comprehension and thinking in unique ways.

Some suggestions for incorporating graphics technology into instruction are as follows:

- incorporate multimedia depictions of information that is learned and read

- incorporate graphics, images, sounds, animation, and pictures with written composition

Visual literacy instruction can support traditional reading comprehension. Utilizing technology to present information or demonstrate learning coincides with our increasingly visual world (Flaum, 2012).

▮ Review Questions

1. A Special Education teacher wants to assess her students' fluency. What is NOT an area she will assess when listening to her students read orally?

    (A) Rate

    (B) Expression

    (C) Accuracy

    (D) Idioms

    The correct response is (**D**). An idiom is a combination of words that has a figurative meaning (for example, "It's raining cats and dogs."). While idioms are a source of trouble for students with disabilities and for English learners, they are not an area related to fluency. (A), (B), and (C) are incorrect as they are all areas charted in fluency assessments. Fluency is a combination of rate or speed, accuracy in pronunciation, and oral expression.

2. Which of the following instructional strategies would be used to activate prior knowledge?

    (A) Having students complete a KWL chart before reading a book on snakes

    (B) Asking students to summarize the book they just read

    (C) Having students write a letter about their favorite book of all time

    (D) Guiding students to find all the instances of an author using a targeted vocabulary word

The correct response is (**A**). A KWL chart has students list what they already "Know" about a topic, what they "Want" to know about the topic, and what they "Learned" after they read about the topic. It is an excellent way to activate prior knowledge about a nonfiction topic as students fill out the K and W columns before they read. (B) is not the correct answer because summarization occurs after reading, not before. (C) is not the correct answer because it involves reflecting on and writing about books that were memorable, but it does not specifically activate knowledge for a book the teacher is planning to have the students read. (D) is an incorrect answer because it is a vocabulary acquisition strategy and is not focused on having students think about the topic of a book prior to reading it.

3. One of the most powerful motivators for engaging reluctant readers in books is

   (A) fear of staying after school.

   (B) round-robin reading.

   (C) highlighting vocabulary words.

   (D) giving students a choice of what they read.

The correct response is (**D**). Choice is a powerful motivator for all students, including reluctant readers. When students get to choose a book or article and can select based on their own interests, they have a built-in reason to persevere as they work to read the text. (A) is not the correct answer because punitive measures are rarely motivational, especially for reluctant readers who frequently also exhibit challenging behaviors as a way of masking their academic difficulties. (B) is incorrect because "round-robin" reading is actually demotivating for struggling readers who do not like being embarrassed when they cannot read well out loud. (C) is not the correct answer because, while vocabulary acquisition is an important part of learning to read, calling attention to a number of words the student may not know can be discouraging.

4. A research-based technique for helping students in the prewriting stage is

   (A) circling spelling errors.

   (B) providing graphic organizers.

   (C) having them memorize the steps for writing an essay.

   (D) providing a punctuation chart.

The correct response is (**B**). Graphic organizers are powerful tools for helping students organize different types of writing. These visual tools help students lay out their thoughts in an organized way so that they are ready to write. (A) is an incorrect answer because identifying spelling errors is a part of the editing stage, not the prewriting stage. (C) is not the correct answer since memorizing the general steps for writing an essay does not help students put together specific thoughts on what they want to write about. (D) is not the correct answer because addressing punctuation is a part of the editing stage, not the prewriting stage.

5.   A seventh-grade teacher works with students who failed the STAAR® reading assessment the previous year. Many of these students have learning disabilities. The teacher has the students work in pairs to create a picture that shows the meaning of a selected word from the story they just read. Partners then share their drawings with the class. What is the purpose of this activity?

(A)   Sight-word recognition

(B)   Symbolic representation of text

(C)   Vocabulary acquisition

(D)   Phonemic awareness

The correct response is (**C**). Pairing a word with a visual image is a powerful strategy to help students remember the word's meaning. By having the students work in pairs and create the drawing themselves, the teacher is helping the students "own" the word and add it to their vocabulary. (A) is not the correct answer because the words selected for an activity like this would not be sight words; they would be words with a clearer meaning. (B) is not correct because the students are not creating pictures of the story itself. Rather, the pictures are related to the specific meanings of the words. (D) is not the correct answer because phonemic awareness is an early emergent-reader skill where students are assessed on their recognition of individual letter and rhyming sounds.

.OS X 100 %.

3/8

3 ÷ 8 = .0378 X 100 = 38%

37.5%

Competency 009

Competency 009

The special education teacher promotes students' performance in mathematics.

Chapter 9 will focus on Competency 009—promoting students' performance in mathematics.

Disabilities and Math Performance

According to (Steedly et al., 2008), several areas of learning disability connect to math performance. Visual processing, visual memory, and visual-spatial abilities, all contribute to the ability to do math. The National Research Council has identified the following abilities as paramount to mathematics achievement:

- **Conceptual Understanding:** comprehension of mathematical concepts, operations, and relations

- **Procedural Fluency:** skill in carrying out procedures accurately, efficiently, and appropriately

- **Strategic Competence:** ability to formulate, represent, and solve mathematical problems

- **Adaptive Reasoning:** a capacity for logical thought, reflection, explanation, and justification

Utilizing Formative Assessment for Math Instruction

In a publication by the National Association of State Directors of Special Education (2005), formative assessment is defined as "a process used by teachers and students during instruction that provides feedback to adjust ongoing teaching and learning to improve students' achievement of intended instructional outcomes." According to the Department of Education's Formative Assessment Probes: Math Trailblazers (2011–2012), effective use of formative assessment in mathematics instruction requires the following tenets:

- **Learning Progressions:** Learning progressions contain clearly articulated subgoals of the ultimate learning goal.

- **Learning Goals**: Learning goals and criteria for success are clearly identified and communicated to students.

- **Descriptive Feedback:** Students receive evidence-based feedback linked to the intended instructional outcomes and criteria for success.

- **Self- and Peer-Assessment:** Substantial student self- and peer-assessments are important for providing students an opportunity to think metacognitively about their learning.

- **Collaboration:** Practitioners establish and support a classroom culture in which teachers and students are partners in learning.

Also, an effective system of assessment gathers and uses data that informs decision-making about the following:

- supporting student learning

- identifying students' strengths and weaknesses

- assessing and informing instructional practices

- assessing the effectiveness of the mathematics standards and curriculum

Quality assessment is when teachers gather student work and materials in order to gauge and advance student learning. This is at the heart of formative assessment in mathematics instruction. Special Education teachers teaching mathematics in Texas must be able to gather, evaluate, and interpret data in order to modify and improve instruction. The overall goal is to assess how one is doing by interpreting your instructional planning, implementation, and assessment so that it is better than it was before assessment occurred.

According to "A Vision of Effective Student Assessment in Mathematics" (2008), this concept is converted into practice when the following happen:

- The mathematics that is taught and how it is assessed are aligned with each other.

- Students' answers, solutions, errors, questions, explanations, homework, quizzes and tests are seen as components of the formative assessment data that are used to make decisions about moving forward, reteaching, intervening, and addressing individual needs.

- Formative assessment are designed, adopted, and/or adapted to generate meaningful evidence of learning.

Progress Monitoring

Monitoring and evaluating students' learning progress allow Special Education teachers to make needed adjustments in instruction. According to "Differentiating Math Instruction so Everyone Learns" (2012), these questions should be asked continually—before, during, and after mathematics instruction:

- Is the student making progress?

- What does the student need to learn next?

- How solid is the student's understanding?

- Does the student need more work with a specific concept?

- Is the student having difficulty maintaining and utilizing specific concepts?

- What misconceptions does the student have?

- Where are the learning gaps?

- Is the student's knowledge incomplete? If so, what is missing?

Differentiated Instruction

Once formative assessment has been conducted, it can be used to create flexible groups for instruction. This is at the heart of differentiated learning. This allows the Special Education teacher to target instruction that is based on academic and developmental levels. Small instructional groups are very effective in differentiating according to strengths and needs. Based on formative assessment, flexible groups can be created to address individual needs.

Targeting Instruction Based on Cognitive Needs

Targeting instruction based on cognitive demand should also be considered. According to "A Vision for Effective Student Assessment in Mathematics" (2008), understanding cognitive demand allows the Special Education teacher to target individual needs. In addition, targeting instruction is more beneficial when it is coupled with adjusting the level of cognitive demand. There is strong evidence for maintaining an increased level of cognitive demand (meaning slightly higher than the skill/knowledge level of students) despite their knowledge and skill gaps. Increasing the level of cognitive demand in appropriate ways increases ownership. The key is to find the appropriate level of cognitive demand and then increase it at appropriate times and places in the curriculum. This is done through conducting effective and ongoing formative assessment.

Determining and adjusting levels of cognitive demand in mathematics instruction is similar to determining and adjusting learning levels based on Bloom's Taxonomy of Cognitive Levels. This is often used for gauging depth of learning in language-based learning; however, it works just as well for mathematical learning.

According to "Differentiating Math Instruction so Everyone Learns" (2012), it is important to keep the following in mind:

- **Lower Levels of Cognitive Demand:** This includes recalling, explaining, reciting, and performing mathematical facts, information, and computation.

- **Medium Levels of Cognitive Demand:** This involves application and analysis of mathematical information, procedures, understanding, comparing and classifying.

- **Higher Levels of Cognitive Demand:** This includes evaluation and synthesis of mathematical thinking and reasoning to problem-solve and create new thinking and ideas.

Teaching Number Sense and Operations

According to Texas Essential Knowledge and Skills (TEKS) , students at the early elementary levels (K–2) use number sense to solve problems requiring precision, estimation, and reason. Through understanding number sense, by the end of second grade, students in Texas will be able to add and subtract numbers efficiently and be able to use numbers accurately during computation problems.

So, what is "number sense"? Bresser and Holtzman, in their *Developing Number Sense: Grades 3–6* (1999), describe it as "understanding the relationships between and among numbers; having the ability to think flexibly about numbers and to break numbers apart and put them back together; being familiar with the properties of single-digit numbers and using this information to calculate efficiently using larger numbers; having the ability to manipulate numbers in their head; and having effective ways to estimate."

Teaching Number Sense, Operations, Reasoning, and Place Value

According to Anghileri (2006), assessment tasks of today have been developed to match the changing requirements of the twenty-first century. This equates to children having to understand numbers and numbers sense beyond just calculation, comparison, and basic place value. Assessments today include complex problem-solving and reasoning, and this is no different for Texas. The Numeracy Taskforce reports that children need an in-depth understanding of numeracy. At the primary level, they should

- have a sense of number size and number systems.

- know by heart number facts and number tables.

- know number facts and tables so that they can compute mentally a variety of mathematical tasks.

- calculate accurately, both mentally and on paper.

Children are expected to extract information from charts, graphs, and visual representations of data of all kinds to perform calculations, discover patterns, and reason and problem-solve. Making appropriate choices about proper procedures is also expected and is being taught at early ages (Anghileri, 2006).

Strategies for Teaching Numbers and Operations

Some strategies that support children in the area of numbers and operations include the following:

- Tally charts and manipulatives are very useful for counting and comparing place values such as number lines, counters, base-10 blocks, or shapes of any kind.

- Any materials that have "real-to-life" connections such as money, time, any kind of measuring devices, toys, balls, or games are often effective.

- Model the use of written numerals, and encourage children to use them and practice them as often as possible.

Teaching strategies for operations, patterns and measurement, geometry and spatial sense, probability and statistics, and for establishing statistical thinking are outlined below.

Teaching Strategies for Operations

Students learn the basic patterns of operations through effective counting. Using manipulatives, number lines, and counting exercises in various ways helps students to identify patterns in numbers. Understanding that the operations are related to one another is developed through these instructional exercises. According to "A Guide to Effective Instruction" (2003), there are several general strategies for teaching operations:

- Problem-solving should be a focus.

- Different ways to solve computational problems is effective.

- Using manipulatives or pictorial strategies is effective.

- Discovering independent strategies and encouraging this is important.

- Open-ended probes and questioning allows students to think beyond basic computation.

- Model effective reasoning and problem-solving strategies and procedures.

Teaching Patterns and Measurement

Using manipulatives to investigate number patterns provides a solid basis for teaching more complex patterns where problem-solving and quantitative reasoning is involved on higher cognitive levels. According to "A Guide to Effective Instruction" (2003), the following are some strategies for teaching patterns and measurement:

- Using music and movement for conceptualizing pattern is very effective.

- Using number lines, charts, counters, and base-10 blocks are effective resources for conceptualizing and then practicing patterns.

- Counters such as money, beads, buttons, or any kind of familiar objects are good resources to teach patterns.

- Arrays help children to visualize patterns.

- Measurement activities with visual quantities such as liquids, amounts, weights, and distances help children to conceptualize measurement.

Teaching Geometry and Spatial Sense

Developing spatial understanding at early ages helps set the stage for improved math achievement at older ages. This helps to internalize more complex concepts in geometry as well. According to "A Guide to Effective Instruction" (2003), some strategies for teaching geometry and spatial sense at the primary level include the following:

- Use geoboards to create different shapes.

- Build structures in three dimensions as activities.

- Use books, puzzles, and environmental awareness of geometric shapes.

- Manipulatives of all sorts are useful (for example, blocks, spheres, grids, and drawings).

- Use software as much as possible that reinforces working with and understanding geometric shapes and spatial sense.

Teaching Probability and Statistics

According to Mary Metz in the *Journal of Statistics Education* (2010), statistics education is no longer relegated just to the few fields where data crunching is prevalent. In today's world of prolific and seemingly perpetual information processing, the gigantic amount of available data affects the decisions we make on different levels—politically, economically, personally, and as consumers.

In this country, statistics education is becoming an increasingly important part of mathematics education and in our daily lives and careers. In order to achieve statistical literacy by adulthood, statistical education must start at the elementary school level.

According to the National Council of Teachers of Mathematics, the data analysis standards enable students do the following:

- formulate questions that can be addressed through relevant data collection and analysis

- select and use appropriate statistical methods

- develop and evaluate inference-based data

- understand and apply basic concepts of probability

Strategies that Establish Statistical Thinking

The following are strategies the help to establish statistical thinking:

- Teach how to ask appropriate questions: How many? What is the most? What is the most popular?

- Model methods of reflecting on questions to formulate ideas about them before and after data collection.

- Teach methods for collecting data (for example, drawing on grid paper, pictorials, manipulatives, and so on).

- Teach visual methods for representing data in various ways.

- Teach methods for interpreting visual representations of data.

- Teach how to distinguish and interpret graphs of different kinds (for example, circle graphs, line graphs, bar graphs, and so on).

- Help students to think about the appropriate questions that stimulate good inferences from data.

- Explore probability by teaching language that supports it (for example, chance, certain, possible, impossible, predict, and so on).

- Use manipulatives to show probability (for example, fraction shapes, counters, blocks, and so on).

- Make predictions based on probability through exercises that use manipulatives.

Review Questions

1. A sixth-grade student with ADHD has been struggling on his mathematics tests particularly on questions that involve solving complex word problems. The most effective strategy to teach this student would be

    (A) benchmarking.

    (B) highlighting vocabulary.

    (C) fact automaticity.

    (D) verbalization.

    The correct response is (**D**). Verbalization is a method that helps students think through the stages of solving a math program, slowing down to say each step aloud as they take it. For students with ADHD who are often impulsive, this method can help them self-regulate the problem-solving process. (A) is incorrect because benchmarking is an assessment procedure. (B) is incorrect because highlighting vocabulary is a technique that helps students think about which operation(s) to use in solving a word problem, but that is only one part of solving a complex word problem. (C) is incorrect because there is no sign that the student does not know his or her operational facts. The issue seems to be with figuring out what to do to solve a complex word problem.

2. A Special Education teacher wants to scaffold mathematics instruction for a group of students with learning disabilities. What kind of examples should the Special Education teacher show students first?

(A)   Abstract examples

(B)   Concrete and real-life examples

(C)   Graphic examples

(D)   Pictorial representations

The correct response is (**B**). Scaffolding learning involves helping students understand mathematical concepts with the most concrete examples first and then moving to the abstract examples. The first step should involve concrete, real-life examples. (A) is incorrect because abstract examples can be the hardest to grasp and should be the last part of a scaffolded sequence. (C) and (D) are incorrect because graphic or pictorial representations are the middle step in a scaffolded lesson.

3.   Mrs. Takei, a third-grade teacher, maintains mathematics performance folders for each of her students. She frequently uses these folders at parent-teacher conferences and individual tutoring sessions. For her Special Education students, she takes these folders to the students' ARDs. The kind of assessment that these performance folders represent is

(A)   formative.

(B)   standardized.

(C)   summative.

(D)   diagnostic.

The correct response is (**A**). An individual performance folder is composed of a collection of a student's work over the course of a school year. Performance folders are great tools for showing student growth over time and for assessing how students are progressing in their goals during the year. This makes them formative assessments. (B) is not correct because performance folders involve teacher judgment. They are not standardized against other students' performances. (C) is not correct because performance folders represent work over time, not just at the end of a unit. (D) is incorrect because performance folders are created as the school year progresses, not at the beginning of the year to show students' baseline skills.

Use this 100-unit square to answer the following two questions.

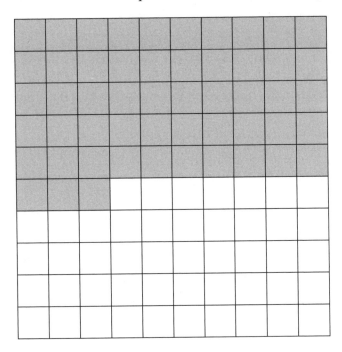

4.   Which of the following number sentences best represents the information in the unit square above?

    (A) $100 + 53 = 153$

    (B) $100 - 35 = 65$

    (C) $100 - 47 = 53$

    (D) $50 + 50 = 100$

The correct response is (**C**). Shading in a 100-unit square is one way to help students understand subtraction. In this case, there are 100 squares total and 47 of them are not shaded. That leaves 53 shaded squares. Therefore, the number sentence $100 - 47 = 53$ represents this information best. (A) is incorrect because there are only 100 squares showing, not 153. (B) and (D) are incorrect because there are 53 shaded squares and 47 unshaded ones, not 65 and 35 or 50 and 50.

5.   In decimal form, the percentage of the 100-unit square that is shaded is

    (A)   0.47.

    (B)   5.3.

(C)   0.053.

(D)   0.53.

The correct response is (**D**). 53 percent of the square is shaded, and this is represented as 0.53 in decimal form, which is read as 53 hundredths. (A) is incorrect because 0.47 represents the unshaded squares, not the shaded ones. (B) is incorrect because 5.3 would indicate 530 shaded squares, not 53. (C) is incorrect because 0.053 would represent 5.3 shaded squares out of 100, not 53.

PART IV: DOMAIN IV

Foundations and Professional Roles and Responsibilities

PART IV: DOMAIN IV

Foundations and Professional Roles and Responsibilities

Part IV: Domain IV consists of three chapters, which focus on Competencies 10, 11, and 12. These chapters discuss the historical events that have led to litigation and the construction of laws that have formed the modern basis for public Special Education in this country. A discussion of the importance of professional collaboration, communication with families of students with disabilities, codes of ethics for Special Education teachers and anyone teaching in the state of Texas, continuum of services, and prevalent models of service delivery are the basis of Domain IV.

However, before this discussion, it is important to reflect on the decisions that have led you to this point: the point of needing to take the EC–12 test to become certified as a Special Education teacher in the state of Texas. It's also important to reflect on what this may mean within the context of Special Education as a whole, its history, its current state, and how you may fit into this discipline.

As a Special Education teacher in Texas, you will join the many who currently teach in this discipline, as well as the thousands who have taught before you. You've chosen to become a Special Education teacher! And chances are that your reason for choosing this discipline is similar to those of others. A commonality is having an understanding of the importance of helping children with learning and/or physical disabilities and wanting to have a part in improving these children's lives. You will be joining a smaller niche group of teachers who possess a common reason for teaching Special Education, and who have a unique skill set that separates this discipline from mainstream or regular pedagogical practices.

So, why this choice? Maybe you've experienced learning struggles yourself, or maybe you know someone close to you that has. The majority of Special Education teachers report choosing this discipline for more personal rather than professional reasons. Whatever your reason, this choice is a good one.

Why is it a good choice? Historically speaking, you may understand that children and adults with physical and intellectual disabilities were widely discriminated against until as recently as the 1970s. Or maybe you are or have been a witness to discriminatory attitudes and practices that continue to this day. Maybe you understand that people with disabilities, or what is deemed as handicapped, have been discriminated against for thousands of years. It's not just a modern or twenty-first-century issue. Maybe you understand that, until as recently as within the past three decades, people with physical and mental disabilities were institutionalized. They were forced to live in places that often became their prisons—places where cruelty, abuse, and, at the very least, indifference, were common practices. These practices stemmed from bureaucratic laziness and a lack of morality.

In order to teach as a Special Education teacher, it is important to understand the beginning and evolution of the history of the rules, laws, philosophies, and models that have shaped current practices. This will help you to maintain a positive perspective that helps this journey forward.

But why is this understanding so important? The answer to this question lies with the past. For many years, the history of Special Education in the United States was bleak. During moments of doubt, it helps to keep in mind that Special Education teachers perform duties that not only are extremely helpful to children with learning disabilities, but to their families as well.

This was not always the case. In the past, many children with disabilities were denied access to public education altogether. In 1970, for example, U.S. schools educated only one in five children with disabilities. In fact, many states had laws that *excluded* children with major disabilities such as deafness and blindness, as well as intellectual disabilities. Throughout most of the history of public schools in America, services to children with disabilities were minimal and were provided at the discretion of local school districts. Up until the mid-1970s, laws in most states allowed school districts to deny enrollment of any students considered "educable." Some children with disabilities were admitted to public schools but were placed in regular education, with no services. Others were placed in special programs in public schools, though the services provided to them were inadequate, to say the least.

It was only after Public Law 94-142, or the IDEA, became effective in 1978 (and, in several states, after federal and state court cases) that the notion of "education for everyone," became a popular practice. Currently, each year, more than 6.5 million children with disabilities have access to free and appropriate education. This is well worth the money spent considering that the alternative for students with disabilities is very little quality education or institutionalization.

Domain IV addresses Competencies 010 to 012.

Competency 010: The special education teacher understands the philosophical, historical, and legal foundations of special education.

The beginning teacher:

A. Knows the historical foundations of special education, major contributors to the literature, major legislation relevant to knowledge and practice in the education of individuals with disabilities and current issues and trends in special education.

B. Applies knowledge of models, theories and philosophies that provide the basis for special education practice.

C. Applies current educational terminology and definitions regarding individuals with disabilities, including professionally accepted classification systems and current incidence and prevalence figures.

D. Analyzes issues relating to definition and identification procedures for individuals with disabilities, including individuals from culturally and/or linguistically diverse backgrounds.

E. Understands factors that influence the overrepresentation of culturally and/or linguistically diverse students in programs for individuals with disabilities.

F. Recognizes various perspectives (e.g., medical, psychological, behavioral, educational) regarding definitions and etiologies of disabilities.

G. Understands cultural variations in beliefs, traditions and values and their effects on the relationships among child, family and school.

H. Applies knowledge of the continuum of placement and services for individuals with disabilities.

Competency 011: The special education teacher applies knowledge of professional roles and responsibilities and adheres to legal and ethical requirements of the profession.

The beginning teacher:

A. Knows how to exercise objective professional judgment, maintain a high level of competence and integrity in professional practice and participate in professional activities and organizations that may benefit individuals with disabilities, their parents/guardians and/or colleagues.

B. Knows consumer and professional organizations, publications and journals relevant to individuals with disabilities and knows how to access information on cognitive, communicative, physical, cultural, social and emotional characteristics and needs of individuals with disabilities.

C. Applies skills for participating effectively in identifying, diagnosing, placing and developing programming for students with disabilities, including using advocacy skills and competencies to support the education of students in least restrictive environments.

D. Applies knowledge of assurances and due process rights related to assessment, eligibility and placement and knows the rights and responsibilities of parents/guardians, students, teachers, other professionals and schools.

E. Knows legal and ethical issues (e.g., liability) relevant to working with individuals with disabilities and knows how to conduct instructional and other professional activities consistent with the requirements of laws, rules and regulations and local district policies and procedures, including complying with local, state and federal monitoring and evaluation requirements.

F. Knows the roles of and relationships among federal, state and local entities with regard to the regulation and provision of special education and related services, including specialized health care services.

G. Applies knowledge of practices that conform to standards and policies of the profession, including the Code of Ethics and Standard Practices for Texas Educators and the Council for Exceptional Children (CEC) Code of Ethics.

H. Demonstrates awareness of personal cultural biases and differences that may affect one's teaching, and knows how to demonstrate respect for the culture, gender, and personal beliefs of individual students.

I. Applies procedures for safeguarding confidentiality with regard to students with disabilities (e.g., by maintaining the confidentiality of electronic correspondence and records, ensuring the confidentiality of conversations) and recognizes the importance of respecting students' privacy.

J. Knows laws, regulations and policies related to the provision of specialized health care in the educational setting.

Competency 012: The special education teacher knows how to communicate and collaborate effectively in a variety of professional settings.

The beginning teacher:

A. Understands the collaborative roles of students, parents/guardians, teachers and other school and community personnel in planning and implementing an individualized program, and applies effective strategies for working collaboratively in various contexts.

B. Applies knowledge of factors that promote effective communication and collaboration with students, parents/guardians, teachers, paraprofessionals and other school and community personnel.

C. Knows how to foster respectful and beneficial relationships between families and professionals in the school and community.

D. Knows typical concerns of families of individuals with disabilities and appropriate strategies to support families in dealing with these concerns.

E. Applies knowledge of strategies for encouraging and assisting parents/guardians in their role as active participants in their children's education and applies procedures for planning and conducting collaborative conferences with parents/guardians.

F. Applies knowledge of effective communication in various professional contexts and knows ethical practices for confidential communication regarding individuals with disabilities.

G. Knows the types of information generally available from parents/guardians, school officials, the legal system and community service agencies.

H. Applies knowledge of the collaborative and consultative roles of special education teachers, paraprofessionals and other school personnel in integrating individuals with disabilities into general educational settings.

I. Knows how to collaborate with teachers in the general educational setting and other school and community personnel to integrate individuals with disabilities into various learning environments.

J. Knows how to serve as a resource person for families, general education teachers, administrators and other school personnel regarding the characteristics and needs of individuals with disabilities.

Competency 010

Competency 010

The special education teacher understands the philosophical, historical, and legal foundations of special education.

Chapter 10 will focus on Competency 010—the philosophical, historical, and legal foundations of Special Education.

History of Federal Special Education Legislation

In the past, many children with disabilities were denied access to public education altogether. As we've said, even in 1970—not very long ago—U.S. schools educated only 20 percent of children with disabilities. In light of the many states that had laws denying access to children with major disabilities, it's not hard to see why.

Throughout most of the history of public schools in America, services to children with disabilities were minimal and were provided at the discretion of local school districts. Until the mid-1970s, laws in most states allowed school districts to deny enrollment of any students considered "uneducable." Some children with disabilities were admitted to public schools but were placed in regular education, with no services. Others were placed in special programs in public schools, though the services provided to them were inadequate.

Only after Public Law 94-142, or the IDEA, became effective in 1978 and, in several states, after federal and state court cases, did the notion of "education for everyone" become a popular practice. Currently, more than 6.5 million children with disabilities have access to free and appropriate education each year.

The Rehabilitation Act at Section 504-1973

Congressional hearings in 1975 revealed that millions of children with disabilities were being shut out of American schools. In fact, 3.5 million children with disabilities in the country were not receiving an education appropriate to their needs, while almost one million more were receiving no education at all. By 1971–72, seven states were still educating fewer than 20 percent of their *known* children with disabilities, and 19 states, fewer than a third. Only 17 states had even reached the halfway mark.

Once state laws and federal court decisions made clear the states' responsibility for providing a free, appropriate, public education to all children, regardless of disability, states joined advocates in seeking the passage of federal legislation to provide consistency, federal leadership, and federal subsidy of the costs of Special Education. Congress's initial response to this national problem was through the Rehabilitation Act, then eventually solidified through Public Law 94-142, or popularly referred to as the IDEA— the Individuals with Disabilities Education Act.

In 1973, Public Law 93-112, the Rehabilitation Act at Section 504, provided that any recipient of federal financial assistance, including state and local educational agencies, must end discrimination in the offering of its services to persons with disabilities. However, Section 504 of the Rehabilitation Act included no funding and no monitoring, and so it was ignored by local and state educational agencies for 20 years. Although parents had the right to bring suit under Section 504 as early as 1973, most preferred to pursue the rights available under Public Law 94-142.

The Individuals with Disabilities Education Act—IDEA

In 1975, Public Law 94-142—the Education for All Handicapped Children Act— was passed by Congress. This act required that all students with disabilities receive a free, appropriate public education and provided mandated funding to assist with the excess costs of offering such Special Education services. The title of the act was changed by

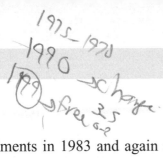

amendments in 1983 and again in 1990 when it was renamed the Individuals with Disabilities Education Act (IDEA).

The IDEA has outlined mandates that local education agencies (school districts) were required to follow or else receive penalties in the form of funding cuts or withholdings. Local education agencies, in order to receive funds, had to put in place a system of *determination of eligibility* for students with disabilities who lived within their specific jurisdictions who were not receiving a free and appropriate education. The agencies were required to perform evaluations of these students to determine the effect of their disabilities on educational performance and prescribe appropriate educational services.

Other Significant Federal Laws

Besides IDEA, there were a number of other significant federal laws that affected students with disabilities:

- Public Law 99-457
- Public Law 101-476
- Public Law 105-17
- Public Law 108-446

Public Law 99-457

Public Law 99-457 was the reauthorization of 94-142, which extended Free and Appropriate Education to children ages 3–5. This reauthorization required states to establish early intervention programs for infants and toddlers ages 0–2 and established the requirement for Individual Family Service Plans.

Public Law 101-476

Public Law 101-476 is the 1990 reauthorization of that law, renamed Public Law 94-142 the Individuals with Disabilities Education Act. It emphasized "family rights" throughout the law, extended eligibility for children with autism and traumatic brain injury, and included the definition of Least Restrictive Environment (LRE) to assure access for all children to the general education curriculum through the means of inclusion wherever possible.

Public Law 105-17

Public Law 105-17 is the 1997 reauthorization that extended the LRE requirement to assure access for all to the general education curriculum. It also required that assistive technology devices and services be considered on every IEP, and included mobility and orientation services for children who are blind or are visually impaired.

Public Law 108-446

Public Law 108-446 is the 2004 reauthorization that effected transition issues and created legal frameworks for student discipline. This law included how teachers needed to be credentialed in order to meet the requirements of "highly qualified." This law also included language around paraprofessionals, and it included terminology that defined scientifically based research that backs instructional practices in No Child Left Behind.

Accepted Classification Systems

There are two accepted classification systems for students with learning disabilities:

- the IQ Discrepancy Model
- the Response to Intervention Model (RTI)

The IQ Achievement Discrepancy Model

According to the IRIS Center (2007), classification of learning disabilities is based on the IQ Achievement Discrepancy Model. This model assesses whether there is a significant difference between a student's scores on a test of general intelligence and scores obtained on achievement tests, such as the Woodcock-Johnson Achievement Test. This is the traditionally accepted approach to determining whether a student is eligible for the classification of *Learning Disabled*.

According to this model, if a student has a discrepancy of 30 points between the student's IQ score and the achievement test, the student is eligible for being classified as having a learning disability. However, there are several reasons for concern over schools using this model to determine eligibility for services as a learning disabled student, such as the following:

- The information gathered from the IQ and achievement test does not indicate each student's learning needs.

- The IQ Achievement Discrepancy Model can create inequitable achievement for students.

- The Response to Intervention Model (RTI) is an alternative to this model.

The Response to Intervention Model (RTI)

The Response to Intervention Model (RTI) is an alternative to the IQ Achievement Discrepancy Model. According to the RTI Action Network, the Response to Intervention Model is a multi-tiered approach to early classification and support of students with learning and behavioral needs. The RTI model is based on three separate tiers:

- **Tier 1—High-Quality Classroom Instruction, Screening, and Group Interventions:** Students receive high-quality, scientifically based instruction provided by quality personnel. This approach ensures that student difficulties are not due to inadequate instruction. Conducting assessments to identify learners who may be struggling or falling behind is achieved through universal screenings.

- **Tier 2—Targeted Interventions and Comprehensive Evaluation:** Students identified as not making progress in Tier 1 are provided with intensive intervention that increases with time. This intervention is meant to match their individual needs. These interventions are mostly provided in small group, in addition to services provided within the general education curriculum. Usually this intervention occurs along the time frame of a grading period. If the student does not show adequate progress, the student is then considered for Tier-3 intervention.

- **Tier 3—Intensive Interventions and Comprehensive Evaluation:** This level involves highly individualized and intensive services. Students who do not achieve the desired level of achievement after these services are then referred to comprehensive evaluation for Special Education services, under the Individuals with Disabilities Education Act (IDEA), 2004.

Current Incidence and Prevalence Figures

These are some up-to-date figures on the prevalence of learning and developmental disabilities from the Centers for Disease Control and Prevention, National Center for Health Statistics:

Specific Developmental Disabilities in U.S. Children Aged 3–17 Years *

Disability	Percent Change between 1997–1999 and 2006–2008
Any developmental disability	17.1%^
ADHD	33.0%^
Autism	289.5%^
Blind/unable to see at all	18.2%
Cerebral palsy	-
Moderate to profound hearing loss	-30.9%
Learning disability	5.5%
Intellectual disability	-1.5%
Seizures, past 12 months	9.1%
Stuttered or stammered, past 12 months	3.1%
Other developmental delay	24.7%^

Centers for Disease Control and Prevention, National Center for Health Statistics, NHIS, 1997–2008

^Statistically significant trend over four time periods (1997–1999, 2000–2002, 2003–2005, and 2006–2008)

Overrepresentation of Minorities Issues

There has been much research and debate on the topic of overrepresentation of minorities in Special Education. The *disproportionality* refers to the uneven placement of certain groups in special education services in comparison to other groups. According to Harry et al. (2002), African American students are much more likely to receive a classification of learning disability, intellectual disability, emotional disturbance, or deaf/blindness. On the other hand, white students are most likely to receive classifications of neurological impairment, health impairment, or autism. The data does show clear ways students from different ethnic backgrounds are identified in certain disability categories. However, it remains unclear as to the exact reasons.

Continuum of Placement of Services

The Individuals with Disabilities Education Act requires that all states extend educational services to the maximum extent that is appropriate in settings where students without disabilities are educated as well. This Continuum of Services, according to (LRE) or Least Restrictive Environment area, is as follows:

- **Regular Education Classrooms/Inclusion:** These are educational settings where regular education, Special Education, paraprofessionals, related service providers, and intervention specialists teach together in settings that have students with Special Education classifications alongside those children who don't have classifications.

- **Small Group/Individual Settings:** These are instructional groups that are either in the general education setting or outside of the general education setting. They are designed for intensive, supplemental instruction that focuses on student IEP objectives and goals.

- **Resource Room:** These settings are strictly pull-out settings that deliver intensive instruction for students with the most significant learning needs.

- **Separate Facility:** Alternative or specialized learning schools are examples of this type of service on the continuum. They are separate programs outside of the mainstream school setting at different locations.

- **Home Instruction:** This is an individualized program provided to children who have disabilities or conditions that require them to stay at home.

- **Institutions and Hospitals:** These are programming and services for children who are institutionalized for mental conditions or have medical conditions that require extended stays at hospitals.

Special Education in Texas

The ARD Committee is the Admission, Review, and Dismissal Committee. It represents the official process for determining eligibility, evaluating children for services, updating progress, and initiating declassification when needed.

According to the ARD, the IEP is a written plan describing the provision of Special Education and related services once a disability has been determined for a student. This written plan describes how a student's needs will be addressed educationally.

The IEP describes what a student can already do and what he or she needs to learn for the next year. It lists the special help a student will receive in order to make progress in the school environment. The ARD committee members must consider a student's strengths and family concerns about a student's education and the results of the initial or most recent full and individual evaluation.

A Student's Individualized Education Program (IEP)

According to *A Guide to the ARD Process* (June 2002), a student's IEP must include the following:

1. Present levels of educational performance: *PLAAFP*

    a. how the disability affects involvement and progress in the general curriculum

    b. for preschool-age students, how the disability affects participation in appropriate activities

2. Measurable annual goals including benchmarks or short-term objectives related to meeting the following:

    a. a student's needs so he or she can be involved and progress in the general curriculum

    b. other educational needs that result from the disability

3. Special Education and related services and other supports and services for a student to do the following:

    a. advance toward annual goals

    b. progress in the general curriculum

    c. participate in extracurricular and nonacademic activities

    d. be educated and participate with disabled and nondisabled students

4. The extent a student will not participate with nondisabled students in regular classes or nonacademic activities, if any.

5. Participation in administration of state or district-wide assessments, including appropriate modifications.

6. If the ARD committee determines that a student cannot participate in such evaluation, a statement must include the following:

    a. why the evaluation is not appropriate

    b. how the student's progress will be assessed

7. Date services and modifications begin, including frequency, location, and duration (minutes per session).

8. How progress toward the annual goals will be measured and how parents will be regularly informed of progress toward the goals of the IEP and if the progress is sufficient to meet the goals. Each annual goal of the student's IEP must be broken down into small steps, called short-term objectives or benchmarks. Benchmarks can be thought of as describing the amount of progress that the student is to achieve within specific segments of the school year. Parents will be provided a report of the student's progress on these short-term objectives at the same intervals as nondisabled peers to ensure the student is making progress toward the IEP annual goals.

Services and Placement Settings

After the IEP goals and objectives are developed, the ARD committee must determine the educational setting or placement where the Special Education and related services will be provided. Students must be educated in the least restrictive environment (LRE). This means students must be placed in the educational setting that provides the most opportunities to be educated with students who do not have disabilities.

Various related service options are available to all students who qualify for Special Education services if that service is required for the student to benefit from Special Education. These services include the following: audiology, counseling, medical evaluation, occupational therapy, orientation and mobility, parent counseling and training, physical therapy, psychological services, recreation therapy, rehabilitation counseling, school health, social work, and transportation. These related services may be provided in a variety of settings.

According to A Guide to the ARD Process (June 2002), education placement decisions must always be based on a student's needs and may include, but are not limited to, the following locations:

- regular education classroom with no support services

- regular education classroom with support services

- resource classroom

- self-contained classroom

- self-contained classroom/separate campus

- hospital/homebound program

- residential program

ARD Considerations of Special Factors as Communicated to Parents

There are several considerations or special factors that the ARD committee needs to consider and communicate to parents, as outlined in their June 2002 Guide to the ARD Process. These include the following:

1. **Behavior:** The ARD committee must consider strategies and supports to address a student's behavior by conducting a functional behavioral assessment. The ARD committee should use the results of this assessment to develop positive behavioral supports and develop a behavior intervention plan (BIP).

2. **Limited Proficiency in English:** If a student has limited proficiency in English, the ARD committee must consider a student's language needs as these needs relate to the IEP. A member of the campus Language Proficiency Assessment Committee (LPAC) should be a member of the ARD committee to help consider a student's language needs.

   a. **Blind or Visually Impaired:** If a student is blind or visually impaired, the ARD committee must provide for instruction in braille, unless the committee determines after an appropriate evaluation (the learning media assessment) that a student does not need this instruction now or for the future. The ARD committee must include a certified vision teacher. The IEP must provide a detailed description of the arrangements made to provide a student with orientation and mobility training; instruction in braille or use of large print; other training to compensate for serious visual loss;

access to special media; and special tools, appliances, aids or devices commonly used by individuals with serious visual impairments. The IEP must also set forth plans and arrangements made for contacts with and continuing services to a student beyond regular school hours to ensure that he or she receives training in and learns the compensatory skills, orientation and mobility, social adjustment skills, and the vocational or career counseling required for a student to succeed in classroom settings and to derive lasting, practical benefits from education in the school district.

b. **Communication Needs:** If a student has communication needs, the ARD committee must consider those language and communication needs.

c. **Deaf and Hard of Hearing:** If a student is deaf or hard of hearing, the ARD committee will consider a student's language and communication needs. This includes a student's opportunities to communicate directly with classmates and school staff in her or his language and communication mode. The ARD committee must include a teacher for the hearing impaired.

d. **Assistive Technology:** The ARD committee must always consider a student's need for assistive technology devices or services.

e. **Autism:** If a student is diagnosed with autism, the ARD committee must address additional considerations: prioritized behavioral objectives, daily schedule reflecting minimum unstructured time, in-home training or viable alternatives, prevocational and vocational needs of students age 12 or older, parent training, suitable staff-student ratio, and extended educational programming.

■ Review Questions

1. As of 1990, the name of Public Law 94-142 is

   (A) Individuals with Disabilities Education Act.

   (B) No Child Left Behind.

   (C) Elementary and Secondary Education Act.

   (D) Rehabilitation Act.

   The correct response is (**A**). Public Law 94-142 is commonly known as the Individuals with Disabilities Education Act, or IDEA. This was the name assigned as part of the 1990 amendment, replacing the earlier name of Education for the Handicapped Act. (B) is incorrect as No Child Left Behind is the name of the 2001 reauthorization of the Elementary and Secondary Education Act. (C) is incorrect because the Elementary and Secondary Education Act is Public Law 89-10. (D) is incorrect because the Rehabilitation Act is Public Law 93-112.

2. Under IDEA, what must local education agencies put in place in order to receive federal Special Education funds?

   (A) Special classrooms for students with disabilities

   (B) Separate campuses with specialized equipment for students with disabilities

   (C) A system of determination of eligibility for students with disabilities

   (D) Tutoring services for students with disabilities

The correct response is (C). Under IDEA, local education agencies must put in place a system of determination of eligibility for students with disabilities so that students can qualify for Special Education services. These services are partially funded by the federal government, provided local education agencies adhere to the IDEA mandates. (A) and (B) are incorrect because both assume segregated environments for students with disabilities. While school districts may create such classrooms or school campuses if they are determined to be the least restrictive environment for a student with disabilities, they are not specifically mandated by IDEA. (D) is incorrect because tutoring services are not specifically outlined as a requirement of IDEA.

3. LRE stands for

   (A) Lessons Ready for Educators.

   (B) Laws of Regular Education.

   (C) Least Restrictive Environment.

   (D) Learning to Read English.

The correct response is (C). LRE stands for Least Restrictive Environment, an extremely important requirement of the Individuals with Disabilities Education Act. A student with disabilities must be educated in the least restrictive environment, the educational setting that provides the most opportunities to be educated with regular education peers while still meeting the needs of the student with disabilities. Therefore, (A), (B), and (D) are all incorrect responses.

4.   According to published guidelines for ARD committees in Texas, which of the following is NOT a special factor that must be considered and communicated to parents?

(A)   Behavior

(B)   Residential preferences

(C)   Assistive technology

(D)   Autism

The correct response is (**B**). The Admission, Review, and Dismissal Committee must consider several special factors and communicate their decisions on these factors to parents as well as document them in the IEP. However, a student's residential preference is not one of those special factors. (A), (C), and (D) are all incorrect because behavior, assistive technology, and autism are all special factors that must be addressed in a student's IEP, according to ARD guidelines.

Competency 011

Competency 011

The special education teacher applies knowledge of professional roles and responsibilities and adheres to legal and ethical requirements of the profession.

Chapter 11 will focus on Competency 011—professional roles and responsibilities and adhering to legal and ethical requirements of the profession.

The IDEA provides mandates for services to all children with disabilities. These children are a large and heterogeneous group. This group of children with disabilities can range from first-grade students with speech impediments to college-bound high school students in wheelchairs to junior-high students with emotional disorders and a history of school suspensions.

Many lawsuits have been brought to determine the responsibilities school districts have for particular types of services within the IDEA's mandates for all children with disabilities. These services begin with requirements for eligibility. The IDEA attempts to make them as clear-cut as possible, as they do for students' and parents' rights.

Special Education Eligibility as Determined by IDEA

A child suspected of having a disability is evaluated to determine the child's eligibility for services. Under the IDEA, school districts are prohibited from planning Special Education programs in advance and offering them to students based on space or any kind of predetermined availability (for example, a predetermined number of spots open for Special Education services).

Under the IDEA, children must be evaluated before school personnel can begin special programming, and parents are to be involved in the process as well. Children must be evaluated in all areas related to suspected disability. Reevaluation is required at least every three years or when a special evaluation is warranted. Most school districts have annual evaluations as well as triennial evaluations. Once found to be disabled and in need of special services, a child is entitled to appropriate services. However, if the school district finds the child to be ineligible, the parents have a right to appeal.

Parental Involvement, Procedural Safeguards, and Due Process

The IDEA provides many specific procedural protections for the parents of children with disabilities. These include notice to parents of proposed actions, attendance at meetings concerning the child's placement or IEP, and the right to appeal school decisions to an impartial hearing officer.

Parental Rights and School District Actions

When a school seeks an initial evaluation or a change in placement of a child with disabilities, the parents are entitled to a full explanation of all procedural safeguards under the IDEA. They are entitled to a description of the action proposed by the school district, along with the reasons for the action and a description of alternatives considered. They are also entitled to a description of each evaluation procedure, test, record, report, or other factors used to determine a change in placement. The school must ensure communication in a form understandable to the parent, such as a written summary that is in the native language of the parent.

Consent to Evaluate

Children must be evaluated under the IDEA regulations before they can be placed in a Special Education program. Parental consent must be obtained before conducting an evaluation of a child who is suspected of having a disability. If parents refuse to consent, school districts may appeal to an impartial hearing officer, who may order evaluation without parental consent. However, Texas state law may override this provision.

Appropriate Evaluation

Evaluation must be selected and administered so as not to be racially or culturally discriminatory, and it needs to be provided and administered in the child's native language by trained personnel. When a test is to be administered to a child with impaired sensory, manual, or speaking skills, the test must be selected and administered to ensure that results accurately reflect the child's aptitude or achievement level or whatever other factors the test seeks to measure.

Choice of Evaluation Materials

No single procedure, such as an IQ test, may be used as the sole measure for determining an educational program or specific specialized service for any child multidisciplinary team, and it must include at least one specialist in the area of the suspected disability. The child must be assessed in all areas related to the suspected disability, which includes health, vision, hearing, social and emotional status, general intelligence, academic performance, communication skills, and motor abilities.

Choice of Independent Evaluations as Procedural Safeguards

If the parent disagrees with the evaluation by the school district, he or she may obtain an independent evaluation conducted by a qualified examiner. Under certain circumstances, the independent evaluation may be obtained at the school district's expense.

Consent to Placement

Parental consent must be obtained before a child with a disability can be placed in a Special Education program. If parental consent cannot be obtained, the school district may appeal to an impartial hearing officer.

Input in Individualized Education Program (IEP)

The IEP states the goals for the child and services to be provided, including the extent to which the child will participate in regular education programs. At each meeting discussing the child's IEP, the school district must ensure that the parents of the child have the opportunity to participate, including advance notification, scheduling the meeting at a mutually agreeable time and place, and providing an interpreter if needed.

Parents' Right to Appeal to an Impartial Hearing Officer

If the parents and school district are unable to agree about placement or about services to be provided, either the parents or the school district may initiate a hearing before an impartial hearing officer. This hearing will have an officer who will issue a binding decision. The hearing officer must not be an employee of a public agency that is involved in the education or care of the child. Any party to the hearing has the right to be accompanied and advised by legal counsel and by individuals with special knowledge regarding the problems of children with disabilities. They may present evidence and cross-examine witnesses. Parents also have the right to have the child attend the hearing and to open the hearing to the public.

The Stay in Place Legal Provision: Placement and Discipline

Once placement has begun, it can only be changed by the IEP committee. If the parents do not consent to a proposed change in placement and request a hearing, the child must *stay put or stay in place* in the current placement until the hearing process is concluded.

Disciplinary sanctions of 10 days or less are not considered a change in placement and are not subject to this restriction unless a series of shorter-term suspensions has the cumulative impact of more than 10 days. Disciplinary sanctions greater than 10 days, such as expulsions, can be proposed by a school district if it finds that a specific misbehavior was not related to the disability. However, if the parents disagree and request a hearing on the issue, the student stays put in the current placement until after the hearing. If the school district believes that maintaining the student in the current placement is likely to cause injury to the student or to others, the school may go to court, and the court can change the placement.

The ARD Process: The IEP Committee in Texas

Federal regulations refer to an IEP committee. In Texas, this committee is referred to as the admission, review, and dismissal (ARD) committee. This committee meets at least once a year to develop, review, and/or revise a child's individualized education program (IEP). Parents are very important members of their child's ARD committee. The ARD committee must include the following members:

1. the parent of the student

2. at least one regular education teacher of the student (if the student is or may be participating in the regular education environment)

3. at least one Special Education teacher of the student, or a Special Education-provider

4. a representative of the school who is:

   a. qualified to provide, or supervise the provision of, specially designed instruction to meet the unique needs of students with disabilities

   b. knowledgeable about the general education curriculum

   c. knowledgeable about the availability of resources of the school district

5. an individual who can interpret the instructional implications of the evaluation results

6. Other individuals, invited by the parent or school, who have any knowledge about the student, including related services providers

7. the student, when appropriate

According to *A Guide to the ARD Process* (June 2002), parents must be provided written notice of the ARD committee meeting at least five school days prior to the meeting. The notice will include the purpose, time, and place of the meeting and a list of those attending. The parents may ask the school to reschedule the meeting if for some reason the date, time, and place are not convenient to the parents. The school must attempt to schedule the meeting at a time and place that is convenient for all participants. Other methods, such as telephone conference calls, can be used to provide participants, including parents, the opportunity to participate.

The ARD committee's first task is to review the full and individual evaluation results and all other information collected to decide if the child meets the federal definition of a student with a disability and needs Special Education services. If the child does need Special Education, then the committee will develop an <u>individualized education program</u> for the child based on the needs determined through the full and individual evaluation.

Maintaining Confidentiality as a Special Education Teacher

According to the Family Education Rights and Privacy Act (FERPA), during the process of determining eligibility, placement, and constructing an individualized education plan, and then implementing that program and services, very personal information about students and families is collected and shared. According to FERPA, this information must be held confidential. This policy is in place solely due to the need for appropriate personal treatment for students and their families.

There are several important things that Special Education teachers should know about handling confidential information and documents. These include the following:

- Personnel who handle confidential information and documents need to be trained to do so.

- All confidential records should be kept secure to prevent access by unauthorized personnel.

- File cabinets and other storage containers that keep confidential records on file must be locked except for access by authorized personnel.

Types of Confidential Documents

There are several types of documents that are considered confidential. These include the following:

- written assessments and diagnostic findings

- official correspondence with families that include sensitive information about the student

- written education, transition, or other treatment plans for the student, including the IEP

- confidential documents provided by other agencies

- written information provided by parents or guardians

Special Education Professional Ethical Principles

According to the Council for Exceptional Children, Special Educators and related professionals are bound to the following code of ethics, which was adopted by the CEC Board of Directors in January 2010:

A. maintaining challenging expectations for individuals with exceptionalities to develop the highest possible learning outcomes and quality of life potential in ways that respect their dignity, culture, language, and background

B. maintaining a high level of professional competence and integrity and exercising professional judgment to benefit individuals with exceptionalities and their families

C. promoting meaningful and inclusive participation of individuals with exceptionalities in their schools and communities

D. practicing collegially with others who are providing services to individuals with exceptionalities

E. developing relationships with families based on mutual respect and actively involving families and individuals with exceptionalities in educational decision making

F. using evidence, instructional data, research, and professional knowledge to inform practice

G. protecting and supporting the physical and psychological safety of individuals with exceptionalities

H. neither engaging in nor tolerating any practice that harms individuals with exceptionalities

I. practicing within the professional ethics, standards, and policies of CEC; upholding laws, regulations, and policies that influence professional practice; and advocating improvements in laws, regulations, and policies

J. advocating for professional conditions and resources that will improve learning outcomes of individuals with exceptionalities

K. engaging in the improvement of the profession through active participation in professional organizations

L. participating in the growth and dissemination of professional knowledge and skills

The Code of Ethics and Standard Practices for Texas Educators

Below is a list of personal and professional ethics from the Texas Code of Ethics for Educators (effective December 26, 2010). They outline professional, ethical, performance, and practice enforceable standards for all educators in the state of Texas.

I. Professional Ethical Conduct, Practices, and Performance

Standard 1.1. The educator shall not intentionally, knowingly, or recklessly engage in deceptive practices regarding official policies of the school district, educational institution, educator preparation program, the Texas Education Agency, or the State Board for Educator Certification (SBEC) and its certification process.

Standard 1.2. The educator shall not knowingly misappropriate, divert, or use monies, personnel, property, or equipment committed to his or her charge for personal gain or advantage.

Standard 1.3. The educator shall not submit fraudulent requests for reimbursement, expenses, or pay.

Standard 1.4. The educator shall not use institutional or professional privileges for personal or partisan advantage.

Standard 1.5. The educator shall neither accept nor offer gratuities, gifts, or favors that impair professional judgment or to obtain special advantage. This standard shall not restrict the acceptance of gifts or tokens offered and accepted openly from students, parents of students, or other persons or organizations in recognition or appreciation of service.

Standard 1.6. The educator shall not falsify records, or direct or coerce others to do so.

Standard 1.7. The educator shall comply with state regulations, written local school board policies, and other state and federal laws.

Standard 1.8. The educator shall apply for, accept, offer, or assign a position or a responsibility on the basis of professional qualifications.

Standard 1.9. The educator shall not make threats of violence against school district employees, school board members, students, or parents of students.

Standard 1.10. The educator shall be of good moral character and be worthy to instruct or supervise the youth of this state.

Standard 1.11. The educator shall not intentionally or knowingly misrepresent his or her employment history, criminal history, and/or disciplinary record when applying for subsequent employment.

Standard 1.12. The educator shall refrain from the illegal use or distribution of controlled substances and/or abuse of prescription drugs and toxic inhalants.

Standard 1.13. The educator shall not consume alcoholic beverages on school property or during school activities when students are present.

II. Ethical Conduct Toward Professional Colleagues

Standard 2.1. The educator shall not reveal confidential health or personnel information concerning colleagues unless disclosure serves lawful professional purposes or is required by law.

Standard 2.2. The educator shall not harm others by knowingly making false statements about a colleague or the school system.

Standard 2.3. The educator shall adhere to written local school board policies and state and federal laws regarding the hiring, evaluation, and dismissal of personnel.

Standard 2.4. The educator shall not interfere with a colleague's exercise of political, professional, or citizenship rights and responsibilities.

Standard 2.5. The educator shall not discriminate against or coerce a colleague on the basis of race, color, religion, national origin, age, gender, disability, family status, or sexual orientation.

Standard 2.6. The educator shall not use coercive means or promise of special treatment in order to influence professional decisions or colleagues.

Standard 2.7. The educator shall not retaliate against any individual who has filed a complaint with the SBEC or who provides information for a disciplinary investigation or proceeding under this chapter.

III. Ethical Conduct Toward Students

Standard 3.1. The educator shall not reveal confidential information concerning students unless disclosure serves lawful professional purposes or is required by law.

Standard 3.2. The educator shall not intentionally, knowingly, or recklessly treat a student or minor in a manner that adversely affects or endangers the learning, physical health, mental health, or safety of the student or minor.

Standard 3.3. The educator shall not intentionally, knowingly, or recklessly misrepresent facts regarding a student.

Standard 3.4. The educator shall not exclude a student from participation in a program, deny benefits to a student, or grant an advantage to a student on the basis of race, color, gender, disability, national origin, religion, family status, or sexual orientation.

Standard 3.5. The educator shall not intentionally, knowingly, or recklessly engage in physical mistreatment, neglect, or abuse of a student or minor.

Standard 3.6. The educator shall not solicit or engage in sexual conduct or a romantic relationship with a student or minor.

Standard 3.7. The educator shall not furnish alcohol or illegal/unauthorized drugs to any person under 21 years of age unless the educator is a parent or guardian of that child or knowingly allow any person under 21 years of age unless the educator is a parent or guardian of that child to consume alcohol or illegal/unauthorized drugs in the presence of the educator.

Standard 3.8. The educator shall maintain appropriate professional educator-student relationships and boundaries based on a reasonably prudent educator standard.

Standard 3.9. The educator shall refrain from inappropriate communication with a student or minor, including, but not limited to, electronic communication such as cell phone, text messaging, email, instant messaging, blogging, or other social network communication. Factors that may be considered in assessing whether the communication is inappropriate include, but are not limited to:

(i) the nature, purpose, timing, and amount of the communication;

(ii) the subject matter of the communication;

(iii) whether the communication was made openly or the educator attempted to conceal the communication;

(iv) whether the communication could be reasonably interpreted as soliciting sexual contact or a romantic relationship;

(v) whether the communication was sexually explicit; and

(vi) whether the communication involved discussion(s) of the physical or sexual attractiveness or the sexual history, activities, preferences, or fantasies of either the educator or the student.

Professional Organizations and Journals Associated with Special Education

During the decades since the advent of legislation, there has been a concerted effort for improving the field of Special Education. There are many outstanding organizations and groups that are dedicated to striving for excellence in Special Education. Here are some examples:

- **Office of Special Education Programs (OSEP):** This group's mission is to provide leadership and financial assistance to states and districts.

- **National Council for Special Education Research (NCSE):** This is a comprehensive forum for Special Education teaching research.

- **International Association for Special Education (IASE):** This association has fostered international connections to bring awareness to Special Education issues and needs on a global level.

- **Coordinated Campaign for Learning Disabilities (CCLD):** This center combines the efforts of six exceptional associations:

  1. The Council for Learning Disabilities

  2. Division of Learning Disabilities

  3. International Dyslexia Association

  4. Schwab Learning Center

  5. National Center for Learning Disabilities

  6. Learning Disabilities Association

- **National Association of Special Education Teachers (NASET):** This is a national membership organization dedicated to Special Education teachers.

- **National Dissemination Center for Children with Disabilities (NICHCY):** This center provides information and research on laws, disabilities, children and youth with disabilities, and basic information on effective practices in the field of Special Education.

- **Council for Exceptional Children (CEC):** This is an excellent organization dedicated to all things Special Education.

- **Journal of Special Education:** This journal provides research articles and scholarly reviews on Special Education for individuals with mild to severe disabilities.

- **The Journal of Teacher Education and Special Education:** This is a scholarly journal from a division of the Council for Exceptional Children.

Review Questions

1. How many days in advance must parents be provided written notice of an ARD committee meeting?

   (A) Three

   (B) Four

   (C) Five

   (D) Six

   The correct response is (**C**). According to law, parents must be provided written notice of an ARD committee meeting five days in advance. Therefore, (A), (B), and (D) are all incorrect as the correct number is five.

2. A Special Education teacher wants to collaborate with other Special Education teachers, share experiences in the classroom, and discuss appropriate teaching strategies for various disabilities. The most appropriate group for this teacher to join would be

   (A) CEC.

   (B) TCEA.

   (C) IRA.

   (D) ASCD.

   The correct response is (**A**). CEC is the Council for Exceptional Children, a national organization for educators and parents that is committed to issues related to children and adults with exceptionalities. Members of CEC can join groups within the organization that are specific to their interests, such as intellectual disabilities or research. Texas has its own state chapter of CEC. (B) is incorrect because TCEA is the Texas Computer Education Association. (C) is incorrect because IRA is the International Reading Association. (D) is incorrect because ASCD is the Association for Supervision and Curriculum Development.

3. Parents of a child who has been referred for Special Education evaluation speak only Mandarin Chinese. No one in the school district knows how to speak this dialect, although there is a custodian who speaks Cantonese. When scheduling the ARD, the school district must

    (A) write everything down in English and give copies of the proceedings to the parents so they can have them translated.

    (B) ask the custodian to attend and orally translate everything into Cantonese.

    (C) have an educational interpreter present, who can translate everything spoken into sign language.

    (D) locate, if at all possible, a Mandarin speaker who can translate during the meeting.

    The correct response is (**D**). When notifying parents of ARD meetings and conducting ARD meetings, it is expected that parents have full access to the information being shared in their native language. A school district, must, if at all possible, have a translator available who can explain the proceedings to the parents in their native language and communicate their thoughts to the rest of the ARD committee. (A) is incorrect because it is the district's responsibility to communicate in the parents' native language, not the parents' responsibility to find their own translator. (B) is incorrect because Cantonese and Mandarin are distinctly different Chinese dialects. Most Mandarin speakers cannot understand spoken Cantonese. (C) is incorrect because the parents, in this case, speak a different language. They are not deaf or in need of sign language.

4. Parents of a child with autism who has just been placed in a self-contained classroom by ARD committee decision are not happy with the teacher and demand that the principal transfer the student back to the regular classroom. What is the appropriate response by the school principal?

    (A) Reconvene the ARD committee, including the parents, to review the situation and discuss placement while leaving the student in the self-contained classroom until the meeting can be held

    (B) Refuse the parents' request and tell the parents it will take time to adjust

    (C) Replace the teacher in the self-contained classroom immediately

    (D) Fulfill the parents' request and transfer the student back to the regular classroom immediately

The correct response is (**A**). The *Stay in Place* legal provision of IDEA is very clear that once an ARD committee has agreed upon a placement for a student, that placement cannot be changed except through another meeting of the ARD committee. The student must stay in place until the ARD committee or a parent-requested hearing has concluded. (B) is incorrect because the principal cannot simply refuse the parents' request. Instead, the principal must tell them that the student cannot be moved immediately but that the ARD committee can be reconvened. (C) is incorrect because there would have to be grounds for moving the teacher that go beyond parents not liking the teacher. (D) is incorrect because the student cannot be moved until the entire ARD committee agrees to an alternative placement.

Competency 012

Competency 012

The special education teacher knows how to communicate and collaborate effectively in a variety of professional settings.

Chapter 12 will focus on Competency 012—communicating and collaborating effectively in a variety of professional settings.

Communicating effectively with families is the utmost priority of any Special Education teacher. It is important to understand the perspectives of the families you work with as an educator in Texas. Effective collaboration not only helps you as the teacher, but it also helps the students you work with by helping their families.

◼ Working with Families with Children with Learning Disabilities

Learning disabilities can be hard on a family. One parent, often the mother, may recognize and face the problem sooner or more readily than the other. Misunderstanding and conflict can result. Brothers and sisters often resent the amount of attention given to a child with special needs and may believe that the child is perfectly capable and therefore "spoiled." Grandparents tend to blame parents for not doing enough, for not being disciplined enough, for not being organized enough, or for not giving enough direct help to the child. Neighbors can be intolerant if the child is very hyperactive or has low frustration tolerance and tends to explode or cry at each hurdle.

Communicating with Parents and Families

Teachers work hard to establish partnerships with parents to support student learning, especially when there are learning issues involved. Strong communication is fundamental to this partnership and to building a sense of trust and rapport between home and school—between families and the children with whom you will be working. Special Education teachers must continue to develop and expand their skills in order to maximize effective communication with parents. There are two basic communication strategies: one-way and two-way.

One-Way Communication Strategy

Several examples of one-way communication include the following:

- **Newsletters:** Newsletters are used to share information to parents and a community.

- **School-to-Home Notebook:** These are communication books to share information with parents. They are used specifically for students with specific learning needs.

- **Home Notes:** Home notes on alternate days or twice weekly are used to engage and update parents on their child's progress.

- **Report Cards:** Report cards are the traditional mode to convey written, evaluative information of student progress.

Two-Way Communication Strategy

Teachers and parents usually communicate together only when concerns are noted about the child. Effective, ongoing dialogue develops out of a growing trust and a mutual concern. Ongoing communication, even when there are no concerns about the child, helps to foster a stronger relationship between parents and teacher, especially when negative concerns eventually need to be communicated. Several examples of two-way communication include the following:

- **Phone Call:** A phone call is often the best way to contact the teacher. Making the initial phone call will open the lines of communication with teachers.

- **Parent-Teacher Conference:** This can create a successful partnership so both parent and teachers are on the same page. Discussion can occur and blame can be avoided by taking a solution-focused approach.

- **Follow-up:** It is important to follow up after parent-teacher conferences to plan specific strategies if needed or discuss issues or concerns further with other teachers.

Using Technology for Communication

Often, using technology allows both parents and teachers to communicate without the limitation of school hours or location. Examples of communication technology include the following:

- voice mail

- email

- video technology

- school websites

If these means are not available to a parent, then teachers can use other forms of communication. Overall, these are quicker and more accessible forms of communication between home and school, and the overall goal is to help you as a Special Education teacher to know a student better. This, in turn, helps their families.

Understanding How to Organize and Conduct a Parent-Teacher Conference

As a Special Education teacher, expect to have some parent-teacher meetings that may become tense. When having to discuss negative behaviors or learning needs with parents, there is always potential for a heightened level of anxiety and frustration that may spill over into the meeting. However, there are definite strategies that will assist a beginning Special Education teacher in maintaining productive and positive meetings.

It is important to select an appropriate meeting time and location and advise participants in advance. Before the meeting, carefully review the student file and IEP and any relating goals or objectives. Develop a clear purpose for the meeting. Identify information to be discussed, including positive aspects of the child's performance, even when you have to dig a little deeper to find these aspects.

Begin the conference with a brief friendly and informal conversation. Then explain the student's progress in a straightforward way, carefully listening to parent input. Ensure that you have enough time to summarize the discussion and plan recommendations. During the meeting, refer to the student file, IEP, and any relating goals or objectives. Ask other related professionals that are on the multidisciplinary team to attend the parent-conference so they can discuss the area of the IEP they are working on with the child. These professionals can be a speech/language therapist, an occupational therapist, a counselor, a psychologist, or even an administrator (if there are disciplinary issues that need to be discussed).

Teachers are encouraged to follow up the meeting by preparing a written conference summary in line with school board policies and Special Education committee policies, if necessary. Additional follow-up activities might involve making appropriate referrals, discussions with relevant teachers, or planning specific instructions or strategies.

Common Barriers to Effective Parent-Teacher Communication

Today, many parents feel unsupported, misunderstood, and overwhelmed by the demands modern living has placed on them. This feeling is often compounded when trying to work with families with students with learning disabilities. To address these barriers, educators in general should appreciate that every positive exchange will serve to increase trust and build stronger relationships. This is especially important when working with families of students with learning disabilities.

Cultural differences can also create significant communication challenges. To address this potential disconnect, teachers need to seek out information to understand the cultural and linguistic diversity reflected in the families of their students. This knowledge and appreciation can be demonstrated by celebrating the various cultural traditions of their students, by incorporating speakers from the community, by appreciating the difficulties faced by immigrant parents, and by seeking out interpreter services as needed. Interpreter services are regularly required when IEP meetings are held. Bilingual hotlines, as well as a bilingual phone tree, have been suggested as creative ways to enhance communication with culturally diverse families regarding upcoming events or meetings. Similarly, it may be appropriate to provide written communication in several languages to ensure the greatest access to communication from school to home.

Special Education teachers must also try to understand the uniqueness of each family based on their own cultural understanding. For example, ability to take parents' perspectives, altering schedules to accommodate parents and families, and providing more explicit information to parents regarding school culture are excellent examples of effective communication with culturally diverse populations.

Economic and time constraints can be and are often barriers to effective parent or family communication. A suggestion is to survey parents at the beginning of the school year to determine parent schedules and availability, and also to provide parents with information regarding how and when to contact you as their child's teacher. Meeting times need to be somewhat flexible to accommodate working parents, including those working shifts and those who commute.

Parents may remember negative experiences they had when in school, especially if they also had learning issues and did not have many or no positive relationships with their teachers. Also, consider that parents may simply not understand how to interact effectively with the educational system. Furthermore, as mentioned earlier, this can be particularly problematic when such a parent is faced with concerns regarding their child's behavior or academic progress. So, it is absolutely essential to make every attempt to bring in parents by effective communication that is positive, honest, and open.

Effective Strategies for Collaborating with General Education Teachers

In order to work effectively on a team, both regular and Special Education teachers need to work together to plan, implement, and evaluate the best possible instructional methods for all children in inclusive settings.

According to Hollingsworth of the Council for Exceptional Children, Special Educators have the responsibility to communicate with general education teachers who have not had a great deal of Special Education preparation. She states that, during the school day, Special Education students may have contact with a host of professionals who fall into this category. These can be teachers in art, music, physical education, health, foreign language, or administrators, paraprofessionals, cafeteria staff, and so on. It is the Special Education teacher's responsibility to reserve time to plan and consult with every professional that teaches or comes in contact with any of their Special Education students.

Hollingsworth also states that the Special Education teacher is the specialist, and it is her or his responsibility to communicate effectively with academic teachers who work with these students. Special education teachers, whether in consultative roles or other roles, need to share their instructional expertise and advocate for these students when needed. This should occur during common planning times and during actual instructional times, where the Special Education teacher can act as a model.

The Importance of Collaboration Between Special Education and Regular Education Teachers

Throughout the past decade, nearly every state in the nation, including Texas, implemented some type of standards-based reform. Sharing a common mission that all students should be held to high standards of learning, Texas has restructured its educational system in an effort to demonstrate greater accountability for student results. As a beginning Special Education teacher in Texas, here are some points to keep in mind:

- General education teachers may not be familiar with all of the specialized resources Special Education teachers know about for matching practice with a student's skill level, which may be far below the grade level.

- Special Education teachers may not be familiar with the rich activities and projects often used to apply learning on grade level.

- Both Special Education and general education teachers may know some techniques to face disciplinary problems. Having two sets of eyes provides more information to notice students being successful as well as to head off problems proactively.

- Either teacher may or may not make effective use of technology as a growing part of today's curriculum.

Suggestions for Effective Collaboration and Team Teaching

The following are several tips for effective collaboration and team teaching:

- Share strengths and needs. Teachers have different strengths and needs. Imagine collaborating together to recognize one another's strengths and to help each other identify your needs.

- Develop simple routines. Organizational routines and templates for routine planning are valuable resources and very helpful for the student. Identify early on what those routines are by talking with other teachers. You'll save time when planning and instructing.

- Create time for mutual planning. Mutual planning is a must. It will make teaching Special Needs students much more difficult if you neglect to plan together.

- Recognize that what you are going through is always a process, and expect your first weeks together to be an adventure. Just as students discover new ideas through you and your ways of teaching over time, your collaborative relationship will undergo its own evolution as well, thus meeting the needs of students in better ways.

Co-Teaching Models

The following are several models for co-teaching:

- **One Teach, One Observe:** This is a model where one co-teacher leads the lesson, while the other co-teacher makes detailed observations of students engaged in the learning process.

- **One Teach, One Drift:** This is a model where one co-teacher takes primary responsibility to lead the lesson, while the other co-teacher circulates around the room assisting students when needed.

- **Station Teaching:** This is a model where both content and students are divided between stations, and students rotate from one co-teacher's station to another.

- **Parallel Teaching:** This is a model where both co-teachers instruct the same information, but they divide the class into two groups and conduct the lessons simultaneously.

- **Alternative Teaching:** This is a model where one co-teacher completes a planned lesson with a large group, while the other co-teacher completes an alternative lesson or the same lesson taught at a different level.

- **Team Teaching:** This is a model where both co-teachers deliver instruction simultaneously, and instruction becomes more than turn-taking.

Co-teaching and collaborating with a team of teachers can be very rewarding. It has several benefits. This type of model for teaching can enable you, as a Special Education teacher, to be among a team of professionals where mutual support is at the center of what you do on a daily basis. Not only does it help to foster teamwork and mutual professional support, it also enables you to assist students effectively with learning disabilities by addressing challenges and in the areas of effective and ongoing assessment, best instructional practices, classroom management, and a sharing of resources, skills, knowledge, and perspectives.

Review Questions

1. A Special Education teacher has been trying to get in touch with the parents of a student with learning disabilities to set up a conference. The teacher has left a message on the parents' home phone and sent a note home with the student. One evening, the teacher runs into the student and his family at the local grocery store. The parents ask the teacher what she wants to talk about. The most appropriate response by the teacher is to

(A) tell the parents about the issues happening with their child at school.

(B) ignore the parents.

(C) greet the parents, tell them how much she enjoys teaching their child, and ask them to schedule a time to talk at school or on the phone.

(D) firmly tell the parents she would never say anything in a public place like the store.

The correct response is (**C**). When meeting parents in a community context, it is critical to greet them warmly. This helps build the parent-teacher relationship by communicating that the teacher cares about the whole child, not just the student at school. However, due to confidentiality laws, it is equally important to not discuss the student's disability or school issues in a public setting. Therefore, setting a time to talk privately at school or on the phone is the best answer in this situation.

(A) is incorrect because it breaches confidentiality laws. (B) is incorrect because ignoring the parents is both rude and communicates a lack of caring on the part of the teacher. (D) is incorrect because firmly telling the parents she would never say anything in a public place makes the parents seem like the ones willing to breach confidentiality. It does not communicate that the teacher cares about the student or the student's family.

2. A Special Education teacher in an ALE classroom has five students with varying intensive disabilities, including autism and Down syndrome. The teacher establishes a communication binder for each student, which is sent home daily in the student's backpack. Each day, the teacher fills out a form detailing the student's behavior, academic work, and eating habits. What type of communication strategy is this teacher implementing?

(A) Two-way

(B) One-way

(C) Group

(D) Parent-centered

The correct response is (**B**). A communication binder is a useful tool for informing parents about the daily progress their children are making. In ALE rooms, where students often have communication challenges, this form of communication is a vital part of keeping parents involved in their children's education. However, it is a one-way communication strategy. The teacher is not necessarily getting any information back from the parents. (A) is incorrect because two-way communication involves information flowing back and forth between a teacher and a student's family. (C) is incorrect because individual binders are going to each student's family, not to a large group. (D) is incorrect because the information is about the student, not the parent, and the information is coming from the teacher, not the parent.

3. A new Special Education teacher is accustomed to texting as a primary means of communication. At school orientation night, he asks all the parents to write down his mobile phone number and text him with any concerns or updates about their children. The teacher assumes if he does not receive a text from a parent that all is well. Halfway through the school year, the principal calls the teacher into her office to discuss complaints from several parents who feel the teacher has been showing favoritism to certain students by communicating frequently with their families, but not others. The teacher notes that the parents who have complained have never texted him, not even once. The teacher could have potentially avoided this situation by

(A) using email as the primary communication rather than texting.

(B)   texting every parent once a week.

(C)   asking each student's parents to tell him their preferred method of communication and using that to communicate with them throughout the year.

(D)   only communicating through official documents, such as report cards, progress reports, and ARD committee meeting notifications.

The correct response is (**C**). Effective teacher-parent communication involves reaching out to parents and finding out their communication preferences. Despite most people having cell phones, not everyone does. And even some who have cell phones do not use texting as a primary means of communication. In this situation, the teacher should have adopted a more balanced and responsive communication style, using texting, email, and written communication to talk to parents. (A) is incorrect because using email as the primary means of communication assumes every parent checks email regularly. Some will not. (B) is incorrect because it is already clear that several parents do not use texting as a means of communication. (D) is incorrect because communicating only through official documents does not allow for proactive discussions about behavior and academic work that can prevent issues before they occur. It also does not communicate a sense of caring on the part of the teacher.

4.   A seventh-grade Texas history teacher and her Special Education co-teacher feel strongly that all students have learning strengths. They plan lessons where each of them presents the same information, but one emphasizes visual and auditory activities, while the other emphasizes tactile and kinesthetic activities. They divide the class by learning modality strengths and simultaneously teach their lessons. What kind of co-teaching model are these two teachers implementing?

(A)   One teach, one drift

(B)   Paired reading

(C)   Station teaching

(D)   Parallel teaching

The correct response is (**D**). Parallel teaching is a co-teaching model where both teachers present the same information simultaneously to two separate groups in the same classroom. (A) is incorrect because the one teach, one drift model involves only one teacher leading the lesson while the other teacher moves around the room assisting individual students. (B) is incorrect because paired reading is a reading strategy where students are paired up and given the same reading assignment. (C) is incorrect because the station teaching model involves each teacher having different content and a different area of the room for instruction. Students rotate from one station to another.

PRACTICE TEST 1

TExES Special Education EC–12 (161)

Also available at the REA Study Center (*www.rea.com/studycenter*)

This practice test is also offered online at the REA Study Center. We recommend that you take the online version of the test to simulate test-day conditions and to receive these added benefits:

- **Timed testing conditions**—helps you gauge how much time you can spend on each question

- **Automatic scoring**—find out how you did on the test, instantly

- **On-screen detailed explanations of answers**—gives you the correct answer and explains why the other answer choices are wrong

- **Diagnostic score reports**—pinpoint where you're strongest and where you need to focus your study

504
Idea.

1.

$\dfrac{1}{135\overline{)260 \times 5 =}}$

300 minutes

270

2 minutes

PRACTICE TEST 1

TIME: 5 Hours
135 Multiple-choice questions

In this section, you will find examples of test questions similar to those you are likely to encounter on the TExES Special Education EC–12 (161) Exam. Read each question carefully and choose the best answer from the four possible choices. Mark your responses on the answer sheet provided on page 289.

1. The first piece of federal legislation to address the civil rights of all people with disabilities was

   (A)   Section 504 of the Rehabilitation Act.
   (B)   Individuals with Disabilities Education Act.
   (C)   Elementary and Secondary Education Act.
   (D)   No Child Left Behind.

2. Marcus is a nine grader with intellectual disabilities. His transition needs evaluation indicates that he likes pets, especially dogs. He does not like doctors and becomes nervous around needles. Marcus is good at carrying out routine tasks. Based on this information, an appropriate supported employment opportunity for Marcus would be

   (A)   taking animals at a veterinarian's office for walks.
   (B)   dealing with customer issues at a customer service counter.
   (C)   completing janitorial services at a local hospital.
   (D)   feeding and washing dogs at an animal shelter.

3. A second grader with autism who is nonverbal gets upset in the cafeteria at lunch and lies down on the ground and begins screaming. This goes on for several minutes, disrupting lunch. Which of the following is NOT a potential cause of this behavior?

   (A)   The noise and confusion in the cafeteria became overwhelming.
   (B)   The child's scheduled lunchtime is normally an hour later and today is a change of routine.
   (C)   The second grader wants everyone to look at him.
   (D)   The child's favorite type of chip was not in his lunch bag today.

4. The primary reason to provide assessment accommodations is to

   (A)   help students with disabilities have an equal opportunity to demonstrate what they know.
   (B)   give an advantage to students with disabilities.
   (C)   make sure students with disabilities pass their classes.
   (D)   make the test administrator's job more challenging.

5. Which of the following transition goals meets IDEA 2004 requirements?

    (A) After high school, Alex will learn janitorial skills for placement in a supported employment position in the local community

    (B) In grade 11, Tina will pass the STAAR Alt

    (C) Juan will apply to community colleges and major in art

    (D) After high school, Mia will live at home

6. A sixth-grade teacher hands out copies of a blank Venn diagram for students to use during prewriting. What form of writing are the students most likely going to be assigned?

    (A) Persuasive

    (B) How-to

    (C) Compare/contrast

    (D) Narrative

Use the information below to answer questions 7 and 8.

In assessing a sixth-grade student's oral reading, a Special Education teacher uses several fictional passages leveled from 1.0 to 6.0. The teacher places each passage in front of the student, starting with the 1.0 passage, and asks the student to read it aloud. The chart below represents the results of the assessment:

Reading Level	Accuracy Percentage
1.0	98%
2.0	96%
3.0	95%
4.0	92%
5.0	85%
6.0	70%

7. Based on the results, what level text would be the most appropriate to use for guided reading instruction?

    (A) Reading Level 2.0

    (B) Reading Level 4.0

    (C) Reading Level 5.0

    (D) Reading Level 6.0

8. Two days after the assessment, the Special Education teacher is with the student's class in the school library. She notices the student looking at an action/adventure book. It is approximately a 6.0 reading level. An appropriate reaction on the part of the teacher would be to

    (A) call the student aside and recommend a similar-themed book that is written at a 3.0 reading level.

    (B) let the student check out the original book.

    (C) walk over to the student and say, "You can't read that. It is too difficult."

    (D) tell the student she will use the original book for the next reading lesson they work on together.

9. Mrs. Benson, a third-grade teacher, has a diverse class that includes students with learning disabilities, English learners, and gifted students. For a reading unit, she pairs the students based on personality (for example, patient fluent readers with struggling readers). She then has the partners complete together every reading assignment in that unit. For text reading, partners decide how they will divide up the text for reading (for example, switching off by paragraphs or pages). For comprehension activities, partners turn in one paper representing work from both students. While partners are working together, Mrs. Benson walks around the classroom observing pairs and assisting with questions. One of the primary advantages of Mrs. Benson's paired reading strategy is that

   (A) struggling students can let their partners do all their work.
   (B) students get a great deal more supported oral reading practice than they would in a group-reading situation.
   (C) Mrs. Benson can take a break from lesson planning.
   (D) students are not paired with their friends so there is less off-task talking.

10. The reason that Section 504 of the Rehabilitation Act was ignored by state and local educational agencies for 20 years after it was passed in 1973 is that the law

   (A) didn't make sense to school boards.
   (B) was discriminatory.
   (C) was never signed by the President of the United States.
   (D) did not include provisions for federal funding or monitoring.

11. A Special Education teacher working with students with intellectual disabilities and autism is teaching one-to-one correspondence. The most appropriate instructional tool for the teacher to use in teaching this concept would be

   (A) a worksheet with symbol-supported text.
   (B) a graphic organizer.
   (C) blocks of different colors.
   (D) a calculator.

12. In Special Education professional circles, the term "disproportionality" refers to

   (A) the overrepresentation of racial, cultural, and linguistic minorities in Special Education.
   (B) a mathematical dilemma with geometric shapes.
   (C) the high number of students with autism in ALE classrooms.
   (D) the low number of Texas schools receiving Special Education funding.

13. Which of the following behaviors would be a potential warning sign for an epileptic seizure?

   (A) Irritability
   (B) Extreme hunger
   (C) Nervous energy
   (D) Unexplained confusion, sleepiness, or weakness

14. Which of the following academic difficulties may characterize a language learning disability?

    (A) Frequent misspelled words
    (B) Difficulty memorizing the multiplication tables
    (C) Frequent missing assignments
    (D) Difficulty working with other students in groups

Use the information below to answer questions 15 and 16.

A teacher presents students with the following number pattern:

1, 3, 9, 27, ___

15. Given this pattern, the next number would be

    (A) 81.
    (B) 45.
    (C) 54.
    (D) 1.

16. What type of number pattern is this?

    (A) Arithmetic sequence
    (B) Fibonacci sequence
    (C) Harmonic sequence
    (D) Geometric sequence

17. Which of the following examples would best serve as a transition for students moving from a concrete to an abstract conceptual understanding of fractions?

    (A) A pie cut into eight pieces
    (B) A pie graph divided into four parts with one part shaded
    (C) An apple cut into 12 slices
    (D) A recipe requiring several ingredients in half and quarter cup or teaspoon measurements

18. A seventh-grade inclusion teacher uses the interactive whiteboard to model persuasive writing for her students. She writes a persuasive essay on why school should be year round. As she writes, she comments on her word choices and talks about points to make, expanding some of them and discarding others. The instructional strategy that this teacher is using is

    (A) think-aloud.
    (B) graphic organizer.
    (C) language experience.
    (D) formula writing.

19. What is the most commonly diagnosed behavioral disorder in children?

    (A) Autism
    (B) Depression
    (C) Attention deficit hyperactivity disorder
    (D) Oppositional disorder

20. A sixth-grade mathematics teacher uses her interactive whiteboard and individual student clickers to administer informal quizzes during her lessons at least twice a week. The most appropriate reason for this teacher to give students regular informal quizzes is to

    (A) get enough individual grades for an accurate average.
    (B) determine if a student should be recommended for Special Education testing.
    (C) utilize the expensive classroom technology.
    (D) identify skills that the teacher should reteach.

21. Two co-teachers choose to use the "One Teach, One Observe" model for a lesson on volcanoes. What would this model look like in action?

    (A) One teacher would pretend to be a reporter on location at a volcanic eruption, reporting what she sees, while the other teacher presents the normal progression of a volcanic eruption.
    (B) One teacher presents the normal progression of a volcanic eruption, using visuals and 3-D models, while the other teacher watches the students in the class and keeps notes on their levels of participation and conceptual understanding.
    (C) One teacher presents information to the boys while the other teacher presents the same information to the girls.
    (D) One teacher sets up a station with a model of an erupting volcano and the other teacher sets up an interactive whiteboard activity that involves labeling the parts of a volcano. Students rotate between the stations.

22. Which of the following student activities is an example of structural analysis?

    (A) Matching words to pictures
    (B) Reading a 100-word passage in less than a minute
    (C) Identifying prefixes and suffixes in a list of words
    (D) Using a graphic organizer for prewriting

23. An initial ARD is held for a student evaluated for Special Education services. The student's parents gave permission for the evaluation, but during the ARD committee meeting, they talk about their concerns regarding Special Education labels and ultimately refuse to sign their agreement to the Special Education placement. The classroom teacher feels strongly that the child needs Special Education services and requests to have a Special Education co-teacher work with the student one-on-one "off-the-record." What is the appropriate response to this suggestion?

    (A) The classroom teacher should be fired for violating the Texas Code of Ethics for Educators.
    (B) Special Education laws require parental consent. The student must be served in the regular classroom for now.
    (C) The classroom teacher should call the parents and let them know her plans.
    (D) The school district will file an appeal to an impartial hearing officer and. In the meantime, the child will receive Special Education services per the teacher's request.

24. A middle-school teacher is working with a small group of below-level readers. He brings in five print advertisements for various consumer products and uses sticky notes to cover all the words. He then displays the advertisements one at a time and asks the students to tell him what each advertisement is trying to tell consumers. The purpose of this activity is to

    (A) convince the students to buy the products.
    (B) show students how visual images in media communicate a message and how to interpret them.
    (C) motivate reluctant readers by removing all the words.
    (D) help students visualize while reading.

25. A student in an ALE classroom has autism and is nonverbal. Symbol-based communication and a picture-based daily schedule are working, but progress is slow. The student has recently shown a fascination with the classroom tablet devices. What type of assistive technology might the teacher recommend the IEP committee consider for this student?

    (A) Communication app for the tablet device
    (B) Talking calculator
    (C) Handwriting guides
    (D) Speech-recognition program for the classroom computer

26. If a child cries easily, does not want to interact with peers, and does not like coming to school on a consistent basis, the best course of action to take would be to

    (A) report it to the school counselor and recommend behavioral observation by a school psychologist.
    (B) ignore the behaviors, as all children sometimes have issues at school.
    (C) seat the child with classmates who will be empathetic.
    (D) suggest to the parents that they should talk to their child.

27. When talking to parents on the phone or at a parent-teacher conference, the most important thing a teacher can do is to

    (A) have documented examples for every problem the teacher has with the student.
    (B) have an answer for every question parents ask.
    (C) praise the parents for their outstanding parenting skills.
    (D) take time to listen to the parents' responses and concerns, and note anything that requires follow-up.

Use the information below to answer questions 28 and 29.

    An elementary ALE teacher uses puff paint and index cards to create flash cards with raised words. The words on the cards are: *and, is, what, I, am, to, have, see, the, you.* The teacher gives each student several minutes to trace the raised words with their fingers. If the student is verbal, the teacher has the student say the word while looking at it and tracing it. If the student is nonverbal, the teacher says the word while the student looks at the word and traces it.

28. What kind of words has the teacher selected for this activity?

    (A) Second-grade words
    (B) Sight words
    (C) Decodable words
    (D) Academic vocabulary

29. The most likely reason that the teacher wants the word spoken at the same time the word is being traced is to

    (A) increase retention through repetition and the combination of learning modalities.
    (B) make the activity fun.
    (C) make sure the words are pronounced correctly.
    (D) decrease disruptive behaviors.

30. Which of the following is NOT an area in which diagnostic assessments to determine eligibility for Special Education services might be given?

    (A) Development
    (B) Social emotional behavior
    (C) Career placement
    (D) Auditory processing

31. A middle-school Special Education teacher reviews a student's grades as part of planning her IEP goals for the next ARD. She sees the following:

Jane Doe Report Card	
Reading	80
Language Arts	60
Mathematics	88
Science	90
Social Studies	65
Physical Education	95
Music	84

When the teacher reflects on the general education teachers the student has, she knows that the Reading teacher incorporates a lot of movement and critical thinking activities into her lesson plans. The language arts teacher requires students to write a paper every week as homework. The social studies teacher assigns chapters and gives open-ended unit tests. The science teacher has students conduct at least two experiments per week. The teacher might conclude that

   (A) the student wants to be an astronaut.
   (B) the student only likes PE.
   (C) the student may be a tactile/kinesthetic learner and needs some explicit reading and writing strategy instruction.
   (D) the student may be an auditory learner and clearly does not like her social studies and language arts teachers.

32. What term best describes an assessment that measures group performance against an established standard at defined points along the path toward the standard?

   (A) Formative
   (B) Benchmark
   (C) Summative
   (D) Alternative

33. A Special Education teacher is working with a small group of students with documented social-skills goals in their IEPs. An appropriate activity for the small group to do would be

   (A) sustained silent reading.
   (B) taking notes as the teacher talks about the benefits of good social skills.
   (C) playing a board game built around conversation skills.
   (D) writing goals about how many friends each student wants to make in the next month.

34. During the first two weeks of school, a first-grade teacher observes his/her students completing various assignments and notes down their strengths and weaknesses. What kind of assessment is the teacher giving?

    (A) Informal
    (B) Norm-referenced
    (C) Summative
    (D) Formal

35. Which reauthorization of IDEA implemented a timeframe of not more than 60 days to conduct initial evaluations for Special Education eligibility?

    (A) Reauthorization of 1990
    (B) Reauthorization of 1997
    (C) Reauthorization of 2004
    (D) Reauthorization of 2009

36. A fourth-grade teacher has a class of 22 students, including four students with IEPs and two English learners. At the beginning of the school year, the teacher administers an inventory with questions about how students approach different learning tasks and what subjects they like best. She also structures a variety of activities, including a memory game similar to Concentration, a classroom scavenger hunt for clues to the answer to a question, and a math game with manipulatives. As students complete the activities, the teacher observes and makes notes on a clipboard. The teacher is most likely

    (A) figuring out who the smartest students are.
    (B) observing and noting each student's learning strengths so that she can plan appropriate activities.
    (C) grouping students by ability.
    (D) making sure every student likes her.

37. A student with an IEP is caught defacing a school wall. Based on the school's written code of conduct, the assistant principal suspends the student from school for three days. The student has not been suspended previously that school year, but the parents protest the suspension, saying that the student's status as a Special Education student prevents him from being suspended. The most appropriate response is that

    (A) the school district should override the suspension since the student receives Special Education services.
    (B) the principal should ask the assistant principal to tell the parents that if they pay for the damages, the student will not be suspended.
    (C) the suspension should be changed to in-school suspension so that the parents do not have to arrange for child care.
    (D) the assistant principal should call a meeting with the parents with another administrator present and point out that disciplinary sanctions of less than 10 days are not considered a change of placement under IDEA and are, therefore, legal.

8-7

38. Mr. Martinez, an eighth-grade social studies teacher, begins a unit on Westward Expansion in the United States by dividing students into "families" and giving each family a destination to reach in the West. Each "family" receives an index card with a list of supplies and transportation. "Family" members must talk together to figure out how they will get to their destination. What is the most likely reason Mr. Martinez begins the unit this way?

(A) To build student engagement in the topic
(B) To prepare students for the test
(C) To foster healthy competition
(D) To make decisions based on data

39. What type of shape is shown below?

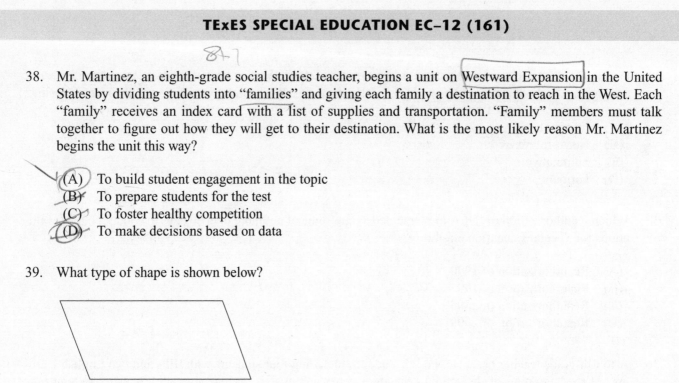

(A) Square
(B) Parallelogram
(C) Isosceles triangle
(D) Oval

40. The purpose of a standardized achievement test is to

(A) identify the best reading method to use with a student.
(B) measure the amount of knowledge and skills a student has acquired in comparison to a larger group.
(C) establish a baseline for learning prior to starting a new unit.
(D) help a teacher form instructional groups.

5th

41. Parents of a fifth grader with learning disabilities have a parent-teacher conference with the student's classroom teacher and Special Education co-teacher. The parents indicate that they would like to learn more about learning disabilities and the potential schools and camps that may be appropriate for their child. An appropriate resource for the teachers to share with the parents would be information about

(A) local camps for children with autism.
(B) local group homes and other residential facilities.
(C) the location of local libraries.
(D) LDA and a link to the organization's website.

LDA

42. For Special Education students with intensive disabilities, school districts must offer public education until age 23. Which of the following curriculum choices would be the most appropriate for students after high school to age 23?

   (A) Intensive reading intervention
   (B) On-the-job coaching and independent living skills
   (C) Academic courses along with two electives
   (D) Social skills training

43. Ms. Silva, a co-teacher in a second-grade classroom, works with a group of three students. She reads a sentence out loud and then has the students repeat the sentence. She instructs them to "mimic" her as closely as possible because she wants them to match her speed and expression. What modeling method is Ms. Silva using?

   (A) Recorded books
   (B) Neurological impress
   (C) Choral reading
   (D) Echo reading

44. According to IDEA 2004 and CFR 300.43, transition services must be based on

   (A) a school's resources.
   (B) local community opportunities for students with disabilities.
   (C) parents' expectations for what their child can accomplish.
   (D) an individual student's needs, taking into account strengths, preferences, and interests.

45. What is the ARD committee in Texas equivalent to in federal regulations regarding Special Education evaluation procedures?

   (A) FAPE committee
   (B) LRE committee
   (C) IEP committee
   (D) CEC committee

46. One week before a geography teacher begins the next unit in the textbook, her co-teacher conducts an activity where he provides each student with half an index card with part of a word on it. Students have to stand and find the student who has the other half of their card. Then they work with their partner to find the definition for the vocabulary word on their card and draw a picture of what the word represents. The purpose of this lesson is to

   (A) give students a break from the textbook.
   (B) preteach vocabulary and thus improve students' ability to read and understand the next chapter.
   (C) show that all geography-related vocabulary words make great pictures.
   (D) give the co-teacher a chance to conduct a lesson.

47. Mr. Osborn, an ALE teacher, works one-on-one with each of his students. Early in the school year, he presents each student with a list of words. He says, "I am going to show you a list of words you may or may not know. If you know the word, read it out loud. If you do not know the word, say pass." As students read the list of words, Mr. Osborn makes notes on a separate checklist. He places a check mark next to any words the student reads correctly in a half second or less. He places an "X" next to any word the student cannot read, hesitates to read, or has to work to sound out. Mr. Osborn is most likely assessing

    (A) students' sight-word automaticity.
    (B) students' grasp of the English language.
    (C) students' ability to follow directions.
    (D) students' reading comprehension.

48. To fulfill the IDEA requirement of least restrictive environment (LRE), which of the following areas must be documented in a Special Education student's IEP?

    (A) The name of the student's Special Education teacher
    (B) The list of medications the student is taking
    (C) The extent to which the student will not participate with nondisabled students in regular classes or nonacademic activities
    (D) The parents' description of the student's home environment

49. A Special Education teacher works with a biology teacher to create a mind map of the upcoming unit on plants. The most likely purpose for this collaboration is

    (A) to help both teachers identify the big ideas and how they are related to each other so that they can identify the key elements to assess as the unit progresses.
    (B) for the biology teacher to be able to teach the Special Education teacher science concepts.
    (C) to show that minds have branches and roots just like plants.
    (D) for the Special Education teacher to show the biology teacher a cool new technique she just learned at a staff development meeting.

50. What details must a written notice of an ARD committee meeting include?

    (A) Purpose, time, and place of the meeting
    (B) Three choices for the date and time of the meeting
    (C) Evaluation results
    (D) The proposed IEP

51. A Special Education teacher has two paraprofessionals assigned to her class. Which of the following would be the best use of these assistants' time?

    (A) Have the paraprofessionals make copies and laminate materials most of the day
    (B) Ask the paraprofessionals to administer medications to the students
    (C) Train the paraprofessionals to help facilitate the instructional programs the teacher is using so that instruction can be divided into individual and small group time
    (D) Have the paraprofessionals monitor the students while the teacher does required paperwork

52. Which of the following is NOT a strategy that will help a teacher conduct productive and positive parent-teacher meetings?

    (A) State at the beginning of the meeting that the teacher has only 10 minutes and will have to end the meeting as soon as those 10 minutes are up

    (B) Develop a clear purpose for the meeting, state the purpose at the beginning of the meeting, and summarize how this purpose was accomplished at the end of the meeting

    (C) Start the meeting by noting some of the positive aspects of the child's performance and behavior

    (D) Schedule the meeting time around the parents' schedule needs

53. The law that mandates that states provide a free appropriate public education to all children with disabilities or risk educational funding cuts or withholdings is

    (A) Public Law 89-10.
    (B) Public Law 93-112.
    (C) Public Law 94-142.   IDEA
    (D) Public Law 94-479.

Use the information below to answer questions 54 and 55.

Mrs. Cullen is a sixth-grade reading teacher. She has both regular and Special Education students in her classroom. At the beginning of the year, she administers a variety of informal assessments and observes students' strengths and weaknesses. She then sets up stations around the classroom where students can work independently or in pairs on reading and writing tasks. Each day, for 15 minutes, Mrs. Cullen teaches a whole group mini-lesson related to the TEKS. Then students are directed to stations. During station time, Mrs. Cullen conducts small-group targeted lessons on various reading skills. While the groups never have more than five students, the students called up each day change depending on the skill being taught.

54. What instructional technique is Mrs. Cullen using?

    (A) Homogenous grouping
    (B) Whole-group instruction
    (C) Self-selected reading
    (D) Flexible grouping

55. Based on the description of Mrs. Cullen's beginning-of-the-year procedures, which of the following statements most likely describes her philosophy?

    (A) Special Education students need to be taught differently
    (B) Teaching to the state standardized test ensures all students will pass
    (C) Data should drive instruction
    (D) There is only one way to teach reading

56. During a reading lesson, a first-grade teacher writes the word "boy" on the board. She points to the letter "b" and asks students to make the sound of the letter. Which of the following concepts is the teacher addressing?

   (A) Phonemic awareness
   (B) Pragmatics
   (C) Fluency
   (D) Letter-Sound correspondence

57. A sixth-grade social studies teacher is having difficulty motivating several students who are tactile/kinesthetic learners. The best way to deal with the problem is to

   (A) show a series of images related to the upcoming unit on the interactive whiteboard.
   (B) have the students read the next chapter in class, with each student expected to read a paragraph out loud.
   (C) play a recording of sounds associated with the content of the next chapter and have students guess what they are.
   (D) place sheets of chart paper around the room. On each one, write an open-ended question about a debatable issue related to the content of the next unit. Have students walk around the room and write their stance on each issue.

58. Which of the following is NOT a stage of the writing process?

   (A) Editing
   (B) Prewriting
   (C) Counting the words
   (D) Publishing

59. At what point should a Special Education teacher in Texas advise parents of a child with intellectual disabilities to apply for state assistance programs (for example, Community Living Assistance and Support Services)?

   (A) At the point when Special Education testing begins
   (B) When the student graduates from high school
   (C) As soon as the student has an official diagnosis
   (D) When parents can no longer care for their child

60. Which of the following situations would be a good reason to provide community-based instruction?

   (A) Ninth-grade students do not see how Algebra relates to the real world
   (B) Students in a high school ALE class have been practicing how to order food off a menu at a restaurant
   (C) Students in a ninth-grade English class all passed the STAAR
   (D) Parents want to know why the district chose a particular reading program

61. What techniques may be used to conduct a functional behavioral assessment?

    (A) Data analysis
    (B) Structured interviews with current teachers
    (C) Standardized behavior assessment
    (D) All of the above

62. A middle-school teacher believes in incorporating movement to help maintain student focus and engagement. Which of the following classroom situations would be an example of that philosophy?

    (A) Students are assigned seats and expected to stay in their seats unless they raise a hand asking for permission to sharpen a pencil or go to the restroom.
    (B) Each student is given an index card and asked to write a question he or she has about the lesson the teacher just presented. The teacher then has the students stand and find partners who are wearing the same color. Once all the students are standing next to their partners, the teacher asks them to exchange cards and answer each other's questions.
    (C) The teacher gives any student who answers a question correctly a high-five.
    (D) Students are asked to draw what they see in their heads as a teacher reads an article aloud to them.

63. A third-grade student is tested for learning disabilities and is found to have memory deficits. Based on this diagnosis, in which area of mathematics is this student likely to have difficulty?

    (A) Math facts
    (B) Geometry
    (C) Graphs and charts
    (D) Fractions, decimals, and percentages

64. A Special Education co-teacher is working with a fifth-grade student with learning disabilities. As the student works through a series of math problems, the teacher observes that word problems, particularly ones with multiple steps, seem particularly challenging for the student. The student often does just the first operation he can figure out and then abandons the problem. Based on this informal assessment, what type of cognitive deficits is the student most likely exhibiting?

    (A) Visual-spatial deficits
    (B) Memory deficits
    (C) Procedural learning deficits
    (D) Number sense deficits

65. Which of the following curriculum development projects would a Special Education teacher be most likely to work with an SLP to develop?

    (A) A rubric for an oral presentation project
    (B) Calculator practice activities
    (C) A fast-food restaurant simulation, practicing how to count money
    (D) A science fair project

66. A container of milk is 3/8 full. What percentage of the container is full?

    (A) 0.5
    (B) 0.38
    (C) 0.75
    (D) 0.375

67. What should precede the development of a Behavior Intervention Plan?

    (A) A tour of the student's home environment
    (B) Functional behavioral assessment
    (C) Review of the discipline policies of the student's teachers
    (D) Review of the student's STAAR scores

68. Researchers look at the strategies successful readers use to help them identify reading strategies to teach explicitly to struggling readers. Which of the following strategies is an example of a strategy most successful readers use during reading, often without consciously thinking about it?

    (A) Reading just to get to the end of the assignment
    (B) Skipping over words they don't recognize
    (C) Reading fiction and nonfiction the same way
    (D) Pausing every few paragraphs and mentally summarizing what just happened in the text

69. One advantage of implementing a research-based Response to Intervention (RTI) program from a Special Education teacher's perspective is that RTI

    (A) is the regular education teacher's responsibility, thus leaving the Special Education department with more time.
    (B) involves less work than Special Education diagnostic testing.
    (C) is easy to implement.
    (D) can potentially reduce overidentification of students with learning disabilities.

70. Mrs. Seville, a seventh-grade mathematics teacher, creates an end-of-unit test for her geometry unit. All of the questions are open-ended and require students to show their work and write their answers. A Special Education co-teacher might modify this test for students with learning disabilities in Mrs. Seville's class by

    (A) making no modifications; all students must take the same test to be fair.
    (B) converting most of the questions to multiple choice, but still require students to show their work on the paper.
    (C) reading the test questions out loud for students.
    (D) providing a calculator.

71.   The purpose of a transition plan in a student's IEP is to

(A)   help the student move from elementary to middle school.
(B)   help the student move from middle school into high school.
(C)   help the student move from high school to postgraduation and adult life.
(D)   help students move from Special Education to general education.

72.   Ms. Tejeda, a Special Education teacher, is assigned to co-teach several classes with an eighth-grade algebra teacher. Which of the following interactions would be the most effective way for Ms. Tejeda to ensure successful collaboration?

(A)   Schedule a time before or after school twice a week to plan lessons together
(B)   Invite the algebra teacher out for appetizers and drinks to "get to know one another"
(C)   Gather all the Special Education resources she uses most and drop them off on the algebra teacher's desk
(D)   Offer to modify all of the algebra teacher's tests for the students with special needs

Use the information below to answer questions 73 and 74.

A third-grade teacher displays the following words on a prominent bulletin board in her classroom: acute, right, obtuse, area, perimeter, symmetry, and volume.

73.   Given these vocabulary words, what kind of math unit is the teacher most likely preparing to present?

(A)   Geometry
(B)   Probability and statistics
(C)   Measurement
(D)   Number sense

74.   Which of the following instructional strategies would be the best use of the mathematical vocabulary words posted on the bulletin board?

(A)   Divide the students in groups of three and assign one word from the bulletin board to each group. Direct the groups to illustrate the meaning of their words on pieces of chart paper. Then have the class play a game of visual charades, where a group presents their illustration to the class, and the class guesses which vocabulary word is illustrated.
(B)   Avoid pointing out the words and let them be a natural part of the classroom environment for the students to absorb.
(C)   Have students refer to the bulletin board when completing math assignments in order to spell words correctly.
(D)   Have students find the same words in magazines and newspapers and staple their environmental print examples to the bulletin board.

75. When formulating instructional objectives for a student's Individualized Education Program (IEP), what should the Annual Review and Dismissal (ARD) committee do?

    (A) Base the objectives exclusively on the grade-level TEKS
    (B) Construct the objectives based on what the student's parents want the child to be able to do
    (C) Let the student choose his or her own objectives
    (D) Review the student's current level of performance, and write reasonable objectives that reflect the grade-level TEKS as closely as possible and promote academic growth

76. For which students was the STAAR Alternate designed?

    (A) Students with learning disabilities
    (B) Students in alternative schools
    (C) Students with ADHD
    (D) Students with significant cognitive disabilities

77. A veteran teacher advises a new colleague in the Special Education department to identify some strengths she sees in each of her students and to call parents in the first few weeks of school to compliment their child on these strengths. What is the primary advantage of this approach to parent-teacher communication?

    (A) It allows the new teacher to ignore all the problems she is going to have with students
    (B) It builds respect with parents who see that the teacher cares about their child and are often pleasantly surprised to be getting a "good" call
    (C) It can be documented on the first evaluation the new teacher receives
    (D) It ensures that the new teacher will believe in herself enough to make it through the school year

78. Why were the Rehabilitation Act of 1973 and Public Law 94-142, passed by Congress in 1975, so important for students with disabilities in the United States?

    (A) These two laws showed the rest of the world that the United States was committed to Special Education
    (B) Prior to these two pieces of federal legislation, individual states were not offering public education to the majority of children with disabilities
    (C) These two laws created a designated day to honor individuals with disabilities
    (D) These two laws made provisions for the federal government to fund over half of the Special Education expenses incurred by school districts

79. Which of the following angles is an obtuse angle?

    (A)   (C)

    (B)   (D)

80. Katie, a fourth-grade student with ADHD, is often off-task. Her regular education teacher places her at a table close to the front of the room with tablemates who are very focused on their work. What is Katie's teacher doing?

    (A) Ignoring Katie's behavior
    (B) Implementing a simple accommodation to improve Katie's performance
    (C) Encouraging Katie's classmates to be watchdogs
    (D) Modifying Katie's assignments

81. A middle-school Special Education teacher is teaching a mathematics class to seventh graders who failed the sixth-grade STAAR math test. The teacher provides highlighters to each student and shows them a list of keywords to look for and highlight in a series of word problems. Each time the students are assigned word problems, the teacher has them highlight keywords. She tells her students that this technique will help them on the test. The strategy that the teacher is providing her students is

    (A) pictorial representation.
    (B) corrective feedback.
    (C) generic problem-solving strategy.
    (D) modeling strategy.

82. As part of the morning circle time in an elementary ALE classroom, the teacher has a small pocket chart with three pockets labeled "hundreds," "tens," and "ones." Each day, a student is selected to place a yellow straw in the "ones" pocket and then count all of the straws in that pocket. If there are 10 straws, the student gets to exchange them for a blue straw, which goes in the "tens" pocket. The mathematical concept the teacher is using to count the days of the school year is

    (A) number sense.
    (B) place value.
    (C) patterns.
    (D) fractions.

83. As part of reading instruction, a Special Education teacher in a self-contained classroom has a student say a word, trace a word, identify a word in text, and complete a worksheet by matching the word to a picture. Which research-based instructional strategy is being demonstrated in this teacher's classroom?

    (A) Repetition and review
    (B) Computer-based instruction
    (C) Positive reinforcement
    (D) Visual teaching

84. A parent tells you her/his child has dyscalculia. In which academic area would you anticipate the student to have difficulties?

    (A) Reading
    (B) Writing
    (C) Mathematics
    (D) Social Studies

85. Which reauthorization of IDEA expanded the definition of disabilities to include children with developmental delays between the ages of three and nine?

    (A) Reauthorization of 1990
    (B) Reauthorization of 1997
    (C) Reauthorization of 2004
    (D) Reauthorization of 2009

86. The best way for dealing with a student who acts silly and talks loudly throughout class time is to

    (A) send the student to time out.
    (B) ignore the behavior.
    (C) create a leadership role for this student.
    (D) make sure all the other students in the class see you reprimanding the student.

87. Look at the following test results.

Standardized Test Results			
Name	Grade	Adjusted Score	Percentile Score
Jane Doe	5	215	65

The percentile score means that

    (A) the student passed the test.
    (B) the student failed the test.
    (C) 65 percent of students who took the test scored equal to or less than the test-taker.
    (D) 35 percent of students who took the test scored less than the test-taker.

88. Which of the following statements is true of autism?

    (A) It is more common among boys than girls.
    (B) It is more common among children born from teenage parents.
    (C) It is more common among girls than boys.
    (D) It is curable.

89. When planning instruction for students with special needs, the best approach is to

    (A) focus on students' weaknesses.
    (B) follow the lessons in textbooks and programs exactly.
    (C) teach to students' strengths.
    (D) teach all students the same way.

90. When writing a Behavior Intervention Plan for a student whose behavior impedes learning, what kind of strategies does IDEA 2004 require the IEP team to consider?

    (A) Positive behavioral interventions and supports
    (B) Behavior logs
    (C) Negative reinforcers
    (D) Parental strategies

91. An elementary school hosts an open house a few days before school starts so that families can meet the teachers. Parents of a new student with autism come to the open house out of breath and scowling. They look around the classroom, and the mother immediately begins asking about types of sensory equipment she would like to see in the classroom. The father interrupts and says the student needs to be treated like every other student with no special equipment. The best way for the teacher to approach these parents is to

    (A) assume they are going to be difficult and maintain a professional but distant approach.
    (B) approach both parents with a warm smile and excitement about the goals for the upcoming school year, and encourage the student to explore the classroom while asking the parents to talk about their son's strengths.
    (C) address the mother and promise to ask the principal to purchase the sensory equipment.
    (D) address the father and assure him that the son will have access to the standard state curriculum.

92. In order to build student's fluency, an appropriate prereading strategy would be to

    (A) have students stop at the end of each page and summarize what happened.
    (B) have students turn to a partner and talk about what they liked and didn't like in the story.
    (C) have students scan the text and then predict what the text will be about.
    (D) have the students look at the title and then name similar titles from other books.

93. A teacher presents students with the following pattern with the third and ninth shapes missing:

○ ○ __ ⊡ △ ○ ○ □ △ __

Based upon this pattern, what would the ninth shape be?

    (A) □
    (B) △
    (C) □
    (D) ○

94. What does OHI stand for?

    (A) Only Healthy Individuals
    (B) Oppositional Hyperactivity Indicator
    (C) Organized Heart Implant
    (D) Other Health Impairment

95. At what age does IDEA 2004 say a transition plan MUST be in place?

    (A) 14 planning
    (B) 15
    (C) 16 . end
    (D) 18

96. A grade 4 student with learning disabilities is struggling with language arts. The student likes to compose stories, but her handwriting is extremely difficult to read and she makes numerous spelling errors. What assistive technology would you recommend the child be evaluated for?

    (A) Recorded books
    (B) Alternative keyboard
    (C) Word processor with a spell checker
    (D) Electronic math worksheets

97. A fourth-grade teacher assigns several three-digit multiplication problems for her students to complete. In reviewing the papers, the teacher finds one with over 50 percent of the answers incorrect. Attempting to see what caused the mistakes, the teacher notices that the student has misaligned many of the numbers. The computation that was done is correct, but the wrong numbers were often multiplied or added together. In reflecting on this student's past math performance, the teacher recalls that geometry also proved difficult for the student. The assumption that would most likely be true about this student is that the student

    (A) hates math and does not put forth effort to do the work neatly.
    (B) seems to be exhibiting visual-spatial deficits that are affecting academic performance.
    (C) has Attention Deficit Hyperactivity Disorder.
    (D) requires handwriting supports.

98. Under the *Individuals with Disabilities Education Act*, which of the following is NOT considered a disability category?

    (A) Speech/language impairment
    (B) Intellectual disability
    (C) Specific learning disability
    (D) Post-traumatic stress disorder

99. Which of the following areas is not a type of assessment accommodation?

    (A) Presentation
    (B) Scheduling
    (C) Content
    (D) Timing

100. A Special Education teacher wants to share study strategies with students with learning disabilities and their families. He organizes an evening hands-on workshop where he presents information about different learning styles and models study strategies that fit each of the learning styles. What is this teacher trying to accomplish?

    (A) Earning a Teacher of the Year nomination
    (B) Showing the general education teachers that the Special Education department does more for students than the academic departments
    (C) Helping parents understand where their students have weaknesses
    (D) Teaching students and their families how to recognize their strengths and use those strengths to achieve success in the regular education environment, no matter who the teacher is

101. According to the Council for Exceptional Children's code of ethics, Special Educators and related professionals are bound to

    (A) maintaining challenging expectations for individuals with exceptionalities.
    (B) using evidence, instructional data, research, and professional knowledge to inform practice.
    (C) advocating for professional conditions and resources that will improve learning outcomes of individuals with exceptionalities.
    (D) all of the above.

102. What is likely an underlying cause of bullying behavior?

    (A) Racism
    (B) Lack of a sense of control
    (C) Dislike of other people
    (D) Overprotective parent

103. A second-grade inclusion teacher arranges her student desks into small groups of four. She places her teacher desk on the right side of the class and an oval table on the left side. Around the oval table, she places four student chairs. She has a teacher chair on one side of the table. On the wall, she places a poster with the following words: *Presenter*, *Researcher*, *Note Taker*, and *Discussion Leader*. Given this classroom arrangement, what types of instruction would you expect to see if you visited?

    (A) Whole-group instruction and leveled groups
    (B) Cooperative learning and targeted small group instruction
    (C) Independent study and project-based learning
    (D) Flexible grouping and sustained silent reading

104. Research on effective math instructional strategies has indicated that explicit instruction is critical. Which of the following lessons is an example of an explicit teaching strategy?

    (A) A teacher has students complete worksheets with operational drills for 20 minutes every day
    (B) A teacher gives students 20 colored squares and then steps back and observes what the students do with the squares
    (C) A teacher demonstrates how to solve an addition problem using a number line, talking out loud through each step of the addition process
    (D) A teacher assigns students homework over the weekend, telling them to find examples of math in the world around them

105. Parents of a child with math learning disabilities want tips on how to help their child with homework. Which of the following Special Education journals would have articles that would be most appropriate to share with these parents?

    (A) *Exceptional Children* from CEC
    (B) *Educational Researcher* from AERA
    (C) *TEACHING Exceptional Children* from CEC
    (D) The *Examiner* newsletter from IDA

106. What ages does an Individual Family Service Plan apply to?

    (A) Birth to 3
    (B) 4–5
    (C) 14–18
    (D) 21 and older

107. A first-grade teacher sets up several math stations for students to rotate through in groups of four to five. The teacher sits at a large table that serves as one station and assigns students to work in pairs or groups of three to represent and solve addition problems using plastic teddy bears. As students solve the problems, the teacher observes and immediately points out mistakes so that students can try again. The teacher praises each pair or small group upon successful completion of the problem. The instructional approach that this teacher is utilizing is

    (A) teacher-directed cooperative learning.
    (B) visual discrimination.
    (C) generic problem solving.
    (D) verbalization.

108. Mr. Garcia has his fourth-grade students read to themselves the following sentence from a Texas history text: "Juneteenth is the oldest known celebration commemorating the ending of slavery in the United States." Mr. Garcia then asks the students what the term "commemorating" means in the sentence. He suggests they look at other words in the sentence to help them find the meaning. What reading comprehension strategy is Mr. Garcia teaching his students to use?

   (A)   Identifying the main idea
   (B)   Using context clues
   (C)   Visualizing
   (D)   Blending

Use the information below to answer questions 109 and 110.

   A third-grade student with learning disabilities turns in the following piece of writing after 40 minutes of classroom writing time:

   I go To th STOR wit mi mom. I lik to pus th kat.

   I wat th koki. mom sa NO. I wat th chip. mom sa Yes!

109. After analyzing the writing, the student's Special Education co-teacher notes strengths to encourage and weaknesses to target. Which of the following aspects of the student's writing would be considered a strength?

   (A)   Syntax
   (B)   Capitalization conventions
   (C)   Writing fluency
   (D)   Punctuation conventions

110. Based on the student's writing sample, at what stage of spelling would the Special Education teacher most likely place this student?

   (A)   Emergent
   (B)   Letter Name-Alphabetic
   (C)   Within-Word Pattern
   (D)   Syllables and Affixes

111. A Special Education teacher working with a student with multiple disabilities moves the student to be part of the class's circle time as part of the student's IEP. The teacher can ensure her own safety and the safety of the student during the lift and transfer by

   (A)   lifting with her legs, not her back.
   (B)   bending at the waist and moving the student quickly.
   (C)   practicing with each student in her class.
   (D)   leaving the student in his or her wheelchair, even though he or she is apart from the other students sitting on the floor for circle time.

112. A fifth-grade student with learning disabilities consistently procrastinates in completing his assignments and is in danger of failing two subjects due to incomplete assignments. The student's teacher has just assigned the class a research paper that will weigh heavily on the language arts grade. An appropriate behavioral intervention for this student would be to

    (A) provide a daily planner and map out partial completion dates as well as the final completion date.

    (B) review the guidelines of the assignment and have the student sign his name, indicating he understands the due date and the consequences of not completing the assignment.

    (C) have the student stay in the classroom during recess every day to write the paper.

    (D) promise the student a candy bar for every paragraph he writes.

113. A five-year-old child and his parents have just moved into the school district's boundaries. The parents bring the child to the school to register for kindergarten and explain that he is not yet speaking. The school psychologist immediately begins the paperwork to refer the child for Special Education evaluation. In selecting assessments for this child to complete, the psychologist and test administrators must keep in mind that

    (A) only paper-and-pencil tests are accepted in determining eligibility.

    (B) tests must be selected and administered so that the child's inability to speak does not interfere with the assessment of the child's aptitude or achievement level, if at all possible.

    (C) there must be an interpreter present during testing who can communicate with the child using sign language.

    (D) the child is only five and will likely learn to speak eventually.

114. Which of the following skills would be an example of a child's gross motor capabilities?

    (A) Drawing with a crayon

    (B) Skipping along a sidewalk

    (C) Talking to a friend

    (D) Solving an addition problem

Use the information below to answer questions 115–117.

Mrs. Miller, a fourth-grade teacher, asks her students to conduct a survey of heights for a sample of fourth-grade boys and girls. Mario surveys 18 students: 9 boys and 9 girls. The following chart shows his results.

Boys	Girls
46	47
49	48
50	49
50	51
51	52
52	54
53	54
54	56
56	58

115. Based on the chart, the median height for the boys is

    (A) 50 inches.
    (B) 51 inches.
    (C) 52 inches.
    (D) 53 inches.

116. Based on the chart, the range of heights for the girls is

    (A) 9 inches.
    (B) 10 inches.
    (C) 11 inches.
    (D) 47 inches.

117. Based on the chart, which of the following statements is true?

    (A) The average height of the girls in this sample is higher than the average height of the boys in this sample
    (B) The mode of the heights of the boys is higher than the mode of the heights of the girls
    (C) Fourth-grade girls are taller than fourth-grade boys
    (D) None of the girls in the sample were 4 foot 8 inches

118. Mr. Boychuk is a seventh-grade mathematics teacher. He is assigned a co-teacher because he has several students with IEPs in his classes. Mr. Boychuk provides step-by-step explanations for each mathematical concept he presents. The co-teacher volunteers to illustrate the explanations on the interactive whiteboard while Mr. Boychuk gives the lesson. After the lesson, the co-teacher pulls together small groups and provides manipulatives. She then asks the students to use the manipulatives to demonstrate the steps Mr. Boychuk explained. She encourages students to narrate the steps as they demonstrate them. What instructional strategy is the co-teacher using?

    (A) Simulation
    (B) Game-based teaching
    (C) Multisensory approach
    (D) Visualization

119. A test administrator, per a student's IEP, administers the test in a location with minimal distractions. What type of assessment accommodation would this be?

    (A) Response
    (B) Presentation
    (C) Setting
    (D) Timing

120. A Special Education teacher has several students who speak Spanish at home, but the teacher is not bilingual. The best approach for this teacher to take when communicating with Spanish-speaking parents is to

   (A) send home written notes in English and instruct students to translate the notes for their parents.
   (B) talk to parents using a lot of gestures to communicate meaning.
   (C) arrange for a bilingual colleague to serve as an interpreter during all parent phone calls and parent-teacher conferences.
   (D) send all communication via emails so the parents can use online translation programs.

121. In a case where the school district and the parents disagree about a student's placement in Special Education or about the services the school district will provide, either the district or the parents may call for a hearing before an impartial hearing officer. Which of the following statements regarding the hearing is true, according to Special Education laws?

   (A) The hearing officer must not be an employee of the school district.
   (B) The hearing officer will listen only to the parents and a school district representative. No one else may attend the hearing.
   (C) The hearing cannot be open to the public.
   (D) The hearing officer can only offer an opinion on the situation. It is up to the parents and the school district to resolve their own differences after the hearing concludes.

122. Which of the following students is most likely to benefit from an assistive technology device like a paper-based computer pen?

   (A) Visual learner with physical disabilities
   (B) Auditory learner with social skills deficits
   (C) Nonverbal learner with behavioral challenges
   (D) Tactile learner with memory challenges

123. A fourth-grade student who recently immigrated to the United States with her family never looks her teacher in the eye. The teacher, after several months of documenting this behavior, refers the student for evaluation by the district's autism team. An important factor for the campus Special Education review team to consider is that

   (A) lack of eye contact is a sign of an autism spectrum disorder.
   (B) autism crosses cultural and linguistic borders.
   (C) it is overwhelming to be an immigrant and that such behaviors are to be expected.
   (D) cultural norms and expectations impact student behavior and teacher interpretation.

124. A Special Education teacher is administering a fluency assessment to a sixth grader. The teacher notes that the student reads 110 words per minute, which is below grade-level expectations. The area of fluency that the teacher is assessing is

   (A) accuracy.
   (B) expression.
   (C) syntax.
   (D) rate.

125. Given the algebraic equation $3x + 4x - 1 = 34$, the value of x is

    (A) 3.
    (B) 4.
    (C) 5.
    (D) 10.

126. Which of the following forms of communication would be considered two-way communication?

    (A) Weekly school newsletters
    (B) Email blasts from the school principal
    (C) Parent-teacher phone call
    (D) Report card

127. How often must a student's transition plan be updated?

    (A) At the beginning of each semester
    (B) Once a year as part of the ARD
    (C) At ages 16, 18, and 21
    (D) Whenever the student gets a new job experience

128. When communicating with parents, what is the best form of communication in today's world?

    (A) Emails
    (B) Texts
    (C) Voice mail
    (D) Any of the above, depending on the parents' preferences

129. A teacher in an autism unit has several students who become frustrated whenever their routines change. Two of them are nonverbal. What is one technique the teacher can use to help her students become more flexible?

    (A) Applied Behavior Analysis
    (B) Floortime
    (C) Circle time with calendar and weather
    (D) Visual schedule

130. According to the National Reading Panel's 2000 report, "Teaching Children to Read," the evidence to support phonemic-awareness instruction is statistically significant. Which of the following strategies represents phonemic awareness instruction?

    (A) A teacher circles all the spelling errors students make in their first drafts.
    (B) A teacher says several rhyming words aloud and asks students what they notice about the words. She then says the word "wet" and asks students to call out words that rhyme with "wet."
    (C) A teacher sits beside a student who is reading out loud and models any word the student stumbles over.
    (D) A teacher reads a book and then asks students to point out their favorite parts.

131. Which of the following choices is NOT one of the purposes of a transition assessment?

   (A) To identify a student's interests and vocational abilities
   (B) To identify a student's level of self-determination skills
   (C) To determine whether a student will pass high school
   (D) To identify a student's strengths, abilities, and potential deficits

Use the information below to answer questions 132 and 133.

   Mr. Aquino, an eighth-grade reading teacher, has his students create summary notebooks. For each chapter they read, they complete a simple chart listing who the main character is, what the main character's objective is, what obstacles stand in the way of the objective, and how the character deals with the obstacle. To help students who are struggling, Mr. Aquino has the students label their charts with the words, "Who Wanted But So." This helps cue students to fill in the applicable information. Here is a sample page from one of the student's notebooks for chapter three of the book she is reading:

Who	Wanted	But	So
Kat	has a crush on Rick and wants him to like her	Rick is busy with basketball and doesn't notice her	Kat decides to go out for cheerleader tryouts

132. Which stage of the reading process is Mr. Aquino's strategy designed for?

   (A) Prereading
   (B) During reading
   (C) After reading
   (D) Emergent reading

133. The primary advantage of Mr. Aquino's summarization framework is to

   (A) prevent students from listing all the details of a story in place of a summary.
   (B) give students a summarization strategy they can use with all texts.
   (C) prevent students from cheating.
   (D) ensure that all students will come up with the same answer.

134. A Special Education teacher arranges her classroom as the diagram shows below:

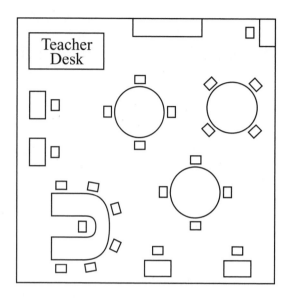

What kind of activities is this classroom best set up for?

    (A)   Whole group lectures
    (B)   Sustained silent reading
    (C)   Physical therapy
    (D)   Small group and individual learning centers or stations

135. Research on effective teaching indicates that students who struggle with math respond positively to mathematics instruction that focuses on

    (A)   improving basic math processing skills.
    (B)   problem-solving.
    (C)   conceptual understanding.
    (D)   all of the above.

1. (A) B	35. (C)	69. (D)	103. (B)
2. (D)	36. (B)	70. (B)	104. (C)
3. (C)	37. (D)	71. (C)	105. (C)
4. (A)	38. (A)	72. (A)	106. (A)
5. (A)	39. (B)	73. (C)	107. (A)
6. (C)	40. (B)	74. (A)	108. (B)
7. (B) C	41. (D)	75. (D)	109. (D)
8. (A)	42. (B)	76. (D)	110. (B)
9. (B)	43. (D)	77. (B)	111. (A)
10. (D)	44. (D)	78. (B)	112. (A)
11. (C)	45. (C)	79. (A)	113. (B)
12. (A)	46. (B)	80. (B)	114. (B)
13. (D) C	47. (A)	81. (C)	115. (B)
14. (A)	48. (C)	82. (B)	116. (C)
15. (A)	49. (A)	83. (A)	117. (A)
16. (D)	50. (A)	84. (C)	118. (C)
17. (B)	51. (C)	85. (B)	119. (C)
18. (A)	52. (A)	86. (C)	120. (C)
19. (C)	53. (C)	87. (C)	121. (A)
20. (D)	54. (D)	88. (A)	122. (D)
21. (B)	55. (C)	89. (C)	123. (D)
22. (C)	56. (D)	90. (A)	124. (D)
23. (B)	57. (D)	91. (B)	125. (C)
24. (B)	58. (C)	92. (C)	126. (C)
25. (A)	59. (C)	93. (D)	127. (B)
26. (A)	60. (B)	94. (D)	128. (D)
27. (D)	61. (D)	95. (C)	129. (D)
28. (B)	62. (B)	96. (C)	130. (B)
29. (A)	63. (A)	97. (B)	131. (C)
30. (C)	64. (C)	98. (D)	132. (C)
31. (C)	65. (A)	99. (C)	133. (A)
32. (B)	66. (D)	100. (D)	134. (D)
33. (C)	67. (B)	101. (D)	135. (D)
34. (A)	68. (D)	102. (B)	

ANSWER EXPLANATIONS

1.   **(A)**   The correct response is (A). Section 504 of the Rehabilitation Act, passed in 1973, was the first piece of federal legislation to address the civil rights of all people with disabilities. Previous federal legislation existed for people with learning disabilities, but not for students with all disabilities. (B) is incorrect because IDEA was passed two years after Section 504. (C) is incorrect because the Elementary and Secondary Education Act did not originally address the civil rights of students with disabilities. (D) is incorrect because No Child Left Behind was the 2001 reauthorization of ESEA.
Competency 010

2.   **(D)**   The correct response is (D). Based on Marcus's interest in pets, particularly dogs, and his aptitude for routine tasks, a supported employment opportunity feeding and washing dogs at an animal shelter would be an appropriate supported employment opportunity. (A) is not an appropriate choice because, while there are pets at a veterinarian's office, there are also needles and medical equipment, which Marcus does not like. (B) is not an appropriate choice because dealing with customer issues requires split-second decision making and constantly changing expectations. Marcus needs a job that is predictable where he can learn the routines. (C) is not an appropriate choice because a hospital will have doctors and needles, both things that make Marcus uncomfortable.
Competency 007

3.   **(C)**   The correct response is (C). Individuals with autism lack "theory of mind," the ability to recognize that other people have different perspectives. They do not do tantrums because they want to be the center of attention or want to manipulate others. Instead, they act out in frustration because they cannot communicate appropriately how they are feeling, and their frustration builds to the breaking point. (A) is a potential cause of the behavior because environmental noise can overwhelm a child with autism who lacks the ability to filter it out and turn it into background noise. (B) is a potential cause of the behavior because children with autism are extremely routine-oriented. Disruptions in the routine can seem "wrong" to the extent that the child acts out in frustration. (D) is a potential cause of behavior for similar reasons. Children with autism often develop limited eating patterns where they only eat certain foods. Changes in these foods can cause mounting frustration, which can then lead to a meltdown.
Competency 006

4.   **(A)**   The correct response is (A). Assessment accommodations do not give students with disabilities an advantage over other students taking the test. Instead, accommodations "level the playing field" so that students have an equal opportunity to demonstrate what they know. (B) and (C) are simply not true. (D) is incorrect because the purpose of accommodations has nothing to do with the test administrator.
Competency 002

5.   **(A)**   The correct response is (A). IDEA 2004 requires that transition goals be "results-oriented" and measurable. The goal should state the intended outcome for the year *after* the student graduates from high school. Only (A) meets all of these criteria. (B) is incorrect because it is a goal for the student *during* high school. Transition goals must focus on postsecondary outcomes. (C) is incorrect because it does not state a time by which the outcome is expected. (D) is incorrect because it does not include employment and education/training. These are expected to be part of any postsecondary goal.
Competency 007

6.   **(C)**   The correct response is (C). A Venn diagram is composed of two circles that intersect. It is perfect for compare/contrast writing as the comparisons can be written inside the circle while the contrasts can be written outside the circle. (A), (B), and (D) are not correct as they represent forms of writing better suited to other graphic organizers.
    Competency 008

7.   **(B)**   The correct response is (B). A student's instructional reading level is considered to be at 90 percent accuracy or one mistake out of every 10 words; 92 percent accuracy is the closest number to 90 percent and falls into the instructional to independent reading range. (A) is incorrect because 96 percent accuracy would mean that reading level 2.0 is an independent reading level. Any percentage 95 percent or higher is considered to be in a student's independent reading range. (C) and (D) are incorrect because reading levels 5.0 and 6.0 are both below 90 percent accuracy and are therefore considered to be at the student's frustration level.
    Competency 008

8.   **(A)**   The correct response is (A). A book at a 6.0 reading level is in this student's frustration level based on the assessment. This means the student will likely run across a number of words he does not know how to read. This can lead to frustration and abandoning the book. Since the Special Education teacher is present in the library and sees the student choose a book on his frustration level, she is able to redirect him toward a book on his independent level. He will get far more enjoyment and reading self-confidence out of a book at his independent level. (B) is incorrect because it sets the student up for a frustrating and potentially self-defeating reading experience. (C) is incorrect because it promotes a negative self-image about the student's ability to read and become a better reader. (D) is incorrect because the level 6.0 book is not on the student's instructional level. It is on the student's frustration level.
    Competency 008

9.   **(B)**   The correct response is (B). Paired reading is an excellent method of providing peer support for reading assignments while freeing the teacher to monitor and work with pairs as needed. In a small group setting, a teacher has to split instructional time as evenly as possible. In paired reading, every student has a partner to read to, and this facilitates more supported oral reading practice than students would receive in a group setting. (A) is incorrect because the teacher is monitoring the partners to ensure that both partners participate in the reading and the postreading assignment. (C) is incorrect because lessons requiring that all the students be engaged in a group task actually take deeper planning to help prevent classroom management issues. (D) is incorrect because pair selection is not based on friendship status; it is based on reading ability and complementary personalities.
    Competency 008

10.   **(D)**   The correct response is (D). Section 504 of the Rehabilitation Act was ignored for 20 years by state and local educational agencies because it did not include provisions for federal funding or monitoring. (A) is incorrect because the law did make sense, but it involved expenditures school boards did not want to make. (B) is incorrect because the law was not discriminatory. In fact, it was clearly a civil rights legislation. (C) is incorrect because it was signed into law; it just was an unfunded mandate.
    Competency 010

11.   **(C)**   The correct response is (C). Students with intellectual disabilities need concepts to be as concrete as possible. Providing manipulatives like colored blocks allows students to place each block as they identify it by number (for example, one block, two blocks). (A) is incorrect because a worksheet is not concrete enough for initial concept development. Symbol-supported text is an accepted way to help nonreaders access content, but the activity itself is still a worksheet. (B) is incorrect because a graphic organizer is a visual representation, and this is a transitional stage in concept development. Initial concept development needs to be more concrete. (D) is incorrect

because a calculator is a useful tool for computation, but it is not a tool to teach the concept of the number one being equivalent to one object, which is the essence of one-to-one correspondence.

Competency 009

12. **(A)** The correct response is (A). The term "disproportionality" in Special Education refers to the overrepresentation of racial, cultural, and linguistic minorities in Special Education. This is a critical issue in Special Education and one that Special Education teachers should constantly watch for in their own evaluations and assumptions. (B), (C), and (D) are all incorrect as they are not true.

Competency 010

13. **(D)** The correct response is (D). Epileptic seizures have a number of potential warning signs. Unexplained confusion, sleepiness, and/or weakness are among those warning signs as are strange tastes or feelings, eyes rolling up, and drooling. (A), (B), and (C) are all incorrect as they are not among the potential warning signs of an epileptic seizure. (A) irritability can be a warning sign for insulin shock for students with diabetes.

Competency 001

14. **(A)** The correct response is (A). Language-learning disabilities involve difficulties or delays with written language, grammar and spelling, and handwriting. Frequent misspelled words would be indicative of a language-learning disability. (B) is incorrect because it is related to mathematics. (C) is incorrect because it is related to either behavioral or attention deficit issues. (D) is incorrect because it is related to social skills or behavioral issues.

Competency 001

15. **(A)** The correct response is (A). The key to this number pattern is that each number is multiplied by 3 to calculate the next number. The final given number is 27, and since 27 multiplied by 3 equals 81, (A) is the correct answer. (B) and (C) are incorrect because while they are multiples of 3, they are not the correct answer to 27×3. (D) is incorrect because it makes the assumption that the pattern is repeating when there is no evidence of this.

Competency 009

16. **(D)** The correct response is (D). A geometric sequence is made by multiplying by a given value each time. This number sequence has a factor of 3. The pattern is continued by multiplying by 3 each time. (A) is incorrect because an arithmetic sequence is made by adding a given value each time. (B) is incorrect because a Fibonacci sequence is made by adding the first two numbers to get the third and then adding the second and third numbers to get the fourth, and so on. (C) is incorrect because a harmonic sequence is a sequence of numbers whose reciprocals form an arithmetic sequence.

Competency 009

17. **(B)** The correct response is (B). The transitional stage of conceptual development involves visual or pictorial representations of objects, so a pie graph is the appropriate choice. (A) and (C) are incorrect because both the pie and the apple are concrete examples, the kind useful for initial conceptual development. (D) is incorrect because a recipe would provide a way to apply a student's understanding of fractions, but it would not be the transitional phase of concept development.

Competency 009

18. **(A)** The correct response is (A). The teacher is modeling a think-aloud, a technique where the facilitator literally thinks out loud the kinds of thoughts that writers or readers think subconsciously during the process of writing or reading. Think-alouds are great strategies for helping students realize that all writers have moments of self-doubt. They are also great opportunities to reveal how writers organize thoughts in their head before writing them down. (B) is not correct because a graphic organizer is a visual planning tool. (C) is an incorrect answer

because language experience is a reading method that integrates writing and reading. (D) is not correct because the teacher is not using a formula constructed to help students achieve on standardized writing tests.

Competency 008

19.　**(C)**　The correct response is (C). Attention deficit hyperactivity disorders are the most commonly diagnosed behavioral disorders in children, affecting 3 to 6 percent. (A), (B), and (D) are incorrect because statistically they do not approach the number of students diagnosed with ADHD.

Competency 001

20.　**(D)**　The correct response is (D). Regular informal quizzes are examples of formative assessment. This assessment is best used to identify skills that students have not yet mastered and that the teacher, therefore, needs to reteach, preferably in a different way. (A) is incorrect as the reason behind quizzes should not be simply to get grades. Quizzes can be excellent tools for using assessment to inform instruction. (B) is incorrect because performance on quizzes should not be the sole qualifier for Special Education testing. (C) is incorrect because an interactive whiteboard, like any classroom tool, exists to help teachers reach their students, not to be used simply for the sake of technology.

Competency 009

21.　**(B)**　The correct response is (B). The "One Teach, One Observe" co-teaching model is ideal for gathering informal observational data on students. While one teacher presents the lesson, the other teacher circulates around the room and makes notes about students' behavior, level of participation, and level of conceptual understanding. (A) is incorrect because it describes a team teaching model. (C) is incorrect because it describes a parallel teaching model. (D) is incorrect because it describes a station-teaching model.

Competency 012

22.　**(C)**　The correct response is (C). Structural analysis involves seeing parts of multisyllabic words in order to decode them. Prefixes and suffixes are word parts that carry a predictable meaning. Being able to see them in long words also means being able to guess at the meaning of those words. (A) is incorrect because matching words to pictures is a comprehension activity. (B) is incorrect because reading a 100-word passage in less than a minute is a fluency activity. (D) is incorrect because using a graphic organizer in writing has nothing to do with breaking a multisyllabic word into its parts.

Competency 008

23.　**(B)**　The correct response is (B). Parental consent must be obtained before a student with a disability can be placed in a school's Special Education program. If parental consent cannot be obtained, a school district may appeal to an impartial hearing officer. A classroom teacher cannot make a decision to ignore this requirement. In the example above, the student must be served in the regular classroom for now. (A) is incorrect because the classroom teacher has not technically violated the Texas Code of Ethics by making her suggestion. As long as she does not actually carry through with her idea, firing the teacher is not the answer. However, educating her on Special Education law is critical. (C) is incorrect because the parents have already refused to give consent. Further discussion on this matter must take place in the context of the ARD committee or the campus administration. (D) is incorrect because when a school district files an appeal to an impartial hearing officer, IDEA provisions state clearly that the student must stay in place in the current placement until the hearing process is concluded.

Competency 011

24.　**(B)**　The correct response is (B). Messages, particularly in our media-rich world, are conveyed with more than just words. Helping students understand this concept through advertisements that have had their words removed or hidden helps students become more critical readers and viewers. It also helps struggling readers learn that they can communicate with more than just words. (A) is incorrect because classroom discussions are never about trying to "sell" a product. (C) is incorrect because the purpose for removing the words is to focus attention on how the visuals alone tell a story. (D) is incorrect because strategies to help students visualize generally involve students drawing their own pictures of what they see when they read.

Competency 008

25. **(A)** The correct response is (A). An ever-increasing number of apps for tablet devices and smart phones are being developed. Many of these are useful in Special Education. For the student described in this scenario, one of the communication apps that allows teachers to build the student's visual schedule and use the voice-over capabilities of the table appears to be an ideal option to motivate the student and help him progress. (B) is incorrect because the student's issue is communication, not mathematics. (C) is incorrect because the student's issue is communication, not handwriting. (D) is not the correct answer because the student is nonverbal, so speech-recognition software has no use in this scenario.

Competency 004

26. **(A)** The correct response is (A). All of the listed symptoms (crying easily, avoiding interactions with peers, and not wanting to come to school) are potential symptoms of a behavioral or emotional disorder. Further observation and testing is called for in this case. (B) is incorrect as the frequency and severity of the behaviors indicate a child in an emotional crisis of some sort. (C) is incorrect because this student's symptoms indicate deeper issues than peers are capable of dealing with. (D) is incorrect because ethically a school employee is required to report behaviors like those listed to school authorities in the interest of the child.

Competency 001

27. **(D)** The correct response is (D). When talking with parents, the most important thing teachers can do is be respectful and responsive listeners. Parents have a wealth of information about their child and can often help problem-solve situations or anticipate where conflicts might occur. In any conversation, when participants feels they have an opportunity to speak and truly be listened to, they tend to feel more positive about the situation and more willing to compromise to find a solution. (A) is incorrect because, while documentation and examples are good things to have, going into a phone call or conference with only problems is likely to lead to negative interactions. (B) is incorrect because teachers do not need to have every answer in a conversation. If a teacher does not have an answer, the best approach is to be honest and then note down the question and promise to follow up and get the answer. (C) is incorrect because praise, when genuine, is a positive aspect to the conversation, but it is not the most important element of a problem-solving parent-teacher conference.

Competency 012

28. **(B)** The correct response is (B). All of the words listed are sight words. In fact, all 10 are from the Dolch sight-word list. (A) is not correct because the words are prekindergarten and kindergarten words according to the commonly referenced Dolch grade-level sight-word lists. (C) is not correct because sight words are often not easily decodable as many are exceptions to standard phonetic rules. (D) is not correct because academic vocabulary is the language of a content area, such as "geometry" in mathematics or "summary" in reading.

Competency 008

29. **(A)** The correct response is (A). By having students simultaneously look at the words, trace the raised letters, and say the word, the teacher is incorporating repetition, specifically repetition through different learning modalities: visual, tactile/kinesthetic, and auditory. This combination of repetition and multisensory learning is a powerful tool for building short- and long-term retention. (B) is not correct because the purpose is not fun, although students do enjoy completing the activity as they learn the sight words. (C) is not correct because the purpose is to have a multisensory approach to improve retention, but as students read the word, the teacher will model correct

pronunciation. (D) is not correct because the purpose is academic, not behavioral. A side benefit of hands-on learning, however, is the decrease in disruptive behavior that often accompanies it.

Competency 008

30. **(C)**   The correct response is (C). When determining eligibility for Special Education services, (A) development, (B) social emotional behavior, and (D) auditory processing may all be assessed. (C) career placement is the only area that would not be part of determining eligibility for Special Education services.

Competency 002

31. **(C)**   The correct response is (C). The student's best grade is PE, and her second-best grade is in a class that emphasizes hands-on experiences; so there are a couple of indications that she may be a tactile/kinesthetic learner. The Special Education teacher would have to confirm that through observation and learning styles inventories. The low grades in the content areas of language arts and social studies are a tip-off to the student's struggles with reading and writing. The fact that the reading teacher incorporates movement into her lesson plans may be part of the reason the reading grade is passing. (A) is incorrect as the student's good grade in science is not indicative of a career choice. (B) is incorrect because a high grade in any class is not definite evidence that a student likes that class exclusively. (D) is incorrect because there is no evidence of the student being an auditory learner, and poor grades do not always translate into dislike.

Competency 005

32. **(B)**   The correct response is (B). A benchmark assessment measures group performance against an established standard at defined points. (A) is incorrect because formative assessments are administered during instruction to guide the teacher in instructional decisions. (C) is incorrect because summative assessments are administered at the end of units to determine student progress. (D) is incorrect because alternative assessments are given when traditional multiple choice formats cannot accurately measure a student's knowledge or skills.

Competency 002

33. **(C)**   The correct response is (C). Improving social skills involves setting up scenarios where students can practice interacting with others. A board game focused on conversation skills provides an activity that encourages students to talk to each other and use questions and comments to carry on a conversation. (A) is incorrect because it is an independent activity with no social-skills practice. (B) is incorrect because taking notes and listening to a teacher does not build the student's own social skills. (D) is incorrect because social-skills instruction should focus on actual practice of the skills that will help students make friends. There should not be an emphasis on how many friends to make, but on how to be at ease striking up a conversation and interacting with others.

Competency 006

34. **(A)**   The correct response is (A). Observations are considered informal assessments. (B) is incorrect since observations are not standardized assessments, but rather professional judgments. (C) is incorrect since the observations were conducted at the beginning of school, not at the end of a unit. (D) is clearly incorrect since observations are not considered formal.

Competency 002

35. **(C)**   The correct response is (C). The IDEA Reauthorization of 2004 includes a timeline of 60 days to conduct initial evaluations for Special Education eligibility. (A) and (B) are incorrect because these reauthorizations did not implement this timeline requirement. (D) is incorrect because there was no reauthorization in 2009.

Competency 010

36. **(B)**   The correct response is (B). The teacher is providing learning activities that cover all of the major modalities: visual, auditory, tactile, and kinesthetic. Between her observations during the activities and the students'

answers to the informal inventory, she will have a good grasp of each student's learning strengths so she can plan instruction accordingly. (A) is not the correct answer because the teacher's purpose is to assess all learners, and her classroom clearly reflects her grasp of Gardner's theory of multiple intelligences. (C) is not the correct answer because she is clearly not grouping by ability. Rather, she is looking at which learners need more visual supports versus which ones need more tactile/kinesthetic activities. (D) is not the correct answer because the informal assessment is not about getting students to like her but instead about understanding her students and their learning strengths.
Competency 004

37. **(D)** The correct response is (D). Under IDEA, disciplinary sanctions are not considered a change in placement and are not subject to this restriction provided the student has not been suspended for more than 10 days cumulatively during the school year. To help ensure a good relationship between the school and parents, the assistant principal should share this information with the parents in a nonconfrontational context with a witness. (A) is incorrect because IDEA makes clear that receiving Special Education services does not prevent a school from implementing disciplinary sanctions, particularly if the misbehavior is not related to the disability. (B) is incorrect because such a proposal would be similar to bribing the parents in order to avoid the suspension. Reparation of damages can be part of the disciplinary sanction, but it is not a replacement for the assistant principal's original decision. (C) is incorrect because the parents' need for childcare is not a factor in the implementation of the disciplinary process.
Competency 011

38. **(A)** The correct response is (A). Mr. Martinez uses the simulation of how it felt to be a family heading west to build anticipation and engagement in the upcoming unit. (B) is incorrect because Mr. Martinez is only kicking off the unit; he has not yet covered the content that will be tested. (C) is incorrect because the activity is cooperative, not competitive. (D) is incorrect because Mr. Martinez is not using data to conduct the activity. He is allowing students to make their own decisions about how their "family" will move out West. This builds ownership.
Competency 003

39. **(B)** The correct response is (B). The shape is a parallelogram. A parallelogram is a four-sided shape with two pairs of parallel sides. The facing sides of a parallelogram are of equal length and the opposite angles are of equal measure. (A) is incorrect because a square is characterized by four right angles and four sides of equal length. (C) is incorrect because an isosceles triangle has three sides and is characterized by two equal sides and two equal angles. (D) is incorrect because an oval is essentially a circle that has been stretched out.
Competency 009

40. **(B)** The correct response is (B). Standardized achievement tests score students in comparison to a larger group. These tests have gone through a series of tests to ensure they are as statistically fair as possible. (A), (C), and (D) are all incorrect as these are not the purpose of standardized achievement tests.
Competency 002

41. **(D)** The correct response is (D). LDA is the Learning Disabilities Association of America. It is an organization of parents and teachers of children with disabilities. Many of its members are individuals with learning disabilities who advocate for themselves. The organization's website is *www.ldanatl.org*. Providing parents with this information and link will give them information about learning disabilities and about a wide variety of schools and camps dedicated to helping individuals with learning disabilities. (A) is incorrect because camps for children with autism will not meet the needs of students with learning disabilities. (B) is incorrect because group homes and other residential facilities are placements for adults with intellectual disabilities. They are not appropriate placements for adults with learning disabilities. (C) is incorrect because it does not help the parents narrow their search for information.
Competency 011

42.   **(B)**   The correct response is (B). The ultimate goal of a post-high school program should be to prepare students for success in their adult life in the community. For this reason, on-the-job coaching and independent living skills should be a curriculum priority. (A) is incorrect because an intensive reading intervention takes a great deal of instructional time. At this point in school, students may still learn to read, but the focus should be on vocational and life skills. (C) is incorrect because once students have completed the typical four years of high school, they are ready for a more specialized program than the typical high school schedule. Again, the focus needs to be on vocational and life skills. (D) is incorrect because it is not comprehensive enough. Social skills are indeed important aspects of preparing students for independent living, but they are only one aspect. They should be a part of a larger vocational and independent living skills curriculum.
Competency 007

43.   **(D)**   The correct response is (D). Echo reading is a modeling method in which a fluent reader takes the lead and reads a sentence or line from a poem and then a developing reader repeats the sentence or line, using the same expression and speed if possible. Like all modeling methods, it provides a level of security for a struggling reader because the fluent reader pronounces all the words before the struggling student has to do so. (A) is incorrect because recorded books are digital recordings of someone reading a book so that students can listen as they follow along. (B) is incorrect because neurological impress is an intervention-modeling method where the teacher whispers the words in the student's ear simultaneously with the student's oral reading. (C) is incorrect because choral reading is when three or more students read text together out loud. It does not include modeling before the student reads, but it does provide peer support.
Competency 008

44.   **(D)**   The correct response is (D). IDEA 2004 and its associated law, CFR 300.43, specifically state that transition services must be based on an individual student's needs and should take into account the student's strengths, preferences, and interests. (A) and (B) are incorrect because, while the availability of school and community resources will impact the transition goals, they should not be the basis for the plan. (C) is incorrect because transition is focused on the student's own desires as much as those can be communicated. The process of transition is ultimately about self-advocacy and the move to adulthood. Parents are part of the transition planning process, but their expectations are not the basis for the plan.
Competency 007

45.   **(C)**   The correct response is (C). The ARD (Admission, Review, and Dismissal) committee is the Texas equivalent to the IEP committee referenced in IDEA regulations. (A) is incorrect because FAPE stands for Free and Appropriate Public Education. (B) is incorrect because LRE stands for Least Restrictive Environment. (D) is incorrect because CEC stands for Council for Exceptional Children, a nonprofit organization that advocates for the rights of students with disabilities and the educators who serve them.
Competency 011

46.   **(B)**   The correct response is (B). Preteaching vocabulary is a research-based strategy for improving reading comprehension. In a content-area class such as geography, students encounter a number of academic vocabulary words that they must understand to grasp central concepts. A hands-on vocabulary strategy like the one described helps students take ownership of the words they will encounter in the unit. (A) is incorrect because, while the activity is a break from the textbook, that is not the reason for the activity. (C) is incorrect because not all geography terms are easily visualized. (D) is incorrect because part of co-teaching is conducting lessons when appropriate and coaching from the side at other times. It all depends on the dynamic between the co-teacher and the general education teacher.
Competency 005

47.   **(A)**   The correct response is (A). Sight-word automaticity is a critical aspect of fluent reading. There are 200 frequently used words that make up over 50 percent of printed text in the English language. Many of these words do not follow typical phonetic conventions. For this reason, educators work to help students recognize these words on sight—thus the term "sight words." Automaticity is achieved when a student can call a word correctly in a half second or less. (B) is incorrect as the English language has many more aspects and nuances than a list of words could represent. (C) is incorrect as the test is focused on how well and how quickly students read the words. The directions will be repeated if students do not understand them. (D) is incorrect because this assessment is focused on fluency, not comprehension.
    Competency 008

48.   **(C)**   The correct response is (C). The extent to which a student will not participate with nondisabled students in regular classes or nonacademic activities must be clearly documented in the student's IEP. This documentation is necessary to ensure that the ARD committee has addressed opportunities for inclusion and has documented decisions to limit inclusion for educationally sound reasons. This documentation is all part of fulfilling the least restrictive environment requirement of IDEA. (A), (B), and (D) are all incorrect as none of those are required for documentation or related to least restrictive environment.
    Competency 010

49.   **(A)**   The correct response is (A). A mind map is a diagram that visually outlines key information. It is an excellent strategy for working through the key ideas of a unit of study. By collaborating on a mind map, the two teachers are figuring out the key concepts they will emphasize in instruction so that they can accurately assess student understanding during and after the unit. (B) is incorrect as this is collaborative planning, not one teaching the other. (C) is incorrect as the decision to use a mind map was not due to the topic being plants. (D) is incorrect as the two teachers are using a common tool to plan together, not showing off a new idea.
    Competency 005

50.   **(A)**   The correct response is (A). A written notice for an ARD (Admission, Review, and Dismissal) committee meeting must include the purpose, time, and place of the meeting. (B) is incorrect because the written notice can specify one time and place. It does not have to offer choices. If parents cannot make that time, they may request that the ARD be rescheduled. (C) is incorrect because evaluation results are shared at the committee meeting, not included in the written notice. (D) is incorrect because the Individual Education Program is written during the ARD committee meeting and agreed upon by all members present.
    Competency 011

51.   **(C)**   The correct response is (C). Special Education classrooms are meant to support individualized and targeted instruction. Paraprofessionals can be excellent instructional resources when trained in the programs students are using. (A) is incorrect because, while paraprofessionals can assist with classroom organization and preparation, their primary use should involve student instruction. (B) is incorrect because no one at a school may administer medications other than the school nurse and the school nurse's staff. (D) is incorrect because it is critical that teachers and paraprofessionals maximize instructional time by engaging with the students and working on IEP goals whenever possible. Generally, paperwork should be left for conference periods and before and after school.
    Competency 004

52.   **(A)**   The correct response is (A). Limiting a parent meeting to 10 minutes and making it clear that the meeting is not the teacher's top priority is a sure way to put parents in a defensive position. Such a short time span makes it difficult to have time for parent questions or for teacher-parent brainstorming and problem solving. When scheduling parent meetings, scheduling a minimum of 20 minutes and being available in case the meeting runs longer will go a long way toward building positive interactions. (B), (C), and (D) are all strategies to promote positive parent-teacher meetings and are, therefore, incorrect.
    Competency 012

53.   **(C)**   The correct response is (C). Public Law 94-142, better known as IDEA, mandates a free appropriate public education for all children with disabilities. States that do not adhere to these mandates risk educational funding cuts or withholdings. (A) is incorrect because Public Law 89-10 is the Elementary and Secondary Education Act. (B) is incorrect because Public Law 93-112 is the Rehabilitation Act, and its Section 504 is an unfunded mandate. (D) is incorrect because Public Law 94-479 gave George Washington the title of General of the United States armies posthumously.
    Competency 010

54.   **(D)**   The correct response is (D). Mrs. Cullen is using flexible grouping to ensure that students receive targeted instruction in the skill areas they most need to improve. (A) is incorrect because homogenous grouping involves placing students in groups by ability and not changing the groups once established. (B) is incorrect because Mrs. Cullen has structured her classroom so that students receive whole-group, small-group, paired, and independent instruction. (C) is incorrect because Mrs. Cullen chooses the members of the small group based on data gathered at the beginning of the year.
    Competency 003

55.   **(C)**   The correct response is (C). Mrs. Cullen's decision to administer a variety of informal assessments at the beginning of the year shows that she values data when planning instruction. (A) is incorrect because Mrs. Cullen has set up a classroom where all students can thrive regardless of disability. (B) is incorrect because Mrs. Cullen does not appear to be focusing on test preparation. Instead, she is targeting students' skill gaps as she works with small groups. (D) is incorrect because Mrs. Cullen has set up a classroom that allows for multiple reading opportunities and represents varied ways to practice reading skills.
    Competency 003

56.   **(D)**   The correct response is (D). The understanding that a written symbol like the letter "b" makes a unique sound /b/ is the essence of letter-sound correspondence. (A) is incorrect because phonemic awareness is the ability to hear and recognize phonemes. It is a precursor to phonics and letter-sound correspondence. (B) is incorrect because "pragmatics" is a term for social conversation skills and is an area that speech-language pathologists address. (C) is incorrect because fluency is the ability to read with appropriate speed and good expression.
    Competency 008

57. **(D)** The correct response is (D). Tactile/kinesthetic learners retain information best when they are learning while moving. For example, a study strategy for a tactile/kinesthetic learner might be running laps while listening to recorded notes. Allowing students to move about the classroom while answering high-interest questions is a great way to motivate tactile/kinesthetic learners. (A) is incorrect because it describes a strategy for visual learners. (B) is incorrect because it describes the round-robin reading strategy, one that tends to demotivate struggling readers because of public embarrassment when they stumble or read too haltingly. (C) is incorrect because it describes a strategy for auditory learners.
    Competency 005

58. **(C)** The correct response is (C). Most educators think of writing as a five-step process: prewriting, drafting, revising, editing (proofreading), and publishing. Counting the words is not a part of this process, although writers are often curious to know how many words they have written. (A), (B), and (D) are all incorrect answers because they are stages of the writing process.
Competency 008

59. **(C)** The correct response is (C). Many of the state assistance programs for individuals with disabilities have waiting lists that can last for years. However, these lists also require an official diagnosis as a qualifier. Advise parents to call the appropriate agencies and get on the waiting lists as soon as a diagnosis is assigned. (A) is incorrect because there is not yet a diagnosis when Special Education testing begins (unless the child has already been diagnosed by a medical professional). (B) is incorrect because some of the lists require waiting 10 years or more before an individual can apply for assistance. Waiting until a student graduates may mean no assistance until the individual is in his or her 30s. (D) is incorrect because parents must plan as far in advance as possible so that proper care can be found when the parents are no longer able to provide it.
Competency 007

60. **(B)** The correct response is (B). Community-based instruction is frequently used in self-contained classrooms as part of preparing students to transition into the community. It makes sense to have an Alternative Learning Environment class (that has been practicing ordering food off a menu) actually go to a restaurant and order off a menu. This allows teachers to assess generalization of skills. (A) is incorrect because a teacher can provide numerous examples of how algebra relates to the real world without leaving the campus. (C) is incorrect because community-based instruction is not a reward, per say. It is a planned part of instruction for students with significant disabilities. (D) is incorrect because community-based instruction has nothing to do with curriculum selection.
Competency 005

61. **(D)** The correct response is (D). When conducting a Functional Behavioral Assessment, data analysis, indirect assessment (including structured interviews), and direct assessment (including standardized assessments) may all be used. However, they are not all required. It is up to the IEP team what techniques they will use to gather the information they need to identify the root cause of the inappropriate behavior.
Competency 006

62. **(B)** The correct response is (B). The teacher's activity in (B) provides for purposeful movement, meeting the needs of kinesthetic learners while also focusing students on the content just taught. (A) is incorrect because students are not encouraged to move at all in this scenario. (C) is incorrect because, while it features positive reinforcement, the movement is all on the teacher's, not on the student's, part. (D) is incorrect because it describes the strategy of visualization, not movement.
Competency 003

63. **(A)** The correct response is (A). Memory deficits often result in math fact memory and retrieval issues. This makes completing math fact drills arduous for students who find themselves frustrated trying to retrieve a math fact they had memorized a few days earlier. (B) is incorrect because geometry issues tend to be a result of visual-spatial deficits. (C) is incorrect because issues with graphs and charts can be due to visual-spatial deficits or reading deficits. (D) is incorrect because issues with fractions, decimals, and percentages can occur for a variety of reasons. The key is identifying at what point in the process of converting fractions to decimals or decimals to percentages the student struggles.
Competency 009

64.   **(C)**   The correct response is (C). Students with procedural learning deficits struggle to apply adequate sequencing when attempting to solve multistep computations or word problems. They are often unsure of which operation to use first or how to structure a problem. It is common for students with procedural learning deficits to use immature strategies like this student does when he completes the first operation and then abandons any further steps. (A) is incorrect because visual-spatial deficits tend to cause issues with geometry as well as number alignment, measurement, and place value. (B) is incorrect because memory deficits tend to result in trouble with math facts and fluency. (D) is incorrect because number sense refers to the most foundational concepts of math such as one-to-one correspondence.
    Competency 009

65.   **(A)**   The correct response is (A). An SLP is a Speech-Language Pathologist, one of the related-services colleagues a Special Education teacher will have the opportunity to work with. An oral presentation project is a wonderful opportunity to develop students' expressive-language skills, and this is an area that an SLP will have specific criteria they expect to see. Creating a rubric to assess the project will provide an opportunity to target specific expressive language skills using the SLP's criteria. (B) and (C) are incorrect because an SLP's focus is communication and language skills, not mathematics skills. (D) is incorrect because an SLP would not be focused on science content.
    Competency 005

66.   **(D)**   The correct response is (D). 3/8 converts to 0.375 in decimal form. This can be found by dividing 3 by 8 on a calculator. (A), (B), and (C) are all incorrect answers. Choosing (B) reveals a conceptual misunderstanding of how to convert fractions to decimals. The numbers in the fraction do not simply transfer over to the decimal form.
    Competency 009

67.   **(B)**   The correct response is (B). Prior to writing a Behavior Intervention Plan, the IEP team should collect data for a functional behavioral assessment in order to identify the cause of the behavior, its frequency, and situations where the student does not exhibit the behavior. Having this data helps the team establish positive supports to redirect and reduce the inappropriate behavior. (A) is incorrect because a tour of the home environment is not necessary when the BIP is addressing inappropriate behaviors at school that interfere with learning. (C) is incorrect because, while reviewing classroom discipline policies may provide useful information in terms of how the student reacts to various disciplinary approaches, it is not a complete picture of the student and the causes of the behavior. (D) is incorrect because STAAR results do not reveal the central cause of the inappropriate behavior.
    Competency 006

68.   **(D)**   The correct response is (D). Successful readers frequently check for understanding as they read a text. Often, they don't even realize they are doing so because it is such a quick mental review of what is happening and an evaluation of whether it makes sense in the context of the passage. (A) is incorrect because reading just to get to the end of the assignment is something struggling readers do. Successful readers read with a purpose. (B) is incorrect because skipping over unrecognized words is something struggling readers do. Successful readers pause and use context clues to determine the meaning of unknown words. (C) is incorrect because reading fiction and nonfiction the same way is something struggling readers do. Successful readers identify the type of text they are about to read and apply appropriate strategies.
    Competency 008

69.   **(D)**   The correct response is (D). RTI provides increasingly intensive intervention as soon as learning deficits are demonstrated without the legal requirements for testing and eligibility that are part of Special Education. This early identification and intervention can correct learning deficits quickly and thus reduce the number of students who will later need Special Education services. (A) is incorrect because RTI is shared between regular education

and Special Education. Neither one should be fully responsible for implementing an RTI program. (B) and (C) are incorrect because a quality RTI program involves a great deal of planning and teacher support.
Competency 010

70. **(B)** The correct response is (B). Students with learning disabilities, particularly language-learning disabilities, will be at a disadvantage with an all open-ended, short-answer assessment. Modifying the questions by making them multiple choice is an appropriate modification. The students are still expected to do the math and show their work; they are just not tasked with composing complete sentences. (A) is incorrect because one of the primary tasks of a Special Education teacher is to make appropriate accommodations and modifications to ensure a "level playing field." Making no modifications would be unfair to the students with learning disabilities. (C) and (D) are incorrect because they are accommodations (changes to the environment) and not modifications.
Competency 005

71. **(C)** The correct response is (C). By IDEA definition, the purpose of a transition plan is to help a student successfully move from high school to postgraduation and adult life. While (A), (B), and (D) all represent times of transition in a student's life, they do not represent the period of time for which IDEA requires the IEP team to document a plan.
Competency 007

72. **(A)** The correct response is (A). When working with a co-teacher, mutual lesson planning is essential to a successful collaboration. Scheduling a time to plan together twice a week and consistently being on time to these planning meetings will ensure that both teachers feel they are being respected and allowed to contribute ideas. (B) is incorrect because it infers that the co-teaching relationship is a casual friendship rather than a collegial collaboration. (C) is incorrect because it places the regular classroom teacher in the position of needing to learn "Special Education" techniques and does not honor the knowledge the classroom teacher brings to the collaboration. (D) is incorrect because offering to modify assessments without first co-planning and agreeing upon key points in the content gives the impression that the co-teacher's role is just to make everything easier for the students with IEPs regardless of the algebra teacher's goals for instruction.
Competency 012

73. **(C)** The correct response is (C). The words displayed on the bulletin board are all math vocabulary related to measurement. The teacher is preparing students for a unit on measurement. (A) is incorrect because a unit on geometry would include terms such as the names of shapes or the types of flips. (B) is not the correct answer since a unit on probability and statistics would include terms such as "mean," "median," and "mode." (D) is incorrect because a unit on number sense would include basic math terms like counting, numbers, and number words.
Competency 009

74. **(A)** The correct response is (A). Using the words as catalysts for peer interaction and discussion of the math vocabulary allows students to internalize the meanings of the words both by visualizing them and by teaching them through the modified game of charades. (B) is incorrect because math vocabulary needs to be taught explicitly to help students truly understand what the words mean. (C) is incorrect because, while the words can be useful spelling references, the power in these words is in students using them and internalizing their meanings. (D) is incorrect because while this strategy helps students recognize how math is used beyond school, it is not as effective as (A) in helping students grasp the meanings of the words.
Competency 009

75. **(D)** The correct response is (D). The ARD committee is responsible for writing and agreeing on reasonable objectives that will foster student growth and development while reflecting the grade-level TEKS as closely as

possible. (A) is incorrect because the purpose of an IEP is to create an educational program that will best meet the student's needs. The TEKS may need to be modified slightly to accomplish this. (B) and (C) are incorrect because a child's IEP objectives must reflect the entire committee's decisions about how to best serve the child. No one stakeholder can dictate the content of the IEP.
Competency 003

76. **(D)** The correct response is (D). The STAAR Alternate was designed for approximately 1% of Texas school-children, specifically those students with such significant cognitive disabilities that they are not able to be tested fairly or accurately using a traditional multiple-choice format. Therefore, (A), (B), and (C) are all incorrect.
Competency 002

77. **(B)** The correct response is (B). Positive phone calls are an excellent way to build respectful relationships with parents at the beginning of the school year. For some parents, it may be the first positive phone call they have ever received from school. By showing parents that a teacher cares about and appreciates students from the beginning, it becomes easier to problem-solve together if negative behaviors emerge later in the year. (A), (C), and (D) are all incorrect as they focus on the teacher only, not on the parent-teacher relationship.
Competency 012

78. **(B)** The correct response is (B). Prior to the Rehabilitation Act of 1973 and Public Law 94-142 (later named Individuals with Disabilities Education Act), the number of students with disabilities receiving free public education was quite low across the United States. These two pieces of federal legislation opened educational opportunities for all students with disabilities by requiring states to offer a free and appropriate public education to all students. (A) is incorrect because the purpose of the federal laws was to change Special Education practices within the states. However, since that time, these laws have indeed helped the United States emerge as one of the premier countries for Special Education programs. (C) is incorrect because these laws did not designate a national day to honor people with disabilities. (D) is incorrect because the Rehabilitation Act provided no funding, and Public Law 94-142 promised some federal funds for Special Education but has never come close to supplying 50 percent of the costs incurred by state and local education agencies.
Competency 010

79. **(A)** The correct response is (A). An obtuse angle is an angle that measures more than 90 degrees but less than 180 degrees. (A) is a 120-degree angle so it is obtuse. (B) is incorrect because it is a 90-degree angle, which is known as a right angle. (C) and (D) are incorrect because they are both less than 90 degrees and are, therefore, acute angles.
Competency 009

80. **(B)** The correct response is (B). Moving Katie closer to the front of the room and choosing tablemates who will not further distract her is a simple accommodation, which may help Katie to concentrate better on schoolwork. If this does not work, more complex accommodations would be developed. (A) is incorrect because ignoring Katie's behavior will only lead to poor grades due to incomplete assignments. (C) is incorrect because a teacher should never use students as part of their discipline plan. (D) is incorrect because Katie is capable of completing the assignments, but she becomes distracted easily because of her documented disability.
Competency 003

81. **(C)** The correct response is (C). Teaching students to highlight keywords every time they encounter a word problem is a generic problem-solving strategy that can help struggling learners slow down and think about the clues the words provide for solving the problem. (A) is incorrect because a pictorial representation is either a graph or an actual drawing of pictures to help set up a problem. (B) is incorrect because corrective feedback is provided by a

teacher as a student is completing a problem. Corrective feedback allows students to correct mistakes as they make them. (D) is incorrect because a modeling strategy involves the teacher or facilitator actually completing a problem step-by-step while students watch and listen.
   Competency 009

82.   **(B)**   The correct response is (B). Any time students are working with "hundreds," "tens," and "ones," they are focused on place value. This example also shows how a concept such as place value can be integrated into a regular routine like circle time and made concrete. (A) is incorrect because number sense involves basic number concepts such as counting and one-to-one correspondence. (C) is incorrect because patterns focus on sequencing numbers or shapes using some kind of repeating rule. (D) is incorrect because fractions focus on parts of a whole like one-half or one-quarter.
   Competency 009

83.   **(A)**   The correct response is (A). By having the student practice the word repeatedly but through different activities, the teacher makes the most of the power of repetition for students with intellectual disabilities. These students often experience retention difficulties and need strategies that provide multiple opportunities to practice without allowing the student to become bored. (B) is incorrect because the students do not use a computer in this instructional scenario. (C) is incorrect because there is no mention of the teacher continuously praising the students as they complete the tasks successfully. (D) is incorrect because the activities represent multiple modalities, not just visual.
   Competency 003

84.   **(C)**   The correct response is (C). "Dyscalculia" means a problem with making calculations. It is a common term for a mathematics learning disability. Therefore, (A), (B), and (D) are all incorrect.
   Competency 001

85.   **(B)**   The correct response is (B). The 1997 Reauthorization of IDEA expanded the definition of disabilities to include children with developmental delays between the ages of three and nine. (A) is incorrect because the 1990 reauthorization is known for the renaming of Public Law 94-142 to IDEA. (C) is incorrect because the 2004 reauthorization is known for its changes to transition and disciplinary requirements. (D) is incorrect because there was no reauthorization in 2009; instead, there was inclusion of Special Education in the distribution of ARRA funds (better known as stimulus funds).
   Competency 010

86.   **(C)**   The correct response is (C). Acting silly and talking loudly are attention-seeking behaviors. This is a student who wants to be noticed. By assigning a leadership role in the class to this student, the teacher is providing an appropriate way for the student to be recognized. Neither (A) nor (B) are the best solutions because they are likely to escalate the attention-seeking behavior as they do not help the student achieve his ultimate goal to be noticed. (D) is not the best solution because it rewards the student's inappropriate behavior by providing him with negative attention.
   Competency 006

87.   **(C)**   The correct response is (C). A percentile rank indicates the percentage of a reference or norm group obtaining scores equal to or less than the test-taker's score. (A) and (B) are incorrect because the purpose of a percentile rank is not to indicate a passing or failing score. (C) is incorrect because a 65 percent ranking would indicate that 35 percent of students who took the test scored better than the test-taker.
   Competency 002

88.   **(A)**   The correct response is (A). Autism spectrum disorders disproportionately affect boys. They are five times more common among boys (1 in 54) than among girls (1 in 252), according to the Centers for Disease Control and Prevention. Therefore, (C) is incorrect. (B) is incorrect because ASD is more common among children of older parents. (D) is incorrect because there is no known cure for autism, although early intervention and therapies can help a child overcome many of his/her communication barriers.
   Competency 001

89.   **(C)**   The correct response is (C). Teaching to a student's strengths will ensure both more rapid success and increased self-esteem. (A) is incorrect because while a teacher may target the skills gaps a student has, focusing solely on weaknesses can be overwhelming and disheartening for a student. (B) is incorrect because part of the role of a Special Education teacher is to make appropriate adaptations to textbooks and programs to meet an individual student's needs. (D) is incorrect because the key to Special Education is not only recognizing but planning for the differences in students' learning patterns.
   Competency 003

90. **(A)** The correct response is (A). IDEA 2004 specifically states that the IEP team should consider positive behavioral interventions and supports to address behaviors that impede learning. The Texas Education Agency fully supports this statement and urges schools to adopt proactive disciplinary approaches. (B) is incorrect because, while behavior logs may be one of the forms of documentation used to justify a Behavior Intervention Plan, they are not specifically required by IDEA 2004. (C) is incorrect because negative reinforcers are discouraged based on the latest research on student behavior. (D) is incorrect because, while some parental strategies work well and the IEP team includes the parents and listens to the parents' viewpoint, the team develops strategies to deal with the child's behavior at school.
   Competency 006

91.   **(B)**   The correct response is (B). Working with families of children with disabilities requires empathy and tact. Many families experience conflict as parents struggle to understand and accept their child's learning difficulties. Teachers play a critical role in helping families access information, listening to families' concerns, and keeping the focus on the child and what is best for her or him. In this example, the teacher should maintain a friendly demeanor and an excitement about the opportunity to work with the child. Refocusing the parents on discussing the child's strengths will provide the teacher with valuable information and turn the event into a more positive outing for everyone. (A) is incorrect because assuming the parents will be difficult leads to an adversarial, defensive relationship from the beginning. (C) and (D) are both incorrect because favoring one parent over another will only lead to further conflict.
   Competency 012

92.   **(C)**   The correct response is (C). The act of scanning or skimming a text allows a reader to get a sense of the topic and words *before* actually reading. Students use this knowledge to make their predictions and build interest in the text. This prereading strategy builds fluency by helping students feel more prepared for the words they encounter. (A) is incorrect because it describes a strategy that is used *during* reading, and it actually works against fluency by requiring the student to pause or stop. (B) is incorrect because it is an *after*-reading strategy. (D) is incorrect because it activates prior knowledge but does not expose students to the text itself. It is the opportunity to skim the words in the text that builds confidence and fluency.
   Competency 008

93.   **(D)**   The correct response is (D). The ninth shape would be a circle since we have established a repeating pattern of two circles, a square, and a triangle. The ninth shape would be the beginning of the third repetition, so it would start with a circle. (A) is incorrect because rectangles have not been introduced into the pattern in question. (B) and (C) are incorrect because neither triangles nor squares begin the pattern.
   Competency 009

94. **(D)** The correct response is (D). OHI stands for Other Health Impairment. This category includes a number of chronic or acute health problems that can adversely affect a child's educational performance.
Competency 001

95. **(C)** The correct response is (C). IDEA 2004 states that a transition plan must be in place by age 16. Many people feel that is too late to appropriately plan for transition, and in 2011, the Texas legislature made 14 the required age for transition planning in Texas. (A), (B), and (D) are all incorrect ages based on IDEA 2004.
Competency 007

96. **(C)** The correct response is (C). Based on the description, the student's primary difficulty with writing appears to be fine motor (poor handwriting) and lack of the alphabetic principle or difficulty with memory (poor spelling). While Special Education testing can give a much better picture of the causes, a simple accommodation such as providing access to a computer or word processor (where the student can type her papers and use a spell checker to identify misspelled words and correct them) can be provided with or without a Special Education designation. (A) is not the correct answer because the challenges indicate an issue with the act of writing, not with reading. (B) is not the correct answer because an alternative keyboard is designed for students with physical disabilities or limited reading skills. This student does not appear to need an adapted keyboard. (D) is incorrect because the issue is with writing, not mathematics.
Competency 004

97. **(B)** The correct response is (B). Visual-spatial deficits cause difficulty with conceptualizing geometric figures and aligning numbers. Based on the teacher's observations of this student, visual-spatial deficits seem likely. (A) is incorrect because the student is clearly trying to do the work, despite frustrations. (C) is incorrect because the nature of the errors points to cognitive deficits, not to lack of attention. (D) is incorrect because the misalignment is not due to poor fine motor skills but to lack of visual/spatial clarity.
Competency 009

98. **(D)** The correct response is (D). Under the *Individuals with Disabilities Education Act*, there are 14 disability categories used by the states to determine whether students aged 3 to 21 are eligible for special education and related services. (A) Speech/language impairments, (B) intellectual disability, and (C) specific learning disability are three of those 13. Only (D) is not a disability category under IDEA.
Competency 001

99. **(C)** The correct response is (C). Content will never be a type of accommodation because accommodations never alter content. (A), (B), and (D) are all ways that accommodations can change the way a test is given.
Competency 002

100. **(D)** The correct response is (D). One of the most important things a Special Education teacher can do is teach students and their families strategies the student can use to succeed on his or her own. Knowing how one learns best allows a student to take control of his or her own learning. In addition, focusing on strengths is so important with students with disabilities who often find people and themselves focusing only on their weaknesses. (A) and (B) are incorrect because the teacher is not acting for himself. (C) is incorrect because the focus of the event is on learning strengths, not weaknesses.
Competency 005

101. **(D)** The correct response is (D). Maintaining challenging expectations for individuals with exceptionalities; using evidence, instructional data, research, and professional knowledge to inform practice; and advocating for professional conditions and resources that will improve learning outcomes of individuals with exceptionalities are all part of CEC's code of ethics for Special Education professionals. (A), (B), and (C) are incorrect because,

although they are all within the code of ethics, none of these answers are correct as single answers.
Competency 011

102. **(B)** The correct response is (B). Exhibiting bullying behavior often stems from a deep feeling of insecurity. Rather than face his own fears, the bully makes others feel bad and exerts power to try and establish a sense of control. (A) is incorrect because, while racism may coexist with bullying behavior, it is not the root cause. (C) is incorrect because, deep down, the bully wants to be liked but doesn't believe it is possible. (D) is incorrect as the root cause is the bully's own feelings of not being in control, not an external person's behavior.
Competency 006

103. **(B)** The correct response is (B). Given the grouping of the desks and the poster specifying individual roles within each group, this classroom is organized for cooperative learning. Furthermore, the oval table on the side with four student chairs and one teacher chair indicates small-group targeted instruction. (A) is not the best answer because there is no sense of all desks facing one direction, and the roles on the poster do not mesh with leveled groups. (C) is not the best answer because independent study and project-based learning would have more individual spaces, like study carrels and work spaces with supplies for projects. (D) is not the best answer because, while there is a sense with the table to the side that the teacher may do some flexible grouping, there is no evidence of an abundance of books and plans for sustained silent reading.
Competency 004

104. **(C)** The correct response is (C). Explicit instruction involves helping students see how a math strategy is applied step-by-step. Modeling and verbalizing each step gives students a concrete picture of how to solve a problem. (A) is incorrect because giving students independent work is not explicitly showing them how to complete problems. (B) is incorrect because stepping back and observing what students do with manipulatives is an implicit approach. Students are expected to come up with what the problem and solution are on their own. (D) is incorrect because asking students to see how math works in the everyday world, while motivating, is not a step-by-step, explicit strategy. This "making connections" exercise is largely implicit.
Competency 009

105. **(C)** The correct response is (C). *TEACHING Exceptional Children* from the Council for Exceptional Children is a practical journal that features research-to-practice information and materials for classroom use. Parents will find articles fairly easy to navigate, and several articles are specific to math strategies. (A) is incorrect because *Exceptional Children* is a scholarly research journal. Parents may find the articles difficult to navigate, and the strategies discussed may be difficult to translate into practice. (B) is incorrect because *Educational Researcher* is the American Educational Research Association's scholarly research journal. Articles are difficult for laypeople to understand and cover topics broader than special needs. (D) is incorrect because *The Examiner* is a newsletter published by the International Dyslexia Association, and it focuses on reading issues, not math issues.
Competency 011

106. **(A)** The correct response is (A). An Individual Family Service Plan is provided for children birth to age 3 as part of early childhood services for children with developmental delays. At age 3, the IFSP is replaced by an IEP. (B), (C), and (D) are incorrect as they all represent ages covered by an IEP.
Competency 007

107. **(A)** The correct response is (A). Teacher-directed cooperative learning is a targeted instruction approach that involves students working in small cooperative groupings while the teacher is nearby and able to observe student strategies and provide direct and immediate feedback. (B) is incorrect because visual discrimination involves presenting students with two or more symbols or shapes and having them distinguish between them based on their

visual differences. (C) is incorrect because generic problem solving involves giving students strategies like high-lighting keywords to use every time they encounter certain problems. (D) is incorrect because verbalization involves talking through each step in a problem-solving process so that the student and others can hear what the student is thinking.

Competency 009

108. **(B)** The correct response is (B). Context clues are the words around an unknown word in a text. By having students find surrounding words that can help them determine the likely meaning of "commemorating," Mr. Garcia is building students' independent reading strategies. (A) is incorrect because the main idea is not related to the meaning of a word in a passage. It is the central message of the entire piece. (C) is incorrect because visualizing is a strategy used during reading to help the reader picture what is happening in the text. (D) is incorrect because blending is an aspect of phonics instruction in which letter sounds are blended together so that students can decode words.

Competency 008

109. **(D)** The correct response is (D). One of the patterns evident in the writing sample is the writer's correct use of punctuation. The fact that every sentence is punctuated correctly is definitely a strength. (A) is incorrect because the syntax of the sample is very simple. Sentences are repetitive and do not have varied beginnings. (B) is not correct because there are seemingly random mistakes in capitalization throughout the sample. (C) is not correct because the fact that the student wrote only 27 words in 40 minutes is a sign of a writer in need of intervention.

Competency 008

110. **(B)** The correct response is (B). Based on the writing sample, the student is in the latter stages of the letter name-alphabetic stage of spelling. The student is generally starting the words with the correct sounding letter and even has some of the inner consonants and vowels correct. However, there are many interior letters missing, and all of the silent "e's" are missing. (A) is incorrect because the student has clearly progressed past the emergent spelling stage where letters do not necessarily correspond to sounds. (C) and (D) are incorrect because the writer has not moved to these higher levels of spelling yet.

Competency 008

111. **(A)** The correct response is (A). Applying knowledge of appropriate body mechanics to ensure safety in transfer, lifting, positioning, and seating is part of Competency 004. Special Education teachers receive training in the proper way to lift students. To prevent injury, it is essential to bend and lift with the legs while maintaining a straight back. (B) is not correct because bending at the waist and lifting with the back can cause serious injury. (C) is not correct because there is no reason to lift a student unless instructed to do so by the student's IEP or because the situation requires it. (D) is incorrect because the student's IEP indicates the need to include the student fully in circle time, and the IEP must be followed by law.

Competency 004

112. **(A)** The correct response is (A). When a student's procrastination behaviors interfere with academic performance, the procrastination must be addressed in as proactive and positive a way as possible. Teaching a student how to use a planner and set smaller deadlines leading up to the final deadline will help the student both in school and beyond. (B) is incorrect because having the student acknowledge the deadline does not actually address the cause of the procrastination or provide a path to change the behavior. (C) is not the correct answer because it is punitive and it assumes the student will miss the deadline. It does not reflect confidence in the student. (D) is incorrect because extrinsic rewards are only good in the moment. Change occurs when students respond to intrinsic rewards. In addition, candy bars are not nutritious and should not be handed out to students as "bribes" for completing work.

Competency 006

113. **(B)** The correct response is (B). When administering diagnostic assessments for Special Education eligibility, diagnosticians and school psychologists must seek out assessments that ensure a student's disability or first language do not interfere with the assessment of the student's aptitude or achievement level where possible. For a child who does not speak, this means that the diagnostic tests must give the child an opportunity to demonstrate aptitude without the necessity of a verbal response. (A) is incorrect because a variety of tests are accepted in determining eligibility, including checklists and observational assessments. (C) is incorrect because the child is nonverbal, not deaf or hard of hearing. Unless the child and his family indicate that sign language is the child's primary means of communication, an interpreter is not necessary. (D) is incorrect because a child who is not speaking at age 5 is demonstrating severe developmental delays. Special Education testing is definitely warranted.
   Competency 011

114. **(B)** The correct response is (B). Gross motor skills involve large body movements. Skipping is a gross motor ability. (A) is incorrect because using one's fingers to hold a crayon and draw involves fine motor skills. (C) and (D) are incorrect because they have nothing to do with large body movements.
   Competency 001

115. **(B)** The correct response is (B). A median number is the middle number in a sorted list of numbers. There are nine boys and the fifth number, directly in the middle, is 51. This is the median height. (A), (C), and (D) are incorrect as they are not the middle number in the sorted list from shortest to tallest boy.
   Competency 009

116. **(C)** The correct response is (C). The range is calculated by finding the difference between the largest number in a data set and the smallest number. For the girls, the largest number is 58 and the smallest number is 47, so if you subtract 47 from 58 (58 − 47 = 11), the range is 11 inches. (A), (B), and (D) are incorrect because they are not the difference between 58 and 47. Choosing (D) indicates a conceptual misunderstanding of range since 47 is the smallest number in the data set.
   Competency 009

117. **(A)** The correct response is (A). The average, or mean, is calculated by adding up all the numbers in a data set and then dividing by the amount of numbers you have. In this case, when we calculate the average heights of the girls and boys, we get 52.111 for the girls and 51.222 for the boys. Thus, the average height of the girls in the sample is higher than the average height of the boys in the sample. (B) is incorrect because mode is calculated by the most common number. For the boys, this is 50 and for the girls this is 54. (C) is incorrect because this is a sample of 18 fourth-grade boys and girls. It is not a large enough sample to be representative of all fourth graders. (D) is incorrect because 4 foot 8 inches is equivalent to 56 inches, and one of the girls in the sample was 56 inches tall.
   Competency 009

118. **(C)** The correct response is (C). By providing visual reinforcements and concrete examples, the co-teacher is providing multiple ways for students to grasp the instructional concepts. (A) is incorrect because a simulation would involve students playing roles in a mock real-world application of the mathematical concepts. (B) is incorrect because the students are not playing a game. (D) is incorrect because the students have not been asked to form a picture in their minds or imagine a situation.
   Competency 003

119. **(C)** The correct response is (C). Administering the test in a place with minimal distractions is an accommodation in the setting or location. (A) is incorrect because an accommodation in response would be a change in how the student indicates his/her answers. (B) is incorrect because an accommodation in presentation would be a change in how the test questions are spaced or in how the directions are presented. (D) is incorrect because an ac-

commodation in timing would mean that a student is given more time to take a test or given more frequent breaks than other students receive.

Competency 002

120. **(C)** The correct response is (C). When working with parents who do not speak English, it is imperative to find a translator at the school or via a translation phone service to ensure that teachers and parents can truly communicate. Making sure to have the translator at all meetings is a way for the teacher to show her respect for the parents and the language they speak. (A) is incorrect because many students, especially students with disabilities, cannot read English well enough to serve as translators for their parents. Notes should be translated and sent home in the parents' native language if at all possible. (B) is incorrect because using a lot of gestures to communicate can be extremely insulting to parents and can lead to major miscommunication. (D) is incorrect because, just like notes, emails should be translated and sent in the parents' native language.

Competency 012

121. **(A)** The correct response is (A). An impartial hearing officer cannot be an employee of a school district or any public agency that is involved in the education or care of the child. (B) is incorrect because any party to the hearing has the right to be accompanied and advised by legal counsel and by individuals with special knowledge regarding the problems of children with disabilities. (C) is incorrect because parents have the right to open the hearing to the public. (D) is incorrect because the hearing officer will issue a binding decision at the conclusion of the hearing.

Competency 011

122. **(D)** The correct response is (D). A paper-based computer pen allows students to take notes and record the teacher's words at the same time. This is a great tool for tactile learners who learn through fine motor activities like writing but who also have memory issues. When the student uses the pen to review the notes, he or she can hear the recording of the classroom discussion simultaneously. (A) is not correct because a visual learner with physical disabilities may not be able to hold the pen and is better served with a multimedia presentation that features visuals. (B) is not correct because an auditory learner with social-skills deficits is likely to remember discussion and lectures but needs a structured approach for interacting with peers. (C) is incorrect because a nonverbal learner with behavioral challenges will not be served by the paper-based computer pen. Generally, nonverbal learners need more hands-on manipulatives to demonstrate understanding since they cannot communicate understanding through speech.

Competency 004

123. **(D)** The correct response is (D). In some cultures, it is disrespectful to look an authority figure in the eye. This may well be a factor in the scenario described. It is critical that Special Education teachers analyze how culturally and/or linguistically diverse backgrounds can impact behavior. (A) is incorrect because, while lack of eye contact can be a sign of an ASD, it can also be a sign of other causes, such as cultural expectations or depression. (B) is incorrect because, while autism does cross all cultural and linguistic borders, that is not the issue that led to this particular referral. (C) is incorrect because the issue here is whether the student has displayed enough potential signs of ASD to warrant a Special Education referral for testing.

Competency 006

124. **(D)** The correct response is (D). Rate is the speed at which a student reads, measured in words per minute. Typically, a sixth-grade student should be reading 120–150 words per minute. (A) and (B) are incorrect because they are different aspects of fluency, related to the number of mistakes a student makes while reading and the tone and emphasis the student uses. (C) is incorrect because syntax refers to the complexity level of the sentences a student speaks or writes.

Competency 008

125. **(C)** The correct response is (C). To solve for x in $(3x + 4x - 1 = 34)$, the first step would be to subtract 1 from the left side of the equation and add it to the right side of the equation, giving us $(3x + 4x = 35)$. We then add $3x$ and $4x$ on the left side of the equation to get $(7x = 35)$. We then divide both sides by 7 to get $(x = 5)$. (A), (B), and (D) are incorrect because they are not the value of x in this equation.
Competency 009

126. **(C)** The correct response is (C). A parent-teacher phone call is an example of two-way communication because both the parent and the teacher have an opportunity to speak and to listen. (A), (B), and (D) are all incorrect because newsletters, email blasts, and report cards are all examples of one-way communication.
Competency 012

127. **(B)** The correct response is (B). IDEA 2004 requires that a student's transition plan be updated annually along with the student's IEP. This is part of the regular ARD process in Texas. (A), (C), and (D) are incorrect choices since they do not account for the annual update requirement.
Competency 007

128. **(D)** The correct response is (D). Mobile technologies have expanded the forms of communication teachers can use and make communication more immediate in many cases. However, the key to positive parent communication is to find out how parents prefer to communicate. Some may have busy careers and not appreciate a phone call on their cell phone during work hours. Others may not be comfortable with texting. At the beginning of the year, teachers can establish positive two-way communication channels by asking parents to indicate their preferred method of communication. (A), (B), and (C) are all incorrect because, although they are each a valid form of communication, none of them can meet every communication need all school year long.
Competency 012

129. **(D)** The correct response is (D). A visual schedule is a research-based technique that helps students with autism understand the plan for the day and what activities have to be completed before others can occur. This is especially helpful when a daily routine changes and a teacher wants to give forewarning. Reviewing the schedule and then removing the card representing each major activity after it is completed allows students to stay on task and have a sense of control over what is happening. (A) is not the correct answer because the purpose of Applied Behavior Analysis is skill acquisition and, by its nature, it relies on routines. It does not teach flexibility. (B) is not the correct answer because the purpose of floortime instruction is to get on the same level as children with autism and engage them. The focus is not on building flexibility but, instead, on building human interaction and social skills. (C) is not the correct answer because circle time with calendar and weather is just one routine activity on a schedule. By itself, circle time does not teach flexibility.
Competency 004

130. **(B)** The correct response is (B). Phonemic awareness is the ability to hear and recognize phonemes. Recognizing rhyming sounds involves recognizing the phoneme that is making the rhyme. Calling out words that rhyme with a target word demonstrates an understanding of a phoneme. (A) is incorrect because circling spelling errors would be a part of the editing phase in the writing process. (C) is incorrect because sitting with a student who is reading and helping with unknown words means the student has progressed far beyond phonemic awareness and is now decoding. (D) is incorrect because it describes a postreading activity that allows students the opportunity to react to the book the teacher just shared.
Competency 008

131. **(C)** The correct response is (C). A transition assessment is built to help educators guide students to post-school jobs and activities that are likely to be most fulfilling to them. It is not used to determine whether a student

graduates from high school or not. (A), (B), and (D) are all purposes of transition assessments and are, therefore, incorrect responses.

Competency 005

132. **(C)** The correct response is (C). Summarization is a strategy used after reading to pinpoint the gist of the storyline in a narrative text. (A) is incorrect because you cannot summarize a story before you read it. (B) is incorrect because you can have a sense of the overall summary as you read, but you cannot summarize the entire piece until you have finished reading it and stepped away to reflect on the text. (D) is incorrect because emergent reading is not a stage of the reading process. It refers to the level of a very beginning reader.

Competency 008

133. **(A)** The correct response is (A). When students are asked to summarize, they frequently make the mistake of just retelling all the high points in the story. The primary advantage of a framework like the one Mr. Aquino uses is that it gives a firm structure for students to build a summary that focuses on the gist of the story, not the details. (B) is not correct because the "Who Wanted But So" strategy only applies to fiction. (C) is not correct because the use of a summarization framework does not specifically prevent cheating. (D) is not correct because, while the frame (Who Wanted But So) is set, the way that frame is filled in is entirely up to the student.

Competency 008

134. **(D)** The correct response is (D). The diagram clearly shows a variety of tables and work stations. This allows the teacher to organize small-group and individual instruction while still maintaining order and classroom control. Success with learning centers and small-group instruction is often contingent on a well-designed environment that allows students to work on projects and tasks without disturbing others. (A) is not the correct answer because whole-group instruction would have all the desks and tables facing one direction. (B) is not the correct answer because the tables and work stations are clearly designed for a variety of tasks. Generally, a room designed for sustained silent reading would have more bookshelves and more individual spaces as well as some informal furniture. (C) is not the correct answer because the setup does not reflect a sensory motor lab.

Competency 004

135. **(D)** The correct response is (D). Evidence-based studies in mathematics instructional strategies have shown positive results from a group of methods that focus on improving math processing skills, problem solving, and conceptual understanding. The key to solid math instruction is to use all of these strategies, not limit instruction to any one area. (A), (B), and (C) are all incorrect because they feature only one area of focus. The correct answer is all three of them in a balanced approach.

Competency 009

ANSWERS SORTED BY DOMAIN AND COMPETENCY

Domain	Competency	Question	Answer	Did You Answer Correctly?
I	1	13	D	
I	1	14	A	
I	1	19	C	
I	1	26	A	
I	1	84	C	
I	1	88	A	
I	1	94	D	
I	1	98	D	
I	1	114	B	
I	2	4	A	
I	2	30	C	
I	2	32	B	
I	2	34	A	
I	2	40	B	
I	2	76	D	
I	2	87	C	
I	2	99	C	
I	2	119	C	
II	3	38	A	
II	3	54	D	
II	3	55	C	
II	3	62	B	
II	3	75	D	
II	3	80	B	
II	3	83	A	
II	3	89	C	
II	3	118	C	
II	4	25	A	
II	4	36	B	
II	4	51	C	
II	4	96	C	
II	4	103	B	

Domain	Competency	Question	Answer	Did You Answer Correctly?
II	4	111	A	
II	4	122	D	
II	4	129	D	
II	4	134	D	
II	5	31	C	
II	5	46	B	
II	5	49	A	
II	5	57	D	
II	5	60	B	
II	5	65	A	
II	5	70	B	
II	5	100	D	
II	5	131	C	
II	6	3	C	
II	6	33	C	
II	6	61	D	
II	6	67	B	
II	6	86	C	
II	6	90	A	
II	6	102	B	
II	6	112	A	
II	6	123	D	
II	7	2	D	
II	7	5	A	
II	7	42	B	
II	7	44	D	
II	7	59	C	
II	7	71	C	
II	7	95	C	
II	7	106	A	
II	7	127	B	
III	8	6	C	

Domain	Competency	Question	Answer	Did You Answer Correctly?
III	8	7	B	
III	8	8	A	
III	8	9	B	
III	8	18	A	
III	8	22	C	
III	8	24	B	
III	8	28	B	
III	8	29	A	
III	8	43	D	
III	8	47	A	
III	8	56	D	
III	8	58	C	
III	8	68	D	
III	8	92	C	
III	8	108	B	
III	8	109	D	
III	8	110	B	
III	8	124	D	
III	8	130	B	
III	8	132	C	
III	8	133	A	
III	9	11	C	
III	9	15	A	
III	9	16	D	
III	9	17	B	
III	9	20	D	
III	9	39	B	
III	9	63	A	
III	9	64	C	
III	9	66	D	
III	9	73	C	
III	9	74	A	
III	9	79	A	
III	9	81	C	
III	9	82	B	
III	9	93	D	

Domain	Competency	Question	Answer	Did You Answer Correctly?
III	9	97	B	
III	9	104	C	
III	9	107	A	
III	9	115	B	
III	9	116	C	
III	9	117	A	
III	9	125	C	
III	9	135	D	
IV	10	1	A	
IV	10	10	D	
IV	10	12	A	
IV	10	35	C	
IV	10	48	C	
IV	10	53	C	
IV	10	69	D	
IV	10	78	B	
IV	10	85	B	
IV	11	23	B	
IV	11	37	D	
IV	11	41	D	
IV	11	45	C	
IV	11	50	A	
IV	11	101	D	
IV	11	105	C	
IV	11	113	B	
IV	11	121	A	
IV	12	21	B	
IV	12	27	D	
IV	12	52	A	
IV	12	72	A	
IV	12	77	B	
IV	12	91	B	
IV	12	120	C	
IV	12	126	C	
IV	12	128	D	

PRACTICE TEST 2

TExES Special Education EC–12 (161)

Also available at the REA Study Center (*www.rea.com/studycenter*)

This practice test is also offered online at the REA Study Center. We recommend that you take the online version of the test to simulate test-day conditions and to receive these added benefits:

- **Timed testing conditions**—helps you gauge how much time you can spend on each question

- **Automatic scoring**—find out how you did on the test, instantly

- **On-screen detailed explanations of answers**—gives you the correct answer and explains why the other answer choices are wrong

- **Diagnostic score reports**—pinpoint where you're strongest and where you need to focus your study

TIME: 5 Hours
135 Multiple-choice questions

In this section, you will find examples of test questions similar to those you are likely to encounter on the TExES Special Education EC–12 (161) Exam. Read each question carefully and choose the best answer from the four possible choices. Mark your responses on the answer sheet provided on page 290.

1.   Which of the following disabilities is an example of a low-incidence disability?

   (A)   Visual impairments, including blindness
   (B)   Speech/language impairment
   (C)   Specific learning disability
   (D)   Dyslexia

2.   What is the area of the triangle below?

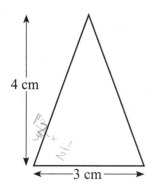

4 cm

3 cm

   (A)   4 cm
   (B)   6 cm
   (C)   7 cm
   (D)   12 cm

3.   Which of the following would be the best activity for teaching budgeting skills to high-school students?

   (A)   Completing budgeting worksheets
   (B)   Watching a video about inflation
   (C)   Providing menus from local restaurants and having students decide what they will order for less than 10 dollars
   (D)   Learning how to use spreadsheet software

4. A Special Education teacher reviews her/his students' IEP objectives and results from the previous year's STAAR assessment to decide which skills to teach. She/he finds three students who need to improve their summarization skills and plans a small-group lesson on summarization just for them. This kind of lesson planning is called

   (A) targeted instruction.
   (B) test-based instruction.
   (C) inclusion.
   (D) errorless discrimination.

5. Before districts can share personal information about students with community agencies providing or paying for transition services, IDEA requires

   (A) a completed transition plan.
   (B) documentation of state certification from the community agency.
   (C) an administrator's approval.
   (D) parental consent, or the consent of an eligible child who has reached the age of majority.

6. What does FAPE stand for?

   (A) First Aid in Physical Education
   (B) Funds for Administrators and Professional Educators
   (C) Free and Appropriate Public Education
   (D) Functional Assessments and Professional Evaluations

7. Tia is an eleventh grader with Downs syndrome. Her transition-needs evaluation indicates that she loves to count coins and can count up to the number 1,000, but she only counts by ones, not fives or tens. Tia is nervous around people she does not know, but she can be quite chatty once she is comfortable with someone. Tia takes some time to learn a routine, but once she has it down, she really knows it. She washes her hands obsessively after using the restroom and sometimes has to be redirected. Tia's Special Education teacher reaches out to a local board-game company to ask about internship opportunities for Tia. The president of the game company supports programs for students with special needs and is open to bringing in Tia for an internship. He suggests the following jobs at his company. Which is the most appropriate for Tia based on her transition-needs evaluation?

   (A) Opening and unpacking boxes with board-game supplies (such as player pieces and six-sided dice) in the warehouse and then sorting the supplies into large bins for each type of game-board component
   (B) Assisting the receptionist at the front desk with greeting visitors and opening and sorting mail
   (C) Assembling board games and making sure each game has the correct number of playing pieces, dice, game cards, and play money
   (D) Working directly with the building custodian, learning how to clean the floors, the bathrooms, and the break room

8. A third-grade student is evaluated for Special Education services, and the assessments indicate she has a reading disability characterized by visual-spatial deficits. At the ARD committee meeting, the parents indicate an interest in learning more about these types of reading disabilities. Which of the following educational organization websites would be the most appropriate to recommend the parents explore?

   (A) www.cec.sped.org
   (B) www.ldanatl.org
   (C) www.interdys.org
   (D) All of the above

9. A third-grade teacher with a diverse class has just attended a professional development session on colored overlays and how reading with a colored background can help some students with reading disabilities because the color does not reflect fluorescent light like white paper does. The teacher has two students in her class who have complained that their eyes hurt when they read or that the print is blurry. The school nurse has checked their eyesight, and it is 20/20. The teacher decides to do a colored overlay experiment with the whole class. Students try each of the colors the teacher provides and write down feedback about whether the text is any easier to read with each color. The teacher is delighted when both of the students who reported trouble with reading in the past find colors that they say "make the words stop moving." Several other students in class also report that the color makes it easier to read. The most likely reason for the teacher deciding to run the experiment with the whole class instead of just the two students is to

   (A) fulfill the requirements of the professional development session.
   (B) be able to count the experiment as a class science lesson.
   (C) give the students something fun to do.
   (D) help the students understand learning differences and ensure that any use of colored overlays by students in the class will not be viewed as "weird."

10. If a teacher assesses a student's rate, accuracy, and expression, what area of reading is being evaluated?

   (A) Comprehension
   (B) Miscue analysis
   (C) Phonics
   (D) Fluency

11. It is important for students to develop procedural fluency in math so students can

   (A) read word problems quickly.
   (B) follow directions easily.
   (C) focus on learning higher order math skills.
   (D) present their ideas clearly in class discussions.

12. Mr. Takei, a regular education earth science teacher, is planning a lesson on why volcanoes erupt and the effects of an eruption on the environment. As he thinks about his students, he reflects that two of his students (Maggie who has an IEP, and Sean who does not) seem to need concrete examples to understand concepts. Another Special Education student, Marcus, seems to retain more information when he has to talk about it himself. Several students need to see a picture to better understand what the teacher is talking about. Which of the following lesson presentation ideas best meets the needs of all of the learners in Mr. Takei's class?

   (A) Make the presentation a multimedia presentation on the classroom's interactive whiteboard.
   (B) Prepare a model of a volcano, and ask Maggie and Sean to be assistants in causing it to erupt. Ask Marcus to serve as narrator for the entire experiment. Place chairs in a semi-circle around the experiment table to allow for a good view.
   (C) Ask Maggie and Sean to sit in the back so they won't be tempted to touch the model volcano. Tell all students, including Marcus, to take careful notes of the steps leading up to the eruption.
   (D) Show a movie about the after-effects of the Mount St. Helens eruption in Washington in 1980.

13. Which of the following practices is an example of assessing students ethically?

   (A) Using culturally and linguistically appropriate assessment procedures
   (B) Testing all students, regardless of disability or background, the same way
   (C) Basing a student's grade on one final exam
   (D) Using a Bell curve to assign grades

14. Which of the following sentences has a syntax error?

   (A) Along the way sees Jesse a cat.
   (B) I ran and ran and ran and ran and ran.
   (C) no! don't go!
   (D) I would like to have a cat.

15. Given the algebraic equation $a = b + 7$, which of the following statements is true?

   (A) a is greater than b
   (B) b is greater than a
   (C) a is equal to b
   (D) It is not possible to know which variable is greater in value.

16. A Special Education teacher in a <u>PPCD</u> (Preschool Program for Children with Disabilities) classroom is assigned a paraprofessional who has never worked with young children before. The paraprofessional states that she is used to supervising children as they complete their work quietly and independently. What would be the most appropriate way for the teacher to respond?

    (A) Explain that young children with disabilities, like all young children, tend to be active learners who need <u>manipulatives</u> and time to practice good social skills. The teacher will be sitting on the floor with the children during circle time and participating in station activities with the children, and she expects the paraprofessional to do the same.
    (B) Ask the school principal to assign a more experienced paraprofessional to the PPCD class.
    (C) Tell the paraprofessional she can do copying and material preparation work primarily while the teacher works with the children.
    (D) Ask the paraprofessional why she took the job if she wasn't comfortable with preschool children.

17. Which of the following shapes is an isosceles triangle?

    (A)

    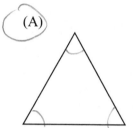

    (B)

    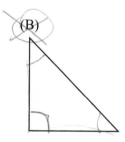

    (C)

    (D)

    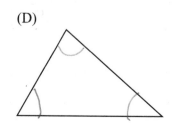

18. Mrs. Tomas, a third-grade teacher, is teaching students to write in cursive. Anna, one of her students, is struggling with this task, and her handwriting is incomprehensible. Which of the following related service providers would be most qualified to evaluate Anna's needs and suggest appropriate accommodations?

    (A) Physical therapist
    (B) Speech-language pathologist
    (C) Occupational therapist
    (D) School psychologist

19. A summative assessment would be administered

    (A) prior to beginning a unit.
    (B) one third of a way through a unit.
    (C) halfway through a unit.
    (D) at the conclusion of a unit.

20. A Special Education teacher is extremely frustrated with one of her students who constantly sneers at her directions and often says, "This class is so boring." Which of the following management strategies would NOT be appropriate with this student?

    (A) Taking the student aside, addressing the behavior directly, and asking what could be wrong
    (B) Ignoring the behavior
    (C) Catching the student being positive and praising the positive behavior (for example, something as simple as praising the student for being on time to class)
    (D) Being clear about consequences for rude behavior and applying those consequences in a calm manner when necessary

21. A teacher presents students with the following number pattern:

$$0, 1, 1, 2, 3, 5, 8, 13, \_\_\_.$$

Given this pattern, the next number would be

    (A) 18.
    (B) 21.
    (C) 25.
    (D) 28.

22. Which of the following factors can affect behavior?

    (A) Cognitive
    (B) Environmental
    (C) Affective
    (D) All of the above

23. A second-grade student with a reading disability has difficulty associating sounds to letters. On which area of reading instruction should the teacher focus?

    (A) Reading comprehension
    (B) Word analysis
    (C) Spelling
    (D) The connection between reading and writing

24. A sixth-grade language arts teacher assigns partners and then gives each pair an index card with a saying on it. Sayings include "It's raining cats and dogs," "He broke my heart," and "Drop Grandma a line." The teacher asks each pair to illustrate the saying on their card as if it was a literal statement. Then she directs partners to talk about the real meaning behind the phrase when used in everyday speech. The type of expression this teacher is introducing is

    (A) idioms.
    (B) metaphors.
    (C) similes.
    (D) symbol-supported text.

25. Which of the following fractions is equivalent to 0.625?

    (A) 3/4
    (B) 6/25
    (C) 5/8
    (D) 2/5

26. A sixth-grade teacher divides her class into two sides. She explains that they are going to have a mock debate in class that day. Side A has to argue for why peanut butter and jelly sandwiches are the best. Side B has to argue for why grilled cheese sandwiches are the best. Each side has 20 minutes to put the arguments together and then present them to the class. The students quickly get to work brainstorming supportive ideas for their side. When the two sides are ready to present, the teacher says she will decide who wins by how hungry she is for their sandwich. After the debate, the teacher assigns homework in the form of a paper each student will write to follow up on the debate. Which form of writing are the students most likely going to use for their homework assignment?

    (A) Persuasive
    (B) How-to
    (C) Compare/contrast
    (D) Narrative

27. How did the reauthorization of the Elementary and Secondary Education Act in 2001 (better known as No Child Left Behind) affect IDEA in the reauthorization of 2004?

    (A) It had no effect on IDEA. They are separate laws
    (B) It combined the two laws into one education initiative
    (C) It required a statement in IDEA that all paraprofessionals, including personal care assistants, meet the requirements of highly qualified personnel
    (D) It influenced language that reflected greater accountability for all students and the selection of research-based instructional programs

28. A student with ADHD has a difficult time maintaining focus in his third-grade classroom. The classroom seating arrangements that would be most appropriate for this student and help him focus is to

    (A) isolate the student in a study carrel in the back of the classroom.
    (B) seat the student at the teacher's desk for proximity control.
    (C) have the student sit with his peers, but make his chair an exercise ball.
    (D) place the student in the middle of the classroom.

29. Two high school ALE teachers plan a trip to the local grocery store for their students. The class works together on a shopping list. Using old magazines and grocery store flyers, students place a picture next to each item on the list. On the day of the trip, students are paired up, and each pair receives a copy of the shopping list. The partners must find all of the groceries on the list and meet at the checkout counter. What kind of instruction is this?

    (A) Game-based learning
    (B) Sheltered instruction
    (C) Community-based instruction
    (D) Scientific experiment

30. What kind of goals must a Special Education student's Individualized Education Program (IEP) include?

    (A) Measurable and annual
    (B) Measurable and semi-annual
    (C) Community-based and annual
    (D) Extracurricular-focused and monthly

31. In Special Education, the term co-morbidity refers to

    (A) terminal illness.
    (B) secondary or tertiary disability that exists alongside a child's primary diagnosis.
    (C) one-to-one aid required for academic tasks.
    (D) allergies to specific foods.

32. Which of the following is NOT a procedural safeguard for parents in the federally mandated Special Education system?

    (A) Written notice of proposed Special Education testing
    (B) Parental consent for Special Education placement
    (C) Right to appeal school decisions to an impartial hearing officer
    (D) Right to select the best teacher for the child

33. According to IDEA guidelines, which of the following elements is NOT required to be included in a Behavior Intervention Plan?

   (A) A measurable description of the behavior changes expected
   (B) A description of when and how information will be shared between home and school
   (C) A description of the interventions that will be used including who will be involved, procedures that will be followed, and an explanation of how data will be collected
   (D) A list of the student's strengths, abilities, academic grades, and standardized test scores

34. FBA stands for

   (A) Federal Bureau of Accommodations.
   (B) Functional Behavior Assessment.
   (C) Focused Behavioral Analysis.
   (D) Fight Bullies Association.

35. A good communication strategy to use when conducting a parent-teacher conference is to

   (A) set a timer for 15 minutes where everyone can see it so the meeting time is kept to a minimum.
   (B) talk about whatever the parents want to talk about.
   (C) start the meeting with a friendly, informal conversation, and share positive details about the student's strengths.
   (D) have the parent sit at the student's desk while the teacher sits at his or her desk.

36. When working with students with disabilities in math, teachers should plan instruction that is primarily

   (A) explicit.
   (B) implicit.
   (C) digital.
   (D) verbal.

37. Which of the following conditions is NOT included in the IDEA definition of OHI?

   (A) Epilepsy
   (B) Leukemia
   (C) Tourette syndrome
   (D) Specific learning disability

38. Which of the following students would likely benefit most from recorded books?

   (A) A student with dyslexia
   (B) A student with dyscalculia
   (C) A student with dysgraphia
   (D) A student with physical disabilities who uses a wheelchair

39. Which of the following assistive technology examples was created specifically to help nonverbal students interact at school, at home, and in the community?

    (A) Talking calculator
    (B) Augmentative communication device
    (C) Speech-recognition program
    (D) Optical character-recognition software

40. What is a common issue for children on all levels of the autism spectrum?

    (A) Communication and social interaction
    (B) Difficulty reading
    (C) Inability to talk
    (D) Depression

41. A teacher in an ALE classroom provides each student with a plastic 10-frame and 10 small plastic rectangles that fit on the 10-frame. The math concept the teacher is most likely planning to teach with this manipulative is

    (A) geometry.
    (B) number patterns.
    (C) probability.
    (D) addition.

42. The primary reason for renaming the Education for all Handicapped Children Act to the Individuals with Disabilities Education Act in 1990 is

    (A) that IDEA is a much cooler acronym than EHA.
    (B) to promote "people first" language, emphasizing the person, not the disability.
    (C) that high-school kids do not like to be called children.
    (D) because Congress updates names of important laws every 15 years.

43. According to the National Reading Panel's 2000 report, "Teaching Children to Read," there are five evidence-based areas of reading instruction. What are the five areas?

    (A) Multisensory awareness, phonemic awareness, choral, comprehension, phonics
    (B) Phonemic awareness, phonics, vocabulary, fluency, comprehension
    (C) Echo reading, vocabulary, shared reading, choral reading, paired reading
    (D) Guided reading, independent reading, whole-group reading, small-group reading, sight words

44. A child must be reevaluated to determine continued eligibility for Special Education services

    (A) every year.
    (B) every two years.
    (C) every three years.
    (D) only when a teacher or related services provider determines a reevaluation is necessary.

45.   One advantage of recorded books is that

  (A)   they keep students quiet during class.
  (B)   they are an old technology.
  (C)   they provide students with a model of fluent reading and can be turned off when the students wants to read on their own.
  (D)   they encourage students to listen instead of read.

Use the information below to answer questions 46 and 47.

When presenting a sight-word lesson to an elementary student with intellectual disabilities, a Special Education teacher introduces a word and then places three word cards in front of the student. The teacher asks the student to point to the target word. When the student points to the incorrect word, the teacher takes away that distractor and repeats the question. The second time, the student points to the correct word, and the teacher praises the student.

46.   What instructional technique is the teacher using to teach sight words?

  (A)   Errorless discrimination
  (B)   Repetition and review
  (C)   Repeated reading
  (D)   Hand over hand

47.   The most likely purpose of praising the student in the sight-word example above is to

  (A)   make the student feel better after missing the word on the first try.
  (B)   provide an instructional accommodation.
  (C)   reinforce the correct answer and build the student's self-esteem.
  (D)   let the student's classmates know that the student is doing good work.

48.   A Special Education teacher in an ALE classroom uses communication notebooks to share information with parents about their children's academic work and behavior each day. She also uses the notebooks to write questions to parents and to request supplies. Two days ago, the teacher wrote in a student's notebook that the student needed a spare set of clothes to have available if he has an accident or gets wet at the water fountain. There has been no reply from the parents, and no spare clothes have been sent. The most appropriate next step for the teacher to take would be to

  (A)   assume the parents don't care about their son, and gather some clothes from a thrift store to have on hand for the child.
  (B)   write another note in the notebook, this time using exclamation points to emphasize that the spare clothes are needed as soon as possible.
  (C)   use another form of communication to contact the parents, such as a phone call or an email.
  (D)   ask the school counselor to reach out to the family since they are not responding to the teacher.

49. Based on United States law, the entity ultimately responsible for providing a free and appropriate public education for all students, including students with disabilities, is

    (A) the federal government.
    (B) the courts.
    (C) the states.
    (D) parents.

50. An eighth-grade U.S. history teacher has a diverse class and wants to ensure that they all gain a deep sense of the causes and effects of the events in our country's past. She asks her co-teacher for some suggestions. Which of the following strategies would be the most appropriate one to suggest given the social studies teacher's goals?

    (A) Use a Venn diagram to illustrate the content
    (B) Have small groups create parts of a multisensory timeline, placing each event in the wall in the sequence it occurred
    (C) Have students make outlines using the headings in their textbooks
    (D) Have students interview their parents about the most memorable historical event in their lives

51. A Special Education teacher in a middle-school ALE classroom sets up student roles in her class that change each week. One of the roles involves filing the class's folder games by skill (indicated by a picture symbol on the file folders). Another role requires students to put homework activities in order and staple them. A third role involves watering the class plants. The teacher's purpose in developing these class roles most likely is to

    (A) assess informally and build students' basic job skills in preparation for the transition plan in their IEP.
    (B) develop cooperative learning skills.
    (C) save the teacher's and paraprofessional's time by getting the students to do the rote classroom chores.
    (D) keep students occupied and less likely to misbehave.

52. A seventh-grade mathematics teacher has several students with learning disabilities in one of his classes and is assigned a co-teacher from the Special Education department to help during that class period. The math teacher sets up a table with five chairs in the back of the room and directs the co-teacher and the four students with learning disabilities to sit there throughout the class. He tells the co-teacher that she can help her kids that way. The most appropriate response by the co-teacher would be to

    (A) thank the math teacher for his consideration.
    (B) explain that working with a small group in the back of the room will distract the other students from their tasks.
    (C) ask the math teacher if she can have a desk instead.
    (D) point out that the table, while a good place to use for flexible group instruction, should not be the permanent seating area for the students with learning disabilities as it segregates them and, therefore, does not meet the legal requirements of least restrictive environment.

53. Which of the following statements about assistive technology is true?

    (A) Assistive technology must have a digital component

    (B) Only a district coordinator can provide assistive technology to a student

    (C) Assistive technology can be as simple as a pencil grip or as elaborate as a multithousand-dollar machine

    (D) Assistive technology gives students with disabilities an unfair advantage over their peers

54. In a ninth-grade algebra class, a student with learning disabilities struggles to complete assignments in a timely manner. The teacher and a Special Education co-teacher spend time analyzing how the student approaches problems, and they find that his reasoning is sound but he is hampered by the fact that he has not memorized his basic math facts. The most appropriate way to help this student is to

    (A) have the student practice his math facts with the co-teacher the first 10 minutes of every class.

    (B) call the student's parents and ask them to help the student practice math facts for 30 minutes every day.

    (C) provide the student with a calculator for completing basic calculations on assignments and tests.

    (D) transfer the student to a remedial math class so he is not so stressed.

Use the information below to answer questions 55–57.

    A first-grade teacher gathers students in a circle and reads them a book with a repetitive phrase. At first, only the teacher reads. The fifth time the phrase appears, the teacher says, "Read with me," and signals the class to read the words aloud with her. The class continues reading the repetitive phrase with the teacher every time it appears. When the story ends, the teacher says "Good reading!" Then she writes the repetitive phrase on the interactive whiteboard and points to it. She says, "Listen to how I read this sentence." She models the sentence and then asks the students to try to read it "just like I did." The students try to match the teacher's voice inflections and speed. The teacher praises the students as they get closer and closer to imitating her.

55. Which of the following reading skills is the teacher addressing?

    (A) Phonemic awareness

    (B) Comprehension

    (C) Fluency

    (D) Phonics

56. When the teacher asks students to do their best to imitate her, she encourages them to match her voice-inflection patterns. Because the key phrase is repetitive, the students have an opportunity to read the phrase 10 times over the course of several minutes. What specific skill is the teacher focusing on when asking students to mimic her?

    (A) Main idea

    (B) Blending

    (C) Prediction

    (D) Expression

57. During the course of the reading time, the three different oral reading methods that the teacher uses fluidly are

   (A) shared reading, echo reading, and choral reading.
   (B) recorded books, neurological impress, and echo reading.
   (C) language experience, phonics, and paired reading.
   (D) choral reading, phonics, and Orton-Gillingham.

58. A tenth grader with reading disabilities wants to join the school newspaper club. The student approaches the journalism advisor and says she really wants to help with the school paper. She is especially interested in covering school sports. The journalism advisor approaches the student's English teacher and asks for her thoughts on the student's capabilities. Based on the Code of Ethics and Standard Practices for Texas Educators, which of the following replies is the most appropriate for the English teacher to make?

   (A) The English teacher relays the student's reading and writing strengths as well as the student's enthusiasm for sports. She also shares a couple of classroom adaptations, such as working with a partner and using colored overlays, which have really helped the student succeed on reading and writing tasks.
   (B) The English teacher tells the journalism advisor that the student has an IEP and struggles to read and write, so the newspaper club is really not appropriate for the student.
   (C) The English teacher tells the journalism advisor that the student has special needs and that extra reading and writing practice would be a good thing for her to do.
   (D) The English teacher offers to make a copy of the student's IEP for the journalism advisor to review.

59. What must be administered to the student with the disability before a transition plan can be written for the student's IEP?

   (A) The STAAR or STAAR Alt
   (B) Age-appropriate transition assessments
   (C) Reading inventory
   (D) A medicare questionnaire

60. A Special Education teacher is planning a lesson on teaching the meaning of common outdoor signs to an Applied Learning Environment (ALE) class. One of the students is nonverbal. One way the teacher can ensure that the nonverbal student can fully participate in the lesson is to

   (A) have a paraprofessional help the student sit quietly.
   (B) provide response cards with pictures of the signs for the student to hold up to indicate his/her answer.
   (C) allow the student to play her/his favorite program on a classroom computer during the lesson.
   (D) talk extra loudly to make sure the student can hear the teacher.

61. What characterizes the work of a late-stage emergent writer?

   (A) Approximated spellings
   (B) Strings of unrelated letters (patterned letters)
   (C) Scribbled pictures
   (D) Complex syntax

62. A Special Education teacher is using miscue analysis to diagnose students' reading difficulties. What would this look like in the classroom?

   (A) Each student reading an independent-level book silently while the teacher moves around the room and talks quietly to individual students

   (B) The teacher and student at a table in the back of the room with the student orally reading short passages and the teacher making marks on a separate copy of the passages

   (C) A small group of students gathered around the teacher at a kidney-shaped table and the teacher holding a big book in her hands and pointing to the first letters of various words

   (D) The teacher standing behind individual students and having them read aloud from an independent-reading-level book while the teacher whispers the words simultaneously in the student's right ear

63. What is a common term for a written language learning disability?

   (A) Dysgraphia
   (B) Dyslexia
   (C) Orthopedic impairment
   (D) Developmental delay

64. Which of the following statements about postsecondary goals is true based on IDEA regulations?

   (A) The postsecondary goals must include independent living skills
   (B) The postsecondary goals must reflect parent expectations
   (C) The postsecondary goals must be measurable
   (D) The postsecondary goals cannot include unpaid employment

65. An appropriate tool for evaluating an authentic assessment task is

   (A) a multiple-choice quiz.
   (B) a norm-referenced test.
   (C) a rubric.
   (D) observation.

66. A Special Education co-teacher is trying to explain to a regular education colleague why classroom time spent on prereading activities will actually improve comprehension. The regular education teacher is concerned about the time that would take away from discussion after the reading is complete. One important reason to spend time on prereading strategies is that

   (A) preparing students to read significantly improves comprehension and teaches students strategies that make them more successful, independent readers in the future.
   (B) prereading strategies are easier than comprehension questions after reading.
   (C) prereading gives the plot away.
   (D) Some students just can't help picking up a book and starting to read.

67. What are generic problem-solving strategies in math instruction?

    (A) Strategies that involve consumer math
    (B) Explicit visual models
    (C) Strategies for memorizing math facts
    (D) Organizational steps that can be applied to a range of math problems

68. Which of the following postsecondary options is NOT included in IDEA 2004's definition of postschool activities?

    (A) Vocational education
    (B) Independent living
    (C) Integrated employment
    (D) Home health

69. A sixth-grade language arts teacher arranges her classroom with desks facing the front and an area in the back with three clipboards on the wall. Masking tape denotes a small area of floor near each clipboard. As the teacher explains her expectations for the school year, she points out the clipboards and the taped-off sections of floor. She says, "During a lesson, if you are having a difficult time paying attention, feel free to stand up and walk quietly to the back and grab a clipboard if one is available. The clipboards will always have paper and pencil so that you can take notes while standing in the taped-off area." What is the teacher most likely trying to accomplish by implementing this classroom arrangement?

    (A) Anticipating and meeting the needs of tactile/kinesthetic learners in her classes
    (B) Rewarding students who finish their work early
    (C) Trying a new writing strategy using clipboards
    (D) Convincing students that she is their coolest teacher

70. A fifth-grade teacher writes the following math problem on the board and tells students to remember the order of operations as they solve it.

    $(2 + 4) \times 5 =$ _____ . The correct answer to this problem is

    (A) 11.
    (B) 14.
    (C) 22.
    (D) 30.

71. The term used to describe a reader who is just beginning to make the letter-sound connection and who recognizes a few sight words is

    (A) decoder.
    (B) reluctant.
    (C) emergent.
    (D) fluent.

72. A Special Education teacher consults with a student's inclusion teacher to plan for the upcoming district assessment. Based on the student's work and behavior in the classroom, they agree to allow the student to mark her/his answers directly in the test booklet, and to provide the student with a study carrel in which to take the test. What are the teachers developing?

    (A) Assessment ethics
    (B) Assessment modifications
    (C) Assessment rules
    (D) Assessment accommodations

73. Fifth-grade students walk into class to find a huge poster on each wall with the word "radius" on it. There is a circular paper spinner on each desk. The teacher has a large cardboard circle taped to his chest with a line from the edge of the circle to the middle of the circle. The teacher is most likely trying to

    (A) draw attention to a new math vocabulary word.
    (B) get students excited about circles.
    (C) provide materials for the students to play an educational game.
    (D) ensure that no student will ever misspell "radius" again.

74. Which of the following examples is NOT a concept of print?

    (A) Book title
    (B) Reading text left to right
    (C) Black marks on a page that are the words being spoken
    (D) Simile

75. A Special Education student is evaluated using a battery of achievement tests, and the results indicate the student has procedural learning deficits. How would these deficits most likely affect the student in math?

    (A) The student has challenges conceptualizing geometric shapes
    (B) The student has difficulty solving multistep word problems
    (C) The student has issues with math fact drills
    (D) The student has difficulty measuring distances

76. A fourth-grade student knows all of his/her multiplication facts and can solve three digit multiplication problems with ease. However, he/she has difficulty solving word problems and is failing mathematics because of his/her poor performance on tests. What skills should the teacher target to best help this student improve his/her performance?

    (A) Mathematics
    (B) Writing
    (C) Reading
    (D) Study skills

77. The purpose of a Behavior Intervention Plan (BIP) is to

 (A) document student behavior for determination of consequences.
 (B) analyze the reasons for a negative behavior.
 (C) explain what behaviors are being targeted for change and how school staff will implement the change.
 (D) satisfy a requirement of the ARD.

78. To prepare students in a middle-school intervention math class for a unit on fractions, a Special Education teacher puts together a Power Point presentation on the interactive whiteboard using videos and images from the Internet. The presentation shows people using fractions at work, at home, and in the community. What is the teacher most likely trying to accomplish with this presentation?

 (A) Involve the visual learners in the class
 (B) Prepare the students for a vocational assessment
 (C) Motivate the students with reasons to learn fractions
 (D) Provide an alternative way to study for the unit test

79. A fourth-grade teacher is new to a school. She has a diverse classroom, and she wants to start the year off on a positive note. Which of the following activities would be the most appropriate way for the teacher to let students know she is excited to be their teacher and that she respects them and their learning needs?

 (A) Hug every student at the beginning of each day
 (B) Smile all day, even when explaining consequences or correcting student behavior
 (C) Play a "name game" to help students learn each other's names while the teacher also learns the name or nickname each student prefers
 (D) As the students pack up to go home each day, give each student a piece of candy with a message like "It's going to be a sweet year" attached

80. Which type of assessment describes qualities of a performance in order to indicate a level of achievement?

 (A) Rating scale
 (B) Parent interview
 (C) Play-based assessment
 (D) Multiple-choice test

Use the information below to answer questions 81–83.

A new Special Education teacher is hired to teach several reading intervention classes at a school-wide Title One middle school. At that school, 90 percent of the students are Hispanic, and 15 percent are English language learners, but these students have their own ESL class. The school has a traditional way of communicating regularly with parents: report cards go home at the end of each quarter, and progress reports go home three weeks before the end of each quarter. The teacher wants to be more progressive in communicating with parents, so she makes a point of sending home hand-written notes about each student once a week. She includes positive observations about the student and always includes one idea for helping the student practice reading skills at home. The teacher is sure these notes will be well-received by parents. One day, she is helping a student find a homework assignment in his backpack and discovers that all of her handwritten notes are in a pile in the bottom of the backpack. The teacher is surprised and looks at the student in confusion. The student looks down at his feet and mumbles something about his parents not being able to read them anyway.

81. What is one flaw in the teacher's communication strategy?

    (A) The teacher's alternate form of communication is one-way communication, just like progress reports and report cards. There is no way for her to know if the notes have been read.
    (B) Students never give their parents notes or official papers from school.
    (C) The teacher's handwriting is sloppy and unreadable, so handwritten notes are a bad idea.
    (D) Handwritten notes are old-fashioned and outdated. Emails would be better.

82. Based on the school's demographic information and the student's response when the teacher finds the note, a likely conclusion to make about the student's parents is that

    (A) the parents have disabilities too.
    (B) English is not the parents' native language.
    (C) the parents are not interested in learning what their son does at school.
    (D) the parents are never home.

83. In this situation, an appropriate response for the teacher to make is to

    (A) discipline the student for not giving the notes to his parents.
    (B) gather all the notes up, and request a parent-teacher conference to show the notes to the parents and explain that their son was supposed to give them the notes.
    (C) stop writing notes to this family and send emails instead.
    (D) ask the school office to help find a bilingual colleague and make a phone call to the parents to relay, with the help of the translator, all the positive things the teacher had written.

84. Instructional modification is

    (A) an extension of time to complete an assignment.
    (B) a change to the content students are learning.
    (C) a complex accommodation.
    (D) a behavioral improvement plan.

85. To determine a child's eligibility for Special Education services, a school district will administer

    (A) a formative assessment.
    (B) parent evaluation.
    (C) formal diagnostic assessments.
    (D) an end-of-chapter test from a textbook used in the child's classroom.

86. A Special Education teacher is working with a ninth-grade biology teacher. The Special Education teacher suggests that for the next chapter in the textbook, they provide the students with five sticky notes each and then have the students read the chapter with a partner. During the reading, partners must stop five times to place a sticky note on the text and write a comment or question about the content. The purpose of the Special Education teacher's suggested activity is to

    (A) teach students to self-monitor for comprehension.
    (B) teach students to activate prior knowledge.
    (C) teach students how to sequence events.
    (D) provide students with an opportunity to converse.

87. Researchers look at the strategies successful readers use to help them identify reading strategies to teach explicitly to struggling readers. Which of the following strategies is an example of an activity most successful readers do after reading?

    (A) Turning to a peer and talk about what was good about the book and what wasn't so good
    (B) Making predictions
    (C) Checking for understanding
    (D) Closing the book, saying "I'm done," and moving on to something else

88. A Special Education co-teacher is working with a small group of students on the concept of "greater than" and "less than." She wants to scaffold their learning, so she uses several different activities to move them toward mastery of the concept. Of the following activities, which one should be last in the teaching sequence?

    (A) Place two liquid measuring cups of equal size in front of students, and fill one to the 1-cup line with fruit punch and the other to the 2-cups line with fruit punch. Have students point to the measuring cup with more fruit punch. Then have students point to the measuring cup with less fruit punch.
    (B) Using a small whiteboard, write down two numbers that students call out randomly. Provide students with cards with the "greater than" and "less than" symbols, and then have a student place the card between the numbers on the whiteboard to show which number is greater. Have the group agree or disagree once the card is placed and explain why.
    (C) Show students a picture of an alligator with its mouth open to help them visualize the greater than/less than symbol.
    (D) Pair students, and provide each pair with a spinner with the numbers 1 to 20 on it and two blank worksheets. Tell students to take turns spinning. The first number spun should go on the left side of the first space on the worksheet, and the second number spun should go on the right side. Once both numbers are written, partners should agree whether the first number is greater than, less than, or equal to the second number, and write the appropriate symbol.

89. What committee did Texas put in place to meet IDEA's requirement for a system of determination of eligibility for students with disabilities?

    (A) PTA
    (B) TEA
    (C) ARD
    (D) RTI

90. A fourth grader is observed exhibiting awkward social behaviors, anxiety, and poor handwriting. After implementing several accommodations recommended by the school's RTI committee, the classroom teacher reports that the student is not showing any improvement in these areas. Special Education testing is recommended, and the parents are notified that the district proposes to conduct evaluations in all academic, emotional, behavioral, and social areas. The district also indicates that they would like to have their autism team evaluate the student for an autism spectrum disorder. The parents give consent for all testing except the autism team's evaluation. They claim that they know their child does not have autism, and they do not want any evaluations in that area. The appropriate response by the school district is to

   (A) conduct all recommended evaluations, as it is the district's purview to decide what assessments will be given.
   (B) conduct only the evaluations for which the parents gave consent.
   (C) tell the parents that if the district cannot conduct all of the recommended evaluations, it will withdraw the offer to evaluate their child in any area.
   (D) have the district's superintendent sign paperwork to override the parent's decision.

91. Which of the following symptoms is NOT an indicator of a hearing impairment?

   (A) The student talks very loudly, even in situations where it not warranted
   (B) The student does not turn and look at a person who is talking behind him/her
   (C) The student puts her/his hands over her/his ears repeatedly
   (D) The student does not speak clearly and mispronounces many words

92. Why is it important to identify the reasons for a student's misbehavior rather than simply administer a punishment?

   (A) To make the punishment stick
   (B) To be able to explain the situation to parents and administrators
   (C) To satisfy teacher union requirements
   (D) To be able to address the cause of the negative behavior and, by extension, eliminate or modify the behavior

93. Which of the following student activities is an example of comprehension?

   (A) Matching words to pictures
   (B) Reading a 100-word passage in less than a minute
   (C) Identifying prefixes and suffixes in a list of words
   (D) Using a graphic organizer for prewriting

94. During a mathematics test, a Special Education teacher provides a student with an MP3 player on which all of the test questions have been recorded. The student has a reading disability. What type of assessment accommodation has the teacher provided?

   (A) Setting
   (B) Presentation
   (C) Timing
   (D) Scheduling

95. An acute angle is

    (A) a 90-degree angle.
    (B) an angle that measures less than 90 degrees but more than 0 degrees.
    (C) an angle that measures more than 90 degrees but less than 180 degrees.
    (D) a 180-degree angle.

96. A teacher in an elementary ALE classroom notices that one of her students with autism is reacting to changes in classroom routine much more emotionally than usual. The student has a 30-minute meltdown when rain prevents the students from going to the playground at their normal recess time. When the third meltdown happens in two days, the teacher calls the preferred contact number on the student's information card and requests a conference with the parents. The teacher does not hear back that day. The next day, there is a message waiting at the front office from the student's mother explaining she is out of town on business and in a time zone that is two hours different from the teacher's. The mother asks if the teacher can call her that evening after 6 p.m. What is the most appropriate response by the teacher?

    (A) Leave another message at the contact number saying, "Never mind. I understand the issue now."
    (B) Call the parent after 6 p.m. and thank her for calling back while being out of town. Explain the situation with the student, and brainstorm ideas with the parent to help the student feel more secure.
    (C) Find a secondary contact number for the student's family, and call that person to arrange a conference.
    (D) Ask an administrator to call the parent back that evening since it is after school hours.

Use the information below to answer questions 97–99.

Ms. Walker, an elementary ALE teacher, has been teaching her students high-frequency sight words along with some basic phonics. One day, Ms. Walker brings in a bag filled with advertisements cut out from magazines and newspapers and printed from the Internet. She pulls the advertisements out one at a time and uses a document camera to project each one on the whiteboard. Then she asks students if they see any of the words they have learned. Tristan, who is nonverbal, nods his head, and Ms. Walker tells him to show her a word on the board. Tristan approaches the board and circles a sight word on the advertisement. Ms. Walker gives him a high five and directs him back to his seat. The lesson continues with other students approaching the board and circling sight words found in the advertisements. Some of the words are in fancy fonts, and some are simple.

97. The reading term for the advertisements that Ms. Walker has brought into the class is

    (A) joint attention.
    (B) primary sources.
    (C) environmental print.
    (D) narratives.

98. Ms. Walker uses the interactive whiteboard and document camera for this lesson

    (A) so that the whole class can easily see the images and watch as peers find the sight words, combining visual and tactile/kinesthetic learning.
    (B) to expose students to technology.
    (C) to practice vocational skills.
    (D) to enable both sight words and phonics reviews.

99.   Ms. Walker's most likely purpose for asking students to find the sight words in the advertisements is to

      (A)   test their long-term retention.
      (B)   check their vision.
      (C)   assess their fluency.
      (D)   see if they can generalize the sight words they have learned.

Use the information below to answer questions 100–102.

      A math teacher writes the following numbers on the board:

      43, 26, 39, 67, 76, 67, 51

100. If the teacher asks the students to find the mean, she is asking them to

      (A)   determine the average of this group of numbers.
      (B)   place the numbers in sequential order.
      (C)   figure out which number is in the middle once the numbers are sorted.
      (D)   identify the lowest number.

101. What is the mode for this group of numbers?

      (A)   26
      (B)   39
      (C)   51
      (D)   67

102. To determine the median for this group of numbers, the students will first have to

      (A)   place the numbers in order, from lowest to highest.
      (B)   find the average.
      (C)   remove any duplicate numbers.
      (D)   complete the number pattern.

103. A fifth-grade teacher is preparing to teach her students order of operations in math. Which of the following ideas would be a good way to help students remember this information?

      (A)   Use the mnemonic PEMDAS
      (B)   Teach the rule "i before e except after c"
      (C)   Have students complete fluency drills with math facts
      (D)   Provide students with several objects, and have them place them in order from smallest to largest

253

Use the information below to answer questions 104 and 105.

A ninth-grade algebra I teacher and his Special Education co-teacher teach one section of their students who were identified as at-risk based on previous math performance. Several of these students have learning disabilities. The two teachers are reviewing students' performance on the section quizzes for the unit just taught on equations and inequalities. They need to prepare for the final review and end of unit test. Here is the data they review:

Section	Percentage Passing	Students who Failed
Using Proportions	90%	Laura, Juan
Equations with Variables on Both Sides	80%	Laura, Tim, Jackson, Emilio
Solving Absolute Value Equations	60%	Laura, Juan, Tim, Jackson, Emilio, Sara, Tia, Tag
Transforming Formulas	85%	Laura, Jackson, Sara

104. Based on the above data, the most appropriate plan for the unit review would be to

   (A)   structure a fun, interactive review in the form of a game using the interactive whiteboard.
   (B)   give all the students who failed extra practice in the appropriate skills in the form of modified worksheets.
   (C)   have the co-teacher tutor Laura and Jackson in the hall while the rest of the class completes the review.
   (D)   reteach the section on "solving absolute value equations" to the entire class using a different approach.

105. Laura, a student with reading disabilities, is always one of the last to finish a quiz. During independent work, she often asks one of the teachers to help with one or more of the words in the directions. Based on the data above and classroom observations of Laura, the most appropriate way to help her would be to

   (A)   make an accommodation for Laura by giving her a dictionary and a calculator to use when she is completing an assignment or taking a quiz.
   (B)   make an accommodation for Laura by administering her quiz in a back corner of the classroom and having the teacher or co-teacher read each quiz question to her.
   (C)   give Laura extra homework so she can get more practice in the skills.
   (D)   transfer Laura to a self-contained Special Education class.

106. If an ARD or IEP Team meeting is called for the purpose of considering postsecondary goals for a student with a disability and the transition services necessary to assist the student in reaching those goals, according to IDEA regulations, the IEP team must invite

   (A)   the student with the disability.
   (B)   a Special Education advocate.
   (C)   a representative from a community agency that pays for transition services.
   (D)   the school counselor.

107. A Special Education teacher in an ALE classroom sets up a classroom store and labels items with various prices from $0.49 to $4.99. She then distributes five play dollars to each student and provides time for each student to "shop" for an item. Once a student has selected an item, the student takes it to the teacher to "pay" for it. The teacher instructs students to look at the price, add 1 to the first number in the price, and give her that many dollars. She calls this the "next dollar" strategy. The most likely reason for teaching this strategy is to

    (A)   avoid having to teach coin values to the students.
    (B)   ensure that students have an easy way to pay for items at stores and will never be cheated out of more than $0.99.
    (C)   fulfill community-based instruction requirements.
    (D)   help students appreciate the value of a dollar.

108. What is Council for Exceptional Children's stance on the involvement of families in the Special Education process, based on the organization's code of ethics?

    (A)   Families should receive training so that they can do a better job addressing the child's deficits.
    (B)   Families deserve respect and should be actively involved in the educational decision-making process.
    (C)   Families do not have the same level of knowledge that educators do. Therefore, educators' opinions should take precedence over families' opinions.
    (D)   Families have enough legal protections in the Special Education process thanks to IDEA, but teachers need more protection.

109. For a social studies unit, a high-school Special Education teacher with an autism class teaches the meanings of a series of indoor and outdoor signs that students will see in the community. Several of the students are nonverbal, so the teacher shows them a large sign, names the sign, and then gives them a card with the same sign on it. As the activities progress, the students who are nonverbal learn to identify the sign when it is paired with one and then two distractors. The teacher also does simulations where she displays the sign and has the students act out how they would react to seeing that sign (for example, mimic washing hands when they see an "All Employees Will Wash Hands" sign or stopping when they see a "Stop" sign). In addition to adapting the social studies content, what required skills is the teacher focusing on with this unit?

    (A)   Reading skills
    (B)   Writing skills
    (C)   Independent-living skills
    (D)   Study skills

110. The primary indicator that a Special Education student needs to have a Behavior Intervention Plan as part of an IEP is that

    (A)   the assistant principal requires it.
    (B)   suspension from school occurs.
    (C)   behaviors are impeding learning.
    (D)   student's least restrictive environment is a self-contained classroom.

111. Which of the following instructional accommodations is most appropriate for a student with visual impairments?

    (A) Seat the student in the back of the classroom
    (B) Provide additional time for the student to complete his/her assignment
    (C) Use an eye gaze board
    (D) Increase the point size and leading between lines for all reading material presented to the student

112. A third-grade student with learning disabilities often cries and complains about her peers disliking her. Her classroom teacher says the student's classmates are not acting inappropriately, but that the student's own behaviors are causing other students to back away from her. Of the following strategies, what would be the most appropriate intervention for this student?

    (A) Obtain parental permission to add her to a small social-skills group with the school counselor where she can role-play how to make friends and react in socially appropriate ways
    (B) Teach her to stand up for herself and tell other students to back off
    (C) Tell her to act her age and never cry in public
    (D) Move her to another third-grade class where the teacher and students are more accepting of her learning disability

113. What are the two most prevalent disabilities for children ages 3–21 in the United States?

    (A) Autism and specific learning disabilities
    (B) Hearing impairments and speech/language impairments
    (C) Emotional disturbance and orthopedic impairments
    (D) Specific learning disabilities and speech/language impairments

114. A Special Education teacher in an ALE classroom is preparing to lift a student with limited mobility. Which of the following guidelines for lifting is NOT true?

    (A) Stand with both feet firmly planted and shoulder width apart
    (B) Approach from the front and place arms underneath the student's arms to lift
    (C) Bend at the knees and hips, not the back
    (D) The lifter's back should remain straight throughout the lift

115. Which of the following types of assessment is informal?

    (A) Criterion-referenced test
    (B) Behavioral checklist
    (C) Achievement test
    (D) Standardized exam

116. IDEA 2004 says a transition plan must be in place in a student's IEP by age 16. The Texas Senate Bill 1788 (passed in 2011) changed the required age for transition planning in Texas schools to

    (A) 12.
    (B) 13.
    (C) 14.
    (D) 15.

117. Public Law 94-142 was passed by Congress in

    (A) 1973.
    (B) 1975.
    (C) 1986.
    (D) 1990.

118. The purpose of the reauthorizations of the Individuals with Disabilities Education Act is to

    (A) clarify, update, revise, and expand the original law.
    (B) meet legal requirements stated in the original law.
    (C) make parents happy.
    (D) respond to federal court cases involving individuals with disabilities.

119. What type of transition information would a teacher expect to see documented in an Individualized Family Services Plan?

    (A) The date the child turns 3 and transitions to IDEA Part B services
    (B) The date the student turns 23 and transitions to independent living
    (C) The student's personal career goals
    (D) The results of the student's vocational assessment

120. A fourth-grade teacher with a diverse class hands each student a piece of paper with a 10-step staircase on it. She then projects a recipe card on the interactive whiteboard using a document camera. She has her students work in their table groups to write down the steps of the recipe on the staircase on their papers. She says, "Each step of the recipe should go on its own step." When the students have completed the assignment, she has them discuss how the staircase helped or didn't help them sequence the events of making the recipe. The teacher then says that the students have just discovered a new graphic organizer for a type of writing they will be learning about. What type of writing would go best with a graphic organizer in the form of steps on a staircase?

    (A) Persuasive
    (B) Compare/contrast
    (C) How-to
    (D) Narrative

121. IDEA defines transition services as

    (A) any service that transports students from school to home or home to school.
    (B) a coordinated set of activities for a child with a disability that improves academic and functional achievement to facilitate the child's movement from school to post-school activities.
    (C) a coordinated set of activities that identifies children ages 0–3 with potential disabilities and arranges for Special Education testing.
    (D) a series of high-school classes that move Special Education students into the regular education environment.

122. According to behavior researchers, when initially working to extinguish an undesirable behavior by not rewarding it, a teacher can expect

    (A) escalation of the behavior.
    (B) repeated apologies from the student.
    (C) total silence from the student.
    (D) reduction of the behavior.

123. A speech-language pathologist works with two students in Mrs. Tuscan's class. She pulls them out twice a week for a half hour each to work on pragmatics. Mrs. Tuscan asks if she can help reinforce the work the students are doing with the SLP. The SLP is thrilled to have the offer since the more generalization of the skills, the better. What would be a good activity for Mrs. Tuscan to structure to practice pragmatics?

    (A) Have students work independently to circle all the contractions in the story they are reading.
    (B) Have students work in small groups to develop a "cheerleading" alphabet and then have groups take turns spelling words kinesthetically with their cheers.
    (C) Ask students to stay in their seats while several different "secret sounds" are played. Students listen carefully and raise a hand if they want to guess the secret sound.
    (D) Pair the students and have them each play the role of a character in the book the class is reading. Ask the students to role-play a conversation between the two characters for five minutes.

124. What characterizes the co-teaching model of alternative teaching?

    (A) Each teacher runs a station in the class, and the students rotate between stations
    (B) One teacher presents the lesson, while the other teacher circulates around the room helping students
    (C) Teachers work together to deliver a lesson, and instruction becomes more than turn-taking
    (D) One teacher presents a lesson to a large group, while the other teacher presents the lesson at a lower level to a smaller group

125. A Special Education teacher working with students with learning disabilities has created her own teacher website, which she updates several times a week. The teacher lists weekly homework assignments and any special projects on the website, and she expects parents to check the information periodically. For the second quarter, the teacher has assigned students a research project on an animal of their choice. Students have several weeks to complete the project, and it will be a large part of their grade. The teacher posts all the project information and due date on the website. Which of the following assumptions would be the best to make to promote positive communication and ensure that students meet the project deadline?

   (A) Parents have all of the information and will be partners with the teacher in ensuring their children get the projects done on time.
   (B) One of the points of a research project is to foster student independence and good work habits, so it is up to the students to meet the project expectations by the deadline. If they don't, they will learn from the consequences of getting a bad grade.
   (C) Parents sometimes need a reminder so the teacher will ask the students to remind their parents to check the website.
   (D) Parents have busy lives and can be easily distracted. They may forget to check the website, or checking a website may not be their preferred method of communication. Since the project will have a significant impact on the students' grades in the class, the teacher will reach out to the parents with alternate forms of communication, including a written note and an email.

126. Which reauthorization of Public Law 94-142 expanded Special Education services to include children ages 0–5 with disabilities, paving the way for the early childhood identification programs every state now has in place?

   (A) Reauthorization of 1983
   (B) Reauthorization of 1986
   (C) Reauthorization of 1990
   (D) Reauthorization of 1997

127. The last stage of the writing process is

   (A) editing.
   (B) publishing.
   (C) revising.
   (D) prewriting.

128. Which of the following statements is true of accommodations in Special Education?

   (A) Accommodations are only used with Special Education students
   (B) Accommodations make the assignment more challenging for a student who is bored
   (C) Accommodations always have to be identified on a student's IEP to be implemented
   (D) Keeping accommodations simple whenever possible makes them more likely to be implemented regularly

259

129. A Special Education teacher is reviewing commercial math programs in order to recommend one for her middle school to purchase for its math intervention courses. In examining the content of the programs, the teacher should be looking for

 (A) an emphasis on basic skills with lots of practice drills.
 (B) a fully digital program.
 (C) a blended program that emphasizes procedural fluency, problem solving, and conceptual understanding with a variety of manipulatives.
 (D) a program that emphasizes cooperative learning for every lesson.

130. When conducting Special Education evaluations with English language learners, which of the following must school district personnel adhere to?

 (A) Evaluations must be provided and administered in the child's native language
 (B) Reading evaluations must be given in English to assess accurately the child's level of English language acquisition
 (C) Parents must be present during the child's evaluation
 (D) English language learners should never be evaluated for Special Education as their challenge is acquiring English, not overcoming a disability

131. A middle-school student with visual impairments is struggling in mathematics, particularly with longer operations. The mathematics teacher has made accommodations by increasing the point size on the student's worksheets and assigning classmates to read the problems aloud to the student. The teacher is convinced a talking calculator is the missing piece in helping this student access the curriculum. A Special Education teacher is called in to review the situation and requests an assistive-technology (AT) evaluation from the district. The Special Education teacher would request an AT evaluation rather than just obtaining a talking calculator for the student because

 (A) the district wants to save as much money as possible.
 (B) IDEA requires documented evaluations for all assistive technology implemented with a student receiving Special Education services.
 (C) the Special Education teacher does not agree with the regular education teacher's opinion.
 (D) an AT evaluation will ensure that AT options are reviewed and will help evaluators judge the likelihood that the student will actually use the selected device.

132. Based on recent reading research, phonemic awareness and phonics need to be taught

 (A) implicitly.
 (B) sparingly.
 (C) explicitly.
 (D) exclusively.

133. An administrator visits a third-grade class during math time. The students are engaged in individual assignments. As the administrator circulates through the room, she notices three different students talking to themselves as they solve their math problems. She hears phrases like, "Now I need to check my answer," and " If he drives 50 miles three times a week, that is three 50s." Which of the following assumptions about this teacher's class would be valid?

    (A)   The three students talking to themselves have learning disabilities
    (B)   The teacher has taught her students the strategy of verbalization
    (C)   The students are working independently because they cannot behave when working in cooperative groups
    (D)   These students need extra math time to get ready for STAAR

Use the information below to answer questions 134 and 135.

    After receiving written notice of the school district's intent to evaluate their second-grade child for learning disabilities, parents approach the head of the Special Education department and ask her to explain the IQ-Achievement Discrepancy Model. The parents express concerns that friends have told them that second graders never qualify for Special Education services because they are too young for the IQ-Achievement Discrepancy Model to identify them.

134. The IQ-Achievement Discrepancy Model is

    (A)   IQ test results.
    (B)   the difference between a student's grades in school and the student's potential as shown on achievement tests.
    (C)   a method that assesses whether a substantial difference exists between a student's scores on an IQ test and his or her scores on one or more academic achievement tests.
    (D)   a picture of the student's brain with highlighting at any areas that are not functioning properly.

135. What can the department head tell the parents about the Special Education evaluation procedure to help allay their concerns?

    (A)   Second graders are not assessed with IQ tests.
    (B)   No assessment may be used as the sole measure for determining eligibility. Parent and teacher interviews, checklists, and observations will also be part of the evaluation process.
    (C)   Because of all of the concerns regarding the IQ-Achievement Discrepancy Model, it is no longer used to determine eligibility in Texas.
    (D)   The department head will personally conduct the tests to make sure they are accurate.

ANSWER KEY

1. (A)	35. (C)	69. (A)	103. (A)
2. (B)	36. (A)	70. (D)	104. (D)
3. (C)	37. (D)	71. (C)	105. (B)
4. (A)	38. (A)	72. (D)	106. (A)
5. (D)	39. (B)	73. (A)	107. (B)
6. (C)	40. (A)	74. (D)	108. (B)
7. (C)	41. (D)	75. (B)	109. (C)
8. (D)	42. (B)	76. (C)	110. (C)
9. (D)	43. (B)	77. (C)	111. (D)
10. (D)	44. (C)	78. (C)	112. (A)
11. (C)	45. (C)	79. (C)	113. (D)
12. (B)	46. (A)	80. (A)	114. (B)
13. (A)	47. (C)	81. (A)	115. (B)
14. (A)	48. (C)	82. (B)	116. (C)
15. (A)	49. (C)	83. (D)	117. (B)
16. (A)	50. (B)	84. (B)	118. (A)
17. (C)	51. (A)	85. (C)	119. (A)
18. (C)	52. (D)	86. (A)	120. (C)
19. (D)	53. (C)	87. (A)	121. (B)
20. (B)	54. (C)	88. (D)	122. (A)
21. (B)	55. (C)	89. (C)	123. (D)
22. (D)	56. (D)	90. (B)	124. (D)
23. (B)	57. (A)	91. (C)	125. (D)
24. (A)	58. (A)	92. (D)	126. (B)
25. (C)	59. (B)	93. (A)	127. (B)
26. (A)	60. (B)	94. (B)	128. (D)
27. (D)	61. (B)	95. (B)	129. (C)
28. (C)	62. (B)	96. (B)	130. (A)
29. (C)	63. (A)	97. (C)	131. (D)
30. (A)	64. (C)	98. (A)	132. (C)
31. (B)	65. (C)	99. (D)	133. (B)
32. (D)	66. (A)	100. (A)	134. (C)
33. (D)	67. (D)	101. (D)	135. (B)
34. (B)	68. (D)	102. (A)	

ANSWER EXPLANATIONS

1. **(A)** The correct response is (A). A low-incidence disability is relatively rare and does not generally exceed 1 percent of the school-aged population. Many of the disability categories under IDEA, including visual impairments, are considered low-incidence disabilities. (B), (C), and (D) are all incorrect because they are high-incidence disabilities, with a much greater percentage of individuals affected among the school-age population.
   Competency 001

2. **(B)** The correct response is (B). The area of a triangle is calculated by taking one half of the product when the base is multiplied with the altitude. In this case, that is ½ × 3 × 4. This is equal to 6 cm. (A) is incorrect because that is the altitude by itself. (C) is incorrect, and choosing that answer indicates that base was added to the altitude. (D) is incorrect, and choosing that answer indicates that the base was multiplied with the altitude and then left alone.
   Competency 009

3. **(C)** The correct response is (C). When teaching a consumer math skill like budgeting, it is best to make the activity as "real" as possible. High school students with disabilities may have opportunities to go on community-based instruction trips outside the school grounds, but when that is not possible, bringing the real world into the classroom works best. With this menu activity, students have an opportunity to practice ordering on a budget, something they will likely do many times in their adult lives. (A) is incorrect because worksheets are rarely engaging and do not reflect real-world interactions. (B) is incorrect because a video is not as powerful as the simulation described in (C). (D) is incorrect because it is not likely that students will need spreadsheet software to manage their budgets, so this activity is not nearly as "real" and "engaging" as (C).
   Competency 009

4. **(A)** The correct response is (A). Targeted instruction is an extremely efficient use of time in the classroom because teachers use data to determine student needs and then teach directly to those needs in small groups. A student who has mastered the skill being taught can work independently or with a partner or paraprofessional on a different skill, while the teacher focuses on the students who do need the targeted skill. (B) is not the correct answer as it is not a common term in education. (C) is incorrect as inclusion is the process of teaching students with disabilities alongside their peers without disabilities. That is not the situation described in this prompt. (D) is not the correct answer because the teacher is not using errorless discrimination to teach the skills. Errorless discrimination is most commonly used with students with significant disabilities who need a great deal of guidance as well as repetition and review.
   Competency 003

5. **(D)** The correct response is (D). IDEA requires districts to have parental consent or the consent of an eligible child who has reached the age of majority before the district shares personal information with community agencies, even if those agencies are providing or paying for transition services. (A), (B), and (C) are therefore not correct answers.
   Competency 007

6. **(C)** The correct response is (C). FAPE stands for Free and Appropriate Public Education, the core promise for all students with disabilities made in the Individuals with Disabilities Education Act. Therefore, (A), (B), and (D) are all incorrect.
   Competency 010

7.   **(C)**   The correct response is (C). Assembling board games and making sure each game is complete fits well with Tia's love of counting, and board game assembly is a routine that she can be taught. Also, in the assembly portion of the warehouse, she is unlikely to encounter strangers. (A) is incorrect because it is not as suited to counting as (C) is. (B) is incorrect because the receptionist's desk is sure to have strangers coming in and out every day, which would make Tia nervous. (D) is incorrect because Tia's obsessive-compulsive behavior over hand washing might be activated if she is doing janitorial work.
Competency 007

8.   **(D)**   The correct response is (D). The three websites listed are for the Council for Exceptional Children, the Learning Disabilities Association of America, and International Dyslexia Association. All of these organizations have websites with pertinent information about reading disabilities. (A), (B), and (C) are incorrect because all three are appropriate and, therefore, no one choice by itself is the correct answer.
Competency 011

9.   **(D)**   The correct response is (D). One of the classroom goals of any teacher should be to foster a positive classroom environment where differences are accepted, not mocked. In this case, the teacher does not want to single out the two students who have complained about reading or have other students ask questions about why those two students get colored overlays. By having the entire class complete the experiment, the teacher also gains the advantage of learning of other students who may have mild issues with reflective light and reading. Since everyone in class tries the colored overlays, all students understand their purpose and will more easily accept that some classmates will use the overlays and some won't. (A) is incorrect because the prompt does not give any hint of an assignment from the professional-development session. (B) is incorrect because the nature of this classroom experiment is acceptance of differences and self-discovery, not about a science grade. (C) is incorrect because, while the activity may be fun, its purpose is a serious one.
Competency 005

10.   **(D)**   The correct response is (D). In reading instruction, fluency indicates that a child can read successfully. This is often assessed through oral reading and evaluated in terms of accuracy, rate, expression, and speed or flow. (A) is not the correct answer because comprehension is assessed in terms of a student's ability to answer questions about the content or to summarize the story. (C) is not the correct answer because phonics assessments focus on a student's ability to connect letter sounds to letters and to decode unknown words. (B) Miscue analysis is not the correct answer because it is a type of reading assessment in and of itself. By noting and analyzing the errors or miscues students make while reading aloud, a teacher can better pinpoint the areas where students need targeted reading instruction.
Competency 002

11.   **(C)**   The correct response is (C). Procedural fluency in math is essentially the ability to complete basic math computations with automaticity. This frees the brain to concentrate on learning new, higher-level concepts. (A) and (B) are incorrect because procedural fluency in math is not related to reading speed or comprehension. (D) is incorrect because procedural fluency in math is not related to speaking skills.
Competency 009

12.   **(B)**   The correct response is (B). The teacher's activity in (B) ensures that the identified concrete learners will be able to interact directly with the concept being taught, while the auditory learner will have a valid reason to talk through the concept out loud. The arrangement of the seats ensures a good view for the visual learners. (A) sounds like a fun idea, particularly for the visual learners, but it does not address the needs of the concrete or verbal/auditory learners. (C) is incorrect because it actually interferes with student learning. The two students who need concrete examples are placed as far away from the action as possible. (D) is incorrect since it does not address the needs of the concrete or verbal/auditory learners.
Competency 003

13. **(A)** The correct response is (A). Assessment ethics refer to a test administrator's responsibility to be as fair and objective as possible when evaluating a student's abilities. Assessment results can have wide-ranging impacts upon a child's future. One way to ensure ethical assessment practices is to use procedures that are culturally and linguistically appropriate. A child's cultural background or native language should not impact the results of an academic achievement test if at all possible. (B) is not the correct answer because ethical test administration involves taking into account a student's disability and/or background and ensuring that the test is a fair representation of the child's abilities despite cultural or linguistic differences. (C) is not the correct answer because a single moment in time is not representative of a quarter's or year's worth of learning and effort. Grades should reflect the many different tasks, projects, and exams a student took over the course of the class. (D) is incorrect because a Bell curve automatically ensures that a percentage of students will fail since they will fall below the curve no matter how many questions they answer correctly.
   Competency 002

14. **(A)** The correct response is (A). A syntax error is an error in the ordering of a sentence. In this case, the verb and the noun are reversed and an awkward and incorrect sentence is left. (B) is incorrect because it is a run-on sentence, but it does not have a syntax error. (C) is incorrect because it has punctuation mistakes, but no words are out of order. (D) is incorrect because there are no errors.
   Competency 008

15. **(A)** The correct response is (A). Since the variable a is equal to the variable b + 7, a is 7 greater than b. (B) is incorrect as b is 7 less than a. (C) is incorrect as the additional 7 on the right side of the equation means a does not equal b. (D) is incorrect as it is clear that a is the variable that is greater in value.
   Competency 009

16. **(A)** The correct response is (A). When working with paraprofessionals, modeling the way a teacher expects adults in the classroom to work with children is essential. Teachers should be clear in their expectations of paraprofessionals while treating the paraprofessionals with respect. (B) is incorrect because the teacher should attempt to work with the paraprofessional before asking an administrator to intervene. (C) is incorrect because the students will benefit most from instructional support in the classroom. Helping the paraprofessional learn the techniques to work with young children will be the key to a successful year. (D) is incorrect because the teacher should always treat the paraprofessional with respect and a sense that the paraprofessional is there to help children.
   Competency 012

17. **(C)** The correct response is (C). An isosceles triangle has two equal sides and two equal angles. (A) is incorrect because it shows an equilateral triangle with three equal sides and three equal angles (60 degrees each). (B) is incorrect because it shows a right triangle with one angle that is 90 degrees. (D) is incorrect because it shows a scalene triangle with no equal sides and no equal angles.
   Competency 009

18. **(C)** The correct response is (C). An occupational therapist works with students on fine-motor and life skills. Since Anna's issue is handwriting, an occupational therapist will be able to evaluate if Anna needs help changing the way she grips the pencil or some other accommodation. (A) is incorrect because physical therapists focus on gross-motor skills (for example, students with limited mobility who need to exercise their legs). (B) is incorrect because speech-language pathologists focus on oral communication skills, particularly articulation and social skills. (D) is incorrect because school psychologists generally administer standardized assessments for a district, evaluating whether students qualify for Special Education services.
   Competency 005

19.   **(D)**   The correct response is (D). A summative assessment is always administered at the conclusion of a unit of study. Its purpose is to evaluate a student's retention and depth of understanding of the key concepts taught in the unit. (A), (B), and (C) are all incorrect answers since, by its very nature, a summative assessment must occur at the end of a unit in order to provide a complete picture of what a student has learned.
    Competency 002

20.   **(B)**   The correct response is (B). When dealing with a disrespectful student, ignoring the behavior is never a good idea. Ignoring disrespectful comments and behaviors sends a message to other students in the class that it is okay to disrespect the teacher. (A), (C), and (D) are all appropriate strategies for dealing with a disrespectful student and are therefore incorrect.
    Competency 006

21.   **(B)**   The correct response is (B). This number pattern is what is referred to as a Fibonacci sequence. In a Fibonacci sequence, the next number is always found by adding the two numbers before it. The two numbers before the blank are 8 and 13. Added together, they make 21. (A), (C), and (D) are all incorrect because they do not follow the Fibonacci pattern established.
    Competency 009

22.   **(D)**   The correct response is (D). Cognitive, environmental, and affective factors can all contribute to behavior. A Functional Behavior Assessment will examine all of these factors in developing a hypothesis regarding the cause of the student's negative behavior. (A), (B), and (C) are all factors, but by themselves, they are incorrect choices.
    Competency 006

23.   **(B)**   The correct response is (B). Word analysis is the process of using phonetic patterns to figure out unfamiliar words. A second-grade student who has difficulty associating sounds to letters is likely to benefit from direct phonics or word analysis instruction. (A) is incorrect because comprehension focuses on word meaning. (C) is incorrect because spelling is highly likely to be a problem for a student who has minimal phonics skills. (D) is incorrect because reading instruction for this student needs to focus on phonetic patterns to meet the student's instructional needs. The connection between reading and writing can still be made; it just is not the main focus of reading instruction based on the student's current skills.
    Competency 001

24.   **(A)**   The correct response is (A). Idioms are expressions that use common words in uncommon ways. They are often very difficult for English learners and students with disabilities who are literal as the students understand only the surface meaning and thus find the idea of cats and dogs raining down rather odd and even frightening. (B) and (C) are incorrect because they are figures of speech used for comparisons. (D) is incorrect because symbol-supported text is a method used to help students who communicate nonverbally.
    Competency 008

25.   **(C)**   The correct response is (C). 0.625 is equivalent to ⅝. If you divide 5 by 8, the answer will always be 0.625. (A) is incorrect because ¾ is equivalent to 0.75. (B) is incorrect because 6/25 is equivalent to 0.24. (D) is incorrect because ⅖ is equivalent to 0.4.
    Competency 009

26.   **(A)**   The correct response is (A). The debate is an example of two sides arguing about an important point. This is the perfect opportunity for a student to take the arguments presented for the two sandwiches and write a persuasive paper about why one sandwich is the best. (B), (C), and (D) are all types of writing, but they do not fit with a persuasive debate.
   Competency 008

27.   **(D)**   The correct response is (D). No Child Left Behind focused on accountability for all students and scientifically research-based interventions. Both of these areas were reflected in the reauthorization of IDEA in 2004. (A) is incorrect as NCLB had a huge influence on the reauthorization of IDEA in 2004. (B) is incorrect, but Congress has talked about the concept of combining the major education laws into one law in the future. Whether the political landscape will allow this to happen remains to be seen. (C) is incorrect as paraprofessionals who are personal-care assistants are exempt from the highly qualified personnel requirements.
   Competency 010

28.   **(C)**   The correct response is (C). Sitting on an exercise ball instead of a chair has been found to improve focus in students with attention issues. Staying upright on the ball necessitates keeping balance and a bit of bouncing which engages the student's body and helps the mind stay on track. Since the exercise ball is not much taller than a chair, it can be used at a student desk with minimal disruptions. (A) is incorrect because isolating a student with ADHD will not provide access to the whole-group instruction, and it denies the student the learning that comes from engaging in discussions with peers. Use of a study carrel can be appropriate when the student is assigned independent work and needs to block out distractions. (B) is incorrect because seating the student at the teacher's desk is another attempt at isolation. It would be seen as a punishment and make the child "stick out" in front of his or her peers. Given that this student has a disability, punishment is not in order. (D) is incorrect because a child with attention issues will have a difficult time surrounded by peers in the middle of the classroom. There would be too many distractions. Seating a student with ADHD at the front of the class would be more appropriate.
   Competency 004

29.   **(C)**   The correct response is (C). Community-based instruction is a powerful tool for engaging student interest and for making real-world connections between the lessons learned in the classroom and the long-term life skills students with disabilities will need as adults to survive and thrive in the community. (A) is not the correct answer because this activity is not set up to be a game. (B) is not the correct answer because it is a strategy used with English learners, not necessarily students with special needs. (D) is incorrect because this is not an activity focused on scientific inquiry.
   Competency 003

30.   **(A)**   The correct response is (A). By law, an IEP must have measurable annual goals that include benchmarks or short-term objectives related to meeting a student's needs so that he or she can be involved and progress in the general curriculum as much as possible. (B) is incorrect as goals must be annual, not semi-annual. (C) is incorrect as goals do not have to be community-based. (D) is incorrect as goals do not have to be extracurricular-focused or monthly.
   Competency 010

31.   **(B)**   The correct response is (B). Co-morbidity is a term Special Education teachers should be familiar with. Technically a medical term, co-morbidity refers to one or more additional disabilities that exist alongside a child's primary diagnosis. For example, ADHD is often co-morbid in students with autism spectrum disorder. (A), (C), and (D) are incorrect answers as they do not reflect the meaning of co-morbidity.
   Competency 001

32. **(D)** The correct response is (D). There are a number of procedural safeguards built into IDEA to protect parents' rights. However, parents do not have the right to select a teacher for their child. Teacher assignment is the purview of the school district and the campus principal. (A), (B), and (C) are all procedural safeguards for parents under IDEA and are, therefore, incorrect responses.
Competency 011

33. **(D)** The correct response is (D). It is a good idea to include information about a student and the student's strengths and abilities as background information in a Behavior Improvement Plan, but it is not required by IDEA guidelines. (A), (B), and (C) are all elements required to be in a Behavior Improvement Plan according to IDEA guidelines and are therefore incorrect.
Competency 006

34. **(B)** The correct response is (B). FBA stands for Functional Behavior Assessment or Functional Behavioral Assessment. FBAs are completed prior to the development of a Behavior Intervention Plan. (A), (C), and (D) are therefore all incorrect.
Competency 006

35. **(C)** The correct response is (C). Starting any meeting with parents on a positive note is an excellent way to build a working relationship built on trust and mutual respect. Parents trust teachers who they sense care about the whole child and the child's family. (A) is incorrect because setting a tight time limit can make parents uncomfortable or afraid to share. (B) is incorrect because letting a meeting wander can make it difficult to cover all the issues that need to be discussed. The teacher should listen to the parents but then be ready to steer the meeting to the issues at hand. (D) is incorrect because seating parents at student desks while the teacher stays at her desk sets up a power differential and does not communicate respect for the family.
Competency 012

36. **(A)** The correct response is (A). Research on effective math strategies is very clear about the power of explicit instruction for students who are struggling. Explicit teaching helps students understand how to approach problems step by step. (B) is incorrect because students with disabilities and students who are struggling with math cannot pick up how concepts work by just watching their effects. (C) is incorrect because the key to good math instruction is a balanced approach, not an exclusively digital one. (D) is incorrect because verbal instruction by itself does not reach all learners, particularly not the tactile/kinesthetic learners who need to work with concrete manipulatives.
Competency 009

37. **(D)** The correct response is (D). The IDEA definition of Other Health Impairment (OHI) is a condition of limited strength, vitality, or alertness caused by a chronic or acute health problem that adversely affects a child's educational performance. A specific learning disability is not a chronic health issue and is therefore not included in the definition of OHI. (A) epilepsy, (B) leukemia, and (C) Tourette syndrome are all conditions included in the definition of OHI and are therefore not correct answers.
Competency 001

38. **(A)** The correct response is (A). Recorded books are assistive-technology tools that allow struggling readers or students with visual impairments to hear a book read by a fluent and expressive narrator. Struggling readers are encouraged to follow along with the narrator. Dyslexia is a common term for a reading disability. A student with dyslexia would likely benefit from a recorded book if she or he followed along and saw the words as she or he heard them pronounced correctly and strung together in expressive phrases. (B) is incorrect because dyscalculia is a term for a math disability. (C) is incorrect because dysgraphia is a term for a writing disability. (D) is incorrect because a student with physical disabilities does not necessarily have trouble reading.
Competency 004

39. **(B)** The correct response is (B). Augmentative communication devices are created to give students who are nonverbal or whose speech is difficult to understand an opportunity to communicate. Augmentative communication devices can be as simple as symbol-based communication books or as complex as extremely expensive electronic machines that "talk" for a student when the student presses a button or types in a phrase. (A) is not correct because talking calculators are primarily used by students with visual impairments, students who are blind, or students who have reading difficulties. (C) is not correct because a speech-recognition program is useless if the student cannot speak. (D) is incorrect because optical character recognition software is used to scan in worksheets and other activities so that they can be viewed in larger point size or read out loud to students with visual impairments or students who are blind.

Competency 004

40. **(A)** The correct response is (A). The core issue for children on the autism spectrum is communication. While autism is a spectrum disorder and will manifest itself in a wide variety of ways, atypical social interaction and communication skills are seen across the ability range. (B) is incorrect because, while some students with ASD struggle to read, others are advanced readers well beyond their grade level. (C) is incorrect because many students with ASD can speak. Some are nonverbal, but this appears to be one extreme in the larger issue of communication. (D) is incorrect because, while depression can be a result of the social isolation, many students on the spectrum feel that it is not the core issue for this disability.

Competency 001

41. **(D)** The correct response is (D). A number of basic math concepts can be taught using a 10-frame, which is essentially a rectangle made up of 10 equal rectangles. Each of the small rectangles stand for one while the larger rectangle stands for 10. For students with significant disabilities, learning to add on a 10-frame allows them to see the process of addition in an extremely concrete way. For 3 + 2, they would place three small rectangles on the 10-frame, and then place two more small rectangles on the 10-frame, so that they could see they now have a total of five small rectangles. (A) is incorrect because a 10-frame is a rectangular shape, but its purpose is to help students understand that 10 ones is the same as the number 10. Its purpose is not to teach students about rectangles. (B) and (C) are incorrect because a 10-frame is not the natural manipulative for understanding number patterns or probability.

Competency 009

42. **(B)** The correct response is (B). The 1990 renaming of the Education for all Handicapped Children Act to the Individual with Disabilities Education Act was part of promoting "people first" language in which the emphasis is on the individual rather than the disability. Not only was the act renamed, but throughout the law, the term "handicapped children" was replaced with "individuals with disabilities." (A) is incorrect because, while the IDEA acronym is "cool," it was not the primary motivator behind renaming Public Law 94-142. (B) is incorrect because it was not the primary reason for renaming the act; however, the term individuals is more representative of the range of ages served by IDEA in public schools (ages 3–23). (D) is incorrect because it is not true.

Competency 010

43. **(B)** The correct response is (B). The National Reading Panel's report and its emphasis on research-based reading methods has led some to talk about the five pillars of reading. They are phonemic awareness, phonics, vocabulary, fluency, and comprehension. (A), (C), and (D) are incorrect because they represent a variety of modeling and flexible grouping options.

Competency 008

44. **(C)** The correct response is (C). By law, a student who qualifies for Special Education services must be reevaluated every three years to determine continued eligibility. (A) and (B) are incorrect because the reevaluation

requirement is at least every three years. (D) is incorrect because a parent or educator can request reevaluation at any time if a special evaluation is warranted, but there will be a reevaluation at least every three years as part of standard procedure.

Competency 011

45. **(C)** The correct response is (C). Recorded books are excellent tools for providing models of fluent, expressive reading. They can also be turned off when the student is ready to read without a "helper." (A), (B), and (D) are all incorrect, and in the case of (D), not true. Used correctly, recorded books stretch readers to try books a bit beyond their level because they provide support and yet leave the student in total control.

Competency 008

46. **(A)** The correct response is (A). The teacher is using errorless discrimination to ensure that the student will eventually select the correct answer and can then be praised for that correct answer. Errorless discrimination has its basis in behavioral theory and is often used with students who have extreme retention issues (for example, students with significant intellectual disabilities or students with traumatic brain injury). (B) is not the correct answer because the description of the activity is focused on guiding students to identify a sight word correctly. Repetition and review could be introduced into this activity by repeating it again and again, but that is not indicated in the description. (C) is an incorrect answer because repeated reading is a technique in which a student is asked to read a passage from start to finish several times to become comfortable with the passage. (D) is not the correct answer because, based on the description, the student is pointing at the word cards on his/her own. Hand over hand is a technique where a teacher or paraprofessional will guide a student's hand to complete the requested task.

Competency 003

47. **(C)** The correct response is (C). Praise is a powerful tool for building student self-esteem and reinforcing desired behaviors. In this scenario, the teacher praises the student every time the student points to the correct sight word. This technique will help the student recall the word and associate a positive feeling with getting the correct answer. (A) is not the correct answer. The teacher ignores mistakes as part of the errorless discrimination procedure described. Only correct choices are praised and paid attention. (B) is an incorrect answer because praise in and of itself is not an accommodation. It is an instructional strategy. (D) is not the correct answer because the focus of this lesson is a targeted, one-to-one interaction. The student is focused on completing the tasks assigned by the teacher and getting feedback, not on the reactions of classmates.

Competency 003

48. **(C)** The correct response is (C). No single form of communication works for every parent. Since the teacher has not heard back in two days, she should assume the parent has not read the notebook and use a different form of communication, preferably a two-way form of communication like a phone call where she can hear the parent's thoughts. (A) is incorrect because it is far more likely that no one has read the notebook and simply does not realize the teacher made a request for a spare change of clothes. (B) is incorrect because it is already clear the parent has not read the notebook, so writing another note in it would be pointless. (D) is incorrect because the teacher should work to establish her own rapport with the parents using different forms of communication before asking a colleague to intervene.

Competency 012

49. **(C)** The correct response is (C). The states have jurisdiction over public education in the United States, although the federal government is able to influence states via funding and monitoring requirements. It was because states were not offering public education to so many children with disabilities that the Rehabilitation Act and IDEA were passed by Congress. These laws make it clear that states are responsible for providing a free and appropriate public education for all students, including students with disabilities. (A), (B), and (D) are all incorrect, although

all of these parties influence the kind of legislation that is passed at the federal and state levels regarding individuals with disabilities.

Competency 010

50. **(B)** The correct response is (B). Given that the teacher wants to emphasize cause and effect in historical events, a multisensory timeline is an excellent way to help students visually see how one event can lead to another or how multiple events can occur in close succession and lead to an unexpected effect. The other advantage of a multisensory timeline is that students make each piece of the timeline themselves, and for learners of all abilities, the act of making a manipulative or illustration increases short- and long-term retention. We remember what we make far longer than we remember what we see or hear. (A) is incorrect because a Venn diagram is used for comparison/contrast. (C) is incorrect because making outlines of headings will emphasize main ideas, but not necessarily cause and effect. (D) is incorrect because interviewing parents will help students personalize history, but it won't necessarily emphasize cause and effect.

Competency 005

51. **(A)** The correct response is (A). When working with students with significant disabilities, like those in ALE classrooms, Special Education teachers have to complete task analyses and break down skills to their most basic levels. These students often learn through a great deal of repetition. Preparing them for vocational opportunities means finding meaningful ways to practice the kind of skills they may use in a workplace once they transition into adult life. Filing, collating, and watering plants are all some of those vocational skills. Since transition plans in Texas are required in the IEP at age 14, exploring vocational skills in middle school is essential. (B) is incorrect because the tasks described are all individual tasks, not cooperative group tasks. (C) is incorrect because the purpose behind the roles is to practice vocational skills. It is not about saving time. In fact, it likely takes more time to help teach these skills to the students and then monitor their completion. (D) is incorrect because, while keeping students focused on tasks does reduce negative behaviors, the purpose here is clearly vocational in nature.

Competency 005

52. **(D)** The correct response is (D). In an inclusion class with a co-teacher, the goal is to facilitate so that the students with learning disabilities do not stand out as different but instead are empowered to achieve alongside their peers. Separating the students with learning disabilities and the co-teacher in the manner suggested by the mathematics teacher would be like having a separate resource class and would not be inclusive. (A) is incorrect because the solution offered is not appropriate for the students and their sense of belonging. (B) is not correct because, while it could be distracting, the main issue is that it is segregating students and labeling them. (C) is not correct because, whether it's a desk or a table, the suggestion is not legally acceptable given the requirements of IDEA in terms of least restrictive environment.

Competency 004

53. **(C)** The correct response is (C). Assistive technology can be almost anything (an item, a software program, a tablet-based app, a multithousand-dollar machine) that is used to help a student learn or to level the playing field so that a disability does not impede learning. (A) is not true because assistive technology does not have to be digital. (B) is not true because, while some districts do have assistive-technology coordinators to help evaluate student needs, many of the simple assistive technologies can be provided at little cost by a classroom teacher. (D) is not true because the purpose of assistive technology is to level the playing field so that students with disabilities are not at a disadvantage in the classroom.

Competency 004

54. **(C)** The correct response is (C). By high school, students are faced with increasingly complex math curriculum like algebra. If a student has not yet mastered math facts, the lack of procedural fluency will slow them

down significantly even if they understand the higher-level concept they are working on. At this point in their lives, teaching students to use a tool like a calculator will provide them with a way to overcome their disabilities. (A) is incorrect because taking the student away from the first 10 minutes of class would result in the student missing key instruction for the algebra concepts being covered. (B) is incorrect because if a student has made it to ninth grade and still has not memorized basic math facts, it is clear there is a memory deficit interfering with mastery of facts. Asking parents to spend 30 minutes a day on math facts would essentially be punishing the student for having a disability. (D) is incorrect because the first course of action is to find accommodations (like the calculator) to allow the student to remain in the least restrictive environment possible. Transferring the student to a remedial class would not be appropriate if the student is able to grasp algebraic concepts.

Competency 009

55. **(C)** The correct response is (C). By providing the students with a repetitive phrase to keep practicing and having the students focus on trying to match the teacher's inflection, the first-grade teacher is providing the perfect instructional opportunity to improve fluency skills. (A) and (D) are incorrect because the focus of the lesson is not on isolated phonemes or sounds. (B) is incorrect because the focus is not on discussing the meaning of the book, but, rather, on the repetitive phrase.

Competency 008

56. **(D)** The correct response is (D). The focus on voice-inflection patterns is a key part of expression. Good expression is part of fluency and has a great impact on comprehension. (A), (B), and (C) are incorrect because those skills are not the focus in this oral-reading lesson.

Competency 008

57. **(A)** The correct response is (A). The teacher reading the book while showing it to the students is shared reading. The students repeating the phrase the teacher reads is echo reading. The students responding with one voice is choral reading. (B), (C), and (D) are incorrect because they do not include all three oral-reading methods that the teacher demonstrates.

Competency 008

58. **(A)** The correct response is (A). The most important thing that the English teacher must keep in mind is that the Texas Code of Ethics is very clear about protecting a student's confidential information. Disabilities are confidential, and no teacher should share information about a student's disability without express consent from the family and school administration. In this case, the English teacher should be positive about the student, emphasizing her strengths to the journalism advisor. (B), (C), and (D) are all incorrect because they all involve sharing confidential information about the student's disability. (D) is particularly wrong because no teacher should copy a student's IEP folder unless there is a specific reason to do so for ARD committee business.

Competency 011

59. **(B)** The correct response is (B). Age-appropriate transition assessments must be administered to the student with the disability so that the assessments can inform the transition plan that will be written in the student's IEP. This ensures that the IEP team has an array of information about the student's vocational strengths and interests. (A), (C), and (D) are all incorrect as none of those documents need to be in a student's IEP folder.

Competency 007

60. **(B)** The correct response is (B). Response cards are powerful tools for students who are nonverbal. They are essentially picture cards that represent key concepts (for example, vocabulary words) that are being taught. By holding up the cards or pointing to them, a student who is nonverbal can fully participate in an interactive lesson. (A) is not the correct answer because the goal is not to have the student sit quietly, but to have the student participate in

the lesson. (C) is incorrect because the goal is to have the student participate in the lesson, not be excused from it. (D) is not the correct answer because a student who is nonverbal is generally not hard of hearing. In fact, students who are on the autism spectrum and are nonverbal may be extremely sensitive to loud voices.

Competency 003

61.   **(B)**   The correct response is (B). A late-stage emergent writer is just about to start writing words that adults can make some sense of, but for the moment, they are content with just stringing random letters together, showing their understanding that letters make up words, but they do not yet associate letters with specific sounds. (A) is incorrect because approximated spellings are a later stage of writing. (C) is incorrect because scribbled pictures are an earlier stage of writing. (D) is incorrect because complete syntax is an advanced stage of writing.

Competency 008

62.   **(B)**   The correct response is (B). Miscue analysis is an assessment method that pinpoints comprehension and other reading issues by listening to students read orally and classifying the errors they make (for example, pronunciation errors or letter reversal errors). Miscue analysis is a one-to-one assessment, so having the student at a table in the back of the classroom is the correct setting. (A) is incorrect as it describes sustained silent reading. (C) is incorrect as it describes a typical phonics lesson. (D) is incorrect as it describes the neurological impress reading method.

Competency 008

63.   **(A)**   The correct response is (A). Dysgraphia is a common name for a written-language learning disability. Dysgraphia makes the act of writing difficult. It can lead to problems with spelling, handwriting, and putting thoughts on paper. (B) is incorrect as dyslexia is a common name for a reading disability. (C) is incorrect because an orthopedic impairment is a bodily impairment. A student who needs to use a wheelchair because she/he cannot walk or has an orthopedic impairment. (D) is incorrect because a developmental delay refers to an issue when a child misses developmental milestones consistently.

Competency 001

64.   **(C)**   The correct response is (C). Based on IDEA regulations, postsecondary goals must be measurable. (A) is incorrect because independent living skills may be taught, but they are not required to be covered. (B) is incorrect because the goals must reflect the student's desires if at all possible, not the parents'. (D) is incorrect because postsecondary goals can include unpaid employment.

Competency 007

65.   **(C)**   The correct response is (C). An authentic assessment is constructed to represent real-world competencies as much as possible. It may be a project or a simulation or a community-based activity. Because an authentic assessment task will have a wide range of factors, a rubric that clearly relays project expectations and potential levels of performance on the task is the most appropriate tool for evaluation. (A) is not the correct answer because an authentic assessment task if complex and cannot be represented by right or wrong answers only. (B) is an incorrect answer because authentic assessment tasks must take into account the local culture and community expectations. A norm-referenced test, by its very nature, takes out unique local factors in favor of finding a norm across a large group. (D) is not the correct answer because observation by itself will not help students understand what is expected of them during the task.

Competency 002

66.   **(A)**   The correct response is (A). Prereading strategies are essential to comprehension. Successful readers implement prereading strategies without even thinking about it, giving the author and title a critical look and flipping through some pages to get a big picture sense of the story. Research suggests that for struggling readers, more

time should be spent on prereading activities than postreading discussion questions, but as a beginning Special Education teacher, just getting some prereading instruction into a content-area class is an accomplishment. (B) is incorrect because prereading strategies can involve some deep thinking. It's all in how the prereading is carried out. (C) is incorrect because prereading sets a reader up with correct strategies; it is not meant to spoil an ending. (D) is incorrect because, while true, it is not the reason to spend time on prereading strategies.
Competency 008

67.   **(D)**   The correct response is (D). Generic problem-solving strategies are steps that students can learn to apply to any math problem they encounter, particularly if it is a word problem or has keywords in the directions. Examples of generic problem solving strategies are "highlight the keywords" or "circle the word that shows the operation." (A) is incorrect because generic problem-solving strategies stretch across all forms of math. (B) is incorrect because generic strategies are general. They are not explicit, although they can be taught alongside explicit instruction. (C) is incorrect because generic problem-solving strategies are generally applied to word problems, not math facts. They are not memory devices.
Competency 009

68.   **(D)**   The correct response is (D). Home health is not included in IDEA's specific list of postschool activities. (A), (B), and (C) are all included in IDEA's list of postschool activities and are therefore incorrect.
Competency 007

69.   **(A)**   The correct response is (A). Tactile/kinesthetic learners (and well over half of students with disabilities are tactile/kinesthetic) retain information best when able to move. This solution is offered to the entire class and, at the beginning of the year, many will try it. But the tactile/kinesthetic learners are likely going to be the students choosing to use it in the long run because it meets their need for some movement and frees them from the restriction of their desk while still providing them with the opportunity to listen and take notes. (B) is not the correct answer because the teacher has offered the standing spaces and clipboards for all students to use as long as they follow the rules. It is not just a reward. (C) is incorrect because this is not a writing strategy; it is a classroom adaptation that helps tactile/kinesthetic learners stay focused. (D) is not the correct answer because the teacher is offering the standing squares based on her understanding of the needs of different learners. She is not looking for kudos for herself.
Competency 004

70.   **(D)**   The correct response is (D). According to the rules of the order of operations, the operation inside parentheses is always completed first. Therefore, the first step to solving this problem is to add 2 and 4. The sum is 6. That leaves 6×5. This is a simple multiplication problem, and the product is 30. (A) is incorrect and choosing that answer indicates that the three numbers were added together. (B) is incorrect, and choosing that answer indicates that the 5 was multiplied by 2 and then 4 was added. (C) is incorrect, and choosing that answer indicates that the 5 was multiplied by 4 and then the 2 was added.
Competency 009

71.   **(C)**   The correct response is (C). An emergent reader is a very beginning reader who may recognize a few sight words and understands that letters make up words and that printed words represent spoken words. However, they are generally just beginning to make the letter-sound connection. (A) is incorrect as it is not even an official term used to describe a reader. (B) is incorrect because a reluctant reader is one who has struggled to read and may have given up on becoming a proficient reader. (D) is not correct because a fluent reader is someone who can read out loud with meaning and expression, using appropriate phrasing and following punctuation.
Competency 008

72. **(D)** The correct response is (D). In this scenario, the teachers are determining changes that may be needed in the way the test is given so that the student in question has a fair opportunity to showcase what he/she knows. Any changes in the way a test is given are considered assessment accommodations. (A) is not the correct answer because ethics are the moral choices surrounding something as high stakes as assessment has become in schools. (B) is incorrect because modifications are changes to the content of an assessment and have nothing to do with how the assessment is administered. (C) is not the correct answer because the rules of any standardized assessment are set by the test's creators to ensure validity of results.
    Competency 002

73. **(A)** The correct response is (A). Drawing attention to a new vocabulary word helps it "stick" in students' memory as they learn the word and what it means. In this example, it is clear that students are about to have a lesson on circles. Knowing what the radius is will help students measure the area of circles. (B) is incorrect since the emphasis is clearly on the word "radius." However, activities like this will also motivate students to learn more about circles. (C) is incorrect because there is no evidence that the students are going to play a game. The spinners are useful because a plastic spinner is often long enough to be a radius. (D) is incorrect because the emphasis in a math class is not on spelling but on meaning of the vocabulary words.
    Competency 009

74. **(D)** The correct response is (D). A simile is a figure of speech, not a concept of print. Concepts of print are foundational understandings of how books are used and the realization that the marks on a page stand for letters and words. (A), (B), and (C) are all concepts of print and are therefore incorrect.
    Competency 008

75. **(B)** The correct response is (B). Procedural learning deficits tend to manifest when students are trying to solve complex, multistep problems like the ones that are often embedded in word problems. Students have a difficult time figuring out how to organize and sequence the steps to solve the problem. (A) is incorrect because challenges conceptualizing geometric shapes are associated with visual-spatial deficits. (C) is incorrect because issues with math drills are associated with memory deficits. (D) is incorrect because difficulty measuring distances is associated with visual-spatial deficits.
    Competency 009

76. **(C)** The correct response is (C). Many students struggle with word problems in mathematics because of below-grade-level reading skills. Since this student is on grade level with his/her computations, we can assume he/she knows how to complete the mathematics problems but is unable to read well enough to understand how to set up the problem. Therefore, targeted instruction in reading will likely also improve this student's mathematics performance. (A), (B), and (D) are incorrect because they do not address the root of this student's academic struggles.
    Competency 001

77. **(C)** The correct response is (C). The purpose of a Behavior Intervention Plan is to describe in concrete and measurable terms what behaviors are being targeted for change and how school staff will implement that change. It is a plan of action that includes clear standards and timelines for measuring success. (A) is incorrect because a BIP is not created to build a case for punishment. It is focused on positive change. (B) is incorrect because analyzing the reasons for behavior is the purpose of the Functional Behavior Assessment, not the Behavior Intervention Plan. The FBA provides the background information from which the BIP is written. (D) is incorrect because an ARD does not require a BIP. An IEP team meeting is called if a BIP needs to be written into an IEP, but the Annual Review and Dismissal hearing does not create the need for a BIP.
    Competency 006

78.   **(C)**   The correct response is (C). When working with students who have struggled with mathematics, one of the most common things a teacher will hear is "When am I ever going to use this stuff?" Lack of motivation to learn the content coupled with learning difficulties often leads to failure. By showing images of fractions in use in the real world, she is helping students see that learning the content is about more than just the grade in school. (A) is incorrect because, while this is a visual presentation, the teacher is taking the time to use this as an anticipatory activity for the entire class. The message that fractions are useful is for the entire class. (B) is incorrect because students are preparing for a math unit, not a vocational assessment. (D) is incorrect because students have not yet learned the content, so they are not yet ready to study for the test.
  Competency 005

79.   **(C)**   The correct response is (C). Learning students' names and (in the case of nicknames) knowing which names they prefer speaks volumes about how much a teacher cares. For many students, the fact that the teacher takes the time to know their names quickly is also a sign of the respect the teacher has for the students. Any kind of "name game" that helps the teacher memorize students' names quickly is a great way to start the school year. (A) is incorrect because teachers should avoid initiating hugs or touching students in general. Some students do not want their personal space invaded and can feel very uncomfortable. (B) is incorrect because smiling at everything sends mixed messages, particularly to any students who have developmental disabilities or autism. Students need to know when a teacher is being serious. (D) is incorrect because supplying students with candy is not a healthy habit, and the concept of giving candy every day will seem more like a bribe to some students. It is not a good way to establish long-term respect and positive feelings.
  Competency 004

80.   **(A)**   The correct response is (A). A rating scale has descriptors of performance that indicate a student's level of achievement on a particular academic, physical, or social task. (B) is not the correct answer because a parent interview involves asking questions and noting answers (often in narrative form) about a child's birth, growth, and development. (C) is not the correct answer because it involves setting up the environment so that children can play or interact with toys, and adults can observe and note the child's typical or atypical interactions. (D) is incorrect because multiple-choice tests are designed with one correct answer per question.
  Competency 002

81.   **(A)**   The correct response is (A). One-way communication strategies are easier than two-way communication strategies because the person distributing the information has time to get it ready before sending it out. There are no unknowns like there are in phone or face-to-face conversations. However, the flaw in one-way communication is that there is no real proof that parents actually read the communication and no way to know if they understood the information. In general, a mix of one-way and two-way communication strategies is preferable to all one-way strategies. (B) is incorrect because many students do pass on papers to their parents. Some do not, but this is where a two-way form of communication can help. (C) is incorrect because there is no sense that the teacher's handwriting is poor. (D) is incorrect because handwritten notes are appreciated by many. Emails will not necessarily solve the problem just because they are digital. In fact, emails can be a problem for families that do not have Internet access.
  Competency 012

82.   **(B)**   The correct response is (B). The teacher knows from the school demographics that a majority of the families are economically disadvantaged, and there is a significant percentage of English learners. Based on the statement by the student that the parents cannot read the notes, the teacher can assume that English is not the parents' native language. (A) is incorrect because there is no evidence that the parents cannot read due to disabilities. (C) is incorrect because the notes were at the bottom of the student's backpack. The parents do not know about the notes. (D) is incorrect because there is no evidence that the parents are never at home.
  Competency 012

83. **(D)** The correct response is (D). Since the teacher can assume that a language barrier exists for these parents, being prepared by having a bilingual colleague to assist with two-way communication if needed is a smart plan. Also, making a point to tell the parents all the positive things that were in the notes will foster a positive relationship with the parents and make it easier in the future if there are issues to resolve. (A) is incorrect because the student is clearly embarrassed about not giving his parents the notes, but it is likely he didn't do so because he didn't want to confront them with their inability to read English. This is not a reason for discipline. (B) is incorrect because a parent-teacher conference with the same notes will not resolve the language barrier. Also, dragging out all the notes would likely get the student in trouble when the real issue here is figuring out how best to communicate with this family. (C) is incorrect because emails in English will not do any better than notes in English. The issue here is to get a translator.
Competency 012

84. **(B)** The correct response is (B). By definition, an instructional modification is a change to the content to make it more accessible to students who are struggling. This change may involve shortening the assignment or re-writing the text to a lower reading level. (A) is not the correct answer because extensions of time are instructional accommodations. (C) is not the correct answer as a modification is distinctly different from an accommodation. (D) is incorrect since behavioral improvement plans are implemented to help students modify harmful or inappropriate behaviors.
Competency 003

85. **(C)** The correct response is (C). School districts administer a variety of formal diagnostic assessments to determine a student's eligibility for Special Education services. Generally, these diagnostic assessments are chosen by school psychologists and cover a range of academic, behavioral, social, and gross and fine motor skills. (A) is not the correct answer because formative assessments are really the domain of a classroom teacher who uses them to determine how well students are learning so that the teacher can make any necessary adjustments in the lesson plans. (B) is incorrect because the parent may be asked to fill out various checklists and background information forms, but the parent is not the one being evaluated. (D) is not the correct answer because end-of-chapter tests are used to assess the level of student learning for one unit and are summative, rather than diagnostic, in nature.
Competency 002

86. **(A)** The correct response is (A). One of the most important skills to teach readers of all abilities is to self-monitor for comprehension. Pausing, even for a moment, and checking for understanding by making a connection or asking a question will greatly increase comprehension. It makes reading an active process. Using sticky notes to physically write comments and questions about the text will slow the process down a bit, but it will make checking for understanding concrete for readers, teaching them how to become more active readers with improved comprehension. Over time, the sticky notes can fade away as students learn to use this strategy subconsciously. (B) is incorrect because activating prior knowledge is a prereading skill that involves making connections between the current topic and previously learned content. (C) is incorrect because students are choosing to stop at points where they have questions or comments. They are putting events in a sequence. (D) is incorrect because the point of the activity is to improve comprehension. Pairing the students is a way to support struggling readers who can hear their partner's opinion on appropriate points to stop in the text as they apply the strategy.
Competency 005

87. **(A)** The correct response is (A). Successful readers don't just forget a book once they finish it and lay it down. If the book sparked something in them, they want to share it. They may do so on a social media site or via text message or in person, but the opportunity to talk immediately about what they just read with someone is quite strong. Structuring the classroom so that these kinds of reactions/reflections can happen naturally after reading will help develop this desire to share in all readers. (B) is incorrect because it is a prereading strategy. (C) is incorrect

because it is a strategy used during reading. (D) is incorrect because it describes the typical action a struggling reader takes after reading a book.

Competency 008

88. **(D)** The correct response is (D). When scaffolding instruction, conceptual activities and independent activities should come last. With the spinner game, students have to apply the concepts of greater than/less than in concert with a partner. (A) is incorrect because it is an introductory, concrete activity. (B) is incorrect because it is a guided group activity with manipulatives, so it is a good transitional activity. (C) is incorrect because it is an introductory visual activity.

Competency 009

89. **(C)** The correct response is (C). In Texas, the Admission, Review, and Dismissal committee (ARD) is the group of educators, diagnosticians, related service providers, administrators, and parents who meet to review test results and determine eligibility for Special Education services. (A) is incorrect as the PTA is the Parent Teacher Association. (B) is incorrect as TEA stands for the Texas Education Agency in Austin. (D) is incorrect because RTI stands for Response to Intervention.

Competency 010

90. **(B)** The correct response is (B). IDEA and Texas state law protect the parent's right to give or withhold consent for a Special Education evaluation. If parents do not want their child tested in a given area, they have the right to refuse consent, and the school district must abide by this or petition an informal hearing officer to make a ruling. (A) is incorrect because parental consent is required; a district cannot just conduct evaluations regardless of the parents' wishes. (C) is incorrect because a district cannot play an all-or-nothing card on parents or pressure the parents to give consent. (D) is incorrect because a district employee, including the superintendent, cannot override a parent's decision. Only an impartial hearing officer who is not a district employee may do this and only after conducting a hearing where both sides have the opportunity to state their case.

Competency 011

91. **(C)** The correct response is (C). Individuals with hearing impairments do not frequently put their hands over their ears. Rather, this is a common gesture seen in individuals with an autism spectrum disorder. (A), (B), and (D) are all commonly seen in individuals with hearing impairments, although this does not mean that an individual with a hearing impairment will exhibit all of these behaviors or speech difficulties. If you see any one of these symptoms exhibited regularly by an undiagnosed student, consult with the school nurse about a hearing test for that student.

Competency 001

92. **(D)** The correct response is (D). Identifying the reasons for a student's misbehavior allows an educator to address the cause of the negative behavior and remove that cause or redirect the student when the cause cannot be eliminated. Essentially, knowing why a student behaves in a negative way allows an educator to put together a plan to prevent the behavior from occurring. This is especially important for many students with severe cognitive or developmental disabilities as they often cannot express the reasons for their behavior and often just react to situations where they feel uncomfortable or out of control. (A) is incorrect because the focus of identifying the reason for behavior is not about punishment. It is about prevention. (B) is incorrect because, while the information in a Functional Behavior Assessment will be shared with parents and administrators at the ARD meeting, they are not the reason behind identifying causality for behaviors. (C) is incorrect because there are no union requirements regarding Functional Behavior Assessment.

Competency 006

93.   **(A)**   The correct response is (A). Matching words to pictures is a common comprehension activity, particularly with younger readers and with students with significant disabilities. Essentially, the reader has to identify what the words "show" through their use or description. (B) is incorrect because it describes fluency. (C) is incorrect because it describes structural analysis. (D) is incorrect because it describes a prewriting skill.
Competency 008

94.   **(B)**   The correct response is (B). Any accommodation that changes how a test is laid out or administered to a student is considered an accommodation in presentation. In this case, recording the questions so that the student can hear them helps ensure that the student has a fair opportunity to showcase her/his knowledge of mathematics despite her/his reading disability. (A) is not the correct answer because setting refers to the environment in which a test is given. (C) is not the correct answer because timing refers to how long a student has to take a test and has nothing to do with delivery of the content. (D) is incorrect because scheduling refers to when a test is administered.
Competency 002

95.   **(B)**   The correct response is (B). An acute angle is an angle that measures less than 90 degrees but more than 0 degrees. (A) is incorrect because a 90-degree angle is called a right angle. (C) is incorrect because an angle that is more than 90 degrees but less than 180 degrees is an obtuse angle. (D) is incorrect because a 180-degree angle is a straight angle.
Competency 009

96.   **(B)**   The correct response is (B). Communicating with parents in a way that produces positive relationships and fosters mutual respect sometimes means calling after school hours. This parent called the school and wants to be involved, so the teacher should foster that involvement. (A) is incorrect because the message does not give any real information and leaves the parent wondering what "the issue" is. (C) is incorrect because the original contact did call back. Communication should continue through the parent who responded unless that parent requests the teacher call someone else. (D) is incorrect because the teacher knows the facts about the student's behavior. Sending in someone else will only confuse the parent. Being willing to talk to parents in the evening shows the teacher's commitment to building the school-home connection.
Competency 012

97.   **(C)**   The correct response is (C). Environmental print is any text on objects or items in the world around us (our environment). The advertisements are a good example of environmental print as we are bombarded each day by media images. (A) is incorrect because joint attention is a term used in early developmental stages to describe how a child follows point and interacts with a parent or other adult figure. (B) is incorrect because primary sources are original documents in a history class setting. (D) is incorrect because narratives are essentially stories.
Competency 008

98.   **(A)**   The correct response is (A). Using the interactive whiteboard allows Ms. Walker to expand the images and words on the advertisements so that they are easier to see and circle. (B) is incorrect because there is a sense that these students use the interactive whiteboard quite frequently as a regular part of Ms. Walker's class. (C) is incorrect because students are practicing sight-word identification, not job skills. (D) is incorrect because there is no phonics review, and the focus of this lesson is clearly discovering known sight words on signs and advertisements in the community.
Competency 008

99.   **(D)**   The correct response is (D). For students in an Alternative Learning Environment classroom, generalization of skills is often challenging because of poor short- and long-term memory and because learners have a tendency to see something only in the way they learn it. By bringing in the advertisements, Ms. Walker gets to see

if her students can generalize and apply their knowledge of the sight words they have been studying. (A) is incorrect because they are identifying isolated sight words, and they are not taking a test to see if they have recall of certain information. (B) is incorrect because a vision test would be completed by the school nurse, not Ms. Walker. (C) is incorrect because students are not being asked to call out the words quickly from a list.

Competency 008

100. **(A)** The correct response is (A). In math, the mean of a group of numbers is the average of those numbers. It is calculated by adding up all of the numbers and then dividing by the amount of numbers in the group. (B) is incorrect because "mean" does not mean sequence. (C) is incorrect because the number in the middle, once numbers are sorted, is the median. (D) is incorrect because "mean" does not refer to the lowest number.

Competency 009

101. **(D)** The correct response is (D). In a group of numbers, the mode is the number that occurs most frequently. If we sort this group of numbers, there is one number that appears twice: 67. That is the mode. (A) and (B) are incorrect because each of them appears only once. (C) is incorrect because 51 appears only once. 51 is the median. It is the middle number when the numbers are sorted from lowest to highest.

Competency 009

102. **(A)** The correct response is (A). To determine the median or middle number in a group of numbers, the first step is to sort the numbers from lowest to highest. (B) is incorrect because the median has nothing to do with the average. (C) is incorrect because the median can be determined no matter how many duplicate numbers there are. (D) is incorrect because there is no predictable number pattern in this group of numbers.

Competency 009

103. **(A)** The correct response is (A). PEMDAS stands for Parentheses, Exponents, (Multiplication and Division), (Addition and Subtraction). This is the order of operations. A mnemonic like PEMDAS makes the order of the steps far easier to remember. The one caution is that teachers need to make it clear that sometimes division will happen before multiplication, and sometimes subtraction will happen before addition. (B) is incorrect because it is a spelling rule. (C) is incorrect because drills improve procedural fluency but don't help students remember the order in which to work a multistep problem. (D) is incorrect because placing objects in order from smallest to largest is a way to practice early concepts regarding size and measurement.

Competency 009

104. **(D)** The correct response is (D). Given that almost half the class failed the section quiz for "solving absolute value equations," the assessment results point to a need to reteach the skills in this section but in a different way than the first time. Assessment is not just about individual student performance; it is an excellent way to tell if teaching has been effective. (A) is incorrect because the assessment results point to the need to do some reteaching before launching into a review. (B) is incorrect because the students who failed need to be shown what they are doing wrong rather than just practice skills they have not yet mastered. (C) is incorrect because Laura and Jackson, while the two that failed three or more sections, are not the only students who failed quizzes. Isolating them while the rest of the class completes a review singles them out in front of their peers and does not address the larger issue of the other students who need some reteaching.

Competency 005

105. **(B)** The correct response is (B). The assessment results show a consistent pattern of failure for Laura. Given her disability and her requests for help in class, making a testing accommodation by reading each question aloud so she clearly understands what is being asked will help level the playing field for Laura. (A) is incorrect because using a dictionary necessitates being able to read well, and Laura has shown that is a challenge for her. A calculator

would be appropriate if completing operations was the issue, but for Laura, evidence show that her difficulty is her inability to set up a problem because of reading comprehension issues. (C) is incorrect because extra homework will not solve Laura's reading issues. (D) is incorrect because IDEA requires least restrictive environment. Any change in assigned setting requires an IEP team meeting with agreement from all parties, including parents. In this case, there is no call to change setting until proper accommodations are implemented and tested out in the current setting.
Competency 005

106. **(A)** The correct response is (A). IDEA regulations were created to ensure, as much as possible, that the individual with special needs has the opportunity to have his or her own say in the transition plan. After all, it's the student's own future. (B), (C), and (D) are all people who could be invited if the parents or student approved, but they are not required to be invited by IDEA mandate, so they are incorrect.
Competency 007

107. **(B)** The correct response is (B). The next dollar-strategy is a survival consumer strategy often taught to students with intellectual disabilities who have a tendency to be too trusting when it comes to transactions at stores. By teaching these individuals to pay always with the "next dollar up," change will never be more than $0.99, which means the individual cannot be "cheated" out of much even if they do not know how to count change. (A) is incorrect because classrooms employing the next-dollar strategy do teach coin values and counting coins, but have the next-dollar strategy in place for students who have difficulty mastering how to make change. (C) is incorrect as the activity described takes place in the classroom, so it cannot be considered a community-based instruction activity. (D) is incorrect as the purpose for the next-dollar strategy is less about teaching the value of a dollar and more about teaching a basic consumer skill.
Competency 009

108. **(B)** The correct response is (B). CEC's code of ethics clearly states that families deserve respect and should be actively involved in the educational decision-making process. (A), (C), and (D) are all incorrect because none of those assertions are in the code of ethics. CEC does support parent training but not with any implication that families are not currently doing a good job when working with their children with disabilities.
Competency 011

109. **(C)** The correct response is (C). Teaching independent-living skills is an essential part of any Special Education teacher's job since successful transition to adult life is the ultimate goal of any IEP. Being able to obey common indoor and outdoor signs is not only an independent-living skill, but also a survival skill. Many of these signs serve as warnings, like "Poison" or "Danger: Electric Current." (A) is not correct because students are identifying the visual signs and memorizing their shape, color, and text. They are not learning to read in the traditional sense. (B) is not correct because the students are not composing sentences. (D) is not correct because the students are not learning how to learn, although the learning tasks the teacher is implementing are sound and research-based for students with significant disabilities.
Competency 005

110. **(C)** The correct response is (C). IDEA 2004 specifically states that a Behavior Intervention Plan must be included in a student's IEP if the student's behaviors are impeding learning. Academic achievement is often tenuous for students with disabilities because of the effects those disabilities can have on learning. Adding behaviors that impede learning onto a learning disability can be disastrous in terms of academic achievement. Therefore, federal law is very clear that action must be taken and documented. (A) is incorrect because federal law requires it, not the assistant principal. (B) is incorrect because a school suspension does not automatically lead to a Behavior Intervention Plan. (D) is incorrect because a student's least restrictive environment placement does not necessarily have

anything to do with behavior. Many students with severe cognitive disabilities are in self-contained classrooms and do not require a Behavior Intervention Plan.

Competency 006

111. **(D)**   The correct response is (D). A student with visual impairments should be given every opportunity to showcase his/her knowledge without being impeded by the disability. By increasing point size and leading between lines, text becomes much easier to see and read. (A) is not the correct answer. A student who has visual impairments will often benefit from sitting near the teacher or near the front of the room to see better what is happening. (B) is incorrect because the issue is not the amount of time a student needs to complete a task. The issue is being able to see the content. (C) is not the correct answer because an eye gaze board is an adaptive tool for students who cannot move their arms or indicate a choice by pointing. These boards are not intended for students with visual impairments.

Competency 003

112. **(A)**   The correct response is (A). The student described in this scenario lacks self-confidence, possibly because of her disability and its impact on learning. Providing this student with direct instruction in social skills could go a long way in helping her understand how she appears to other students and how she can initiate positive interactions. (B) is incorrect because, based on teacher observations, the other students are not actually bullying her. The problem appears to be in the student's own perception of their actions. Telling the other students to back off would only add to the off-putting behaviors she is already exhibiting. (C) is incorrect because it is a negative reaction and inappropriate advice. There are appropriate times when people cry in public. The student just needs some guidance on what those times can be. (D) is incorrect because current reports from the student's teacher do not indicate a toxic classroom environment. In fact, just the opposite appears to be true.

Competency 006

113. **(D)**   The correct response is (D). Specific learning disabilities and speech/language impairments are the two most prevalent disabilities for children ages 3–21 in the United States. Together, they account for almost 60 percent of the diagnosed disabilities in this group. (A) is incorrect because autism is still statistically a low-incidence disability. (B) is incorrect because hearing impairments are low-incidence disabilities. (C) is incorrect because orthopedic impairments are low-incidence disabilities, and emotional disturbance ranks as the third most prevalent disability.

Competency 001

114. **(B)**   The correct response is (B). Applying knowledge of appropriate body mechanics to ensure safety in transfer, lifting, positioning, and seating is part of Competency 004. Special Education teachers receive training in the proper way to lift students. When lifting a student from a wheelchair, a teacher should place one arm behind the student's back and the other arm under the student's knees. Approaching from the front and placing arms underneath a student's arms will not support the student's body properly and may cause the teacher injury because of the bending and twisting necessitated. (A), (C), and (D) are all true guidelines for lifting a student with limited mobility and are, therefore, incorrect answers.

Competency 004

115. **(B)**   The correct response is (B). Any type of checklist is considered an informal assessment since it involves observing and noting student behaviors or academic strengths and weaknesses and therefore relies on human judgment. (A), (C), and (D) are all incorrect answers because criterion-referenced tests, achievement tests, and standardized exams are all examples of formal assessments that have been used on a large group of people and developed with clear right and wrong answer choices.

Competency 002

116. **(C)**   The correct response is (C). Texas Senate Bill 1788 changed the required age to have a transition plan in place to 14. (A), (B), and (D) are all incorrect ages based on Texas Senate Bill 1788.
Competency 007

117. **(B)**   The correct response is (B). Public Law 94-142, later renamed the Individuals with Disabilities Education Act, was passed by Congress in 1975. It was put into effect in 1978. (A) is incorrect because 1973 was the year the Rehabilitation Act was passed. (C) and (D) are incorrect because both 1986 and 1990 were years when Public Law 94-142 was reauthorized.
Competency 010

118. **(A)**   The correct response is (A). There have been several reauthorizations of Public Law 94-142, known today as the Individuals with Disabilities Education Act. Each of the reauthorizations allowed Congress to clarify, update, revise, and expand the original law based on feedback from constituents, states, local education agencies, and disability advocacy groups. (B) is incorrect as the original law does not specifically mandate all of the reauthorizations that have occurred. (C) is incorrect as the reauthorizations have been crafted by joint committees of Congress and are responsive to all constituents and affected agencies, not just to parents. (D) is incorrect because federal court cases have informed changes drafted into reauthorizations, but they are not the purpose behind the reauthorizations.
Competency 010

119. **(A)**   The correct response is (A). An Individual Family Service Plan is provided for children birth to age 3 as part of early childhood services for children with developmental delays. At age 3, the IFSP is replaced by an IEP. If students with an IFSP qualify for Special Education services through their local school district, these students can begin school in the district the day they turn 3. (B), (C), and (D) are incorrect as they all represent transition information that would be in an IEP once a student's Transition Plan is added at age 14.
Competency 007

120. **(C)**   The correct response is (C). A staircase is a great way to show a sequence of events, and a how-to paper explains, step-by-step, how to do something. (A) is incorrect because a persuasive paper would need a graphic organizer that shows two sides of an issue. (B) is incorrect because a compare/contrast paper is best plotted on a Venn diagram or something similar. (D) is incorrect because a narrative is a story and works best on a storyboard of some type.
Competency 008

121. **(B)**   The correct response is (B). IDEA defines transition services as a coordinated set of activities that improve both academic and functional skills while facilitating the move from school to postschool activities. IEPs must include a Transition Plan once a child turns 14 in Texas because of the Senate Bill that was passed in 2011. (A) is incorrect because transition has nothing to do with school bus transportation. (C) is incorrect because it describes the Early Childhood Intervention initiative in the state of Texas. (D) is incorrect because it describes the process of inclusion, not transition.
Competency 007

122. **(A)**   The correct response is (A). Behavioral theory is predicated upon the fact that behavior can be changed or directed by an outside force. This change in behavior begins when the outside force (the teacher, in this case) recognizes what a student is gaining from the behavior and removes that reward. To get the reward back, the student will often escalate in the original behavior, confused as to why it is no longer working. This escalation can be intense, but it is relatively short-lived provided the reward is not granted. (B), (C), and (D) are all incorrect as they do not represent how a student initially responds to behavior modification.
Competency 006

123. **(D)** The correct response is (D). Pragmatics describes typical social skills such as the ability to hold a pleasant and polite conversation. The role play suggested in (D) will allow students to practice their pragmatics while helping them better grasp the characters in the book the class is reading. (A) is incorrect because it does not allow for any conversation. (B) is incorrect because its focus is on a tactile/kinesthetic activity, not conversation. (C) is incorrect because it describes an auditory activity.

Competency 008

124. **(D)** The correct response is (D). The alternative teaching model involves one teacher presenting the lesson to most of the students while the other teacher works with a small group of students to present the same material in a different way or on a different level. (A) is incorrect because it describes the station teaching model. (B) is incorrect because it describes the "One Teach, One Drift" model. (C) is incorrect because it describes the team teaching model.

Competency 012

125. **(D)** The correct response is (D). Teacher websites are wonderful tools for distributing information to every family at once. However, websites are a one-way form of communication, and teachers have no idea whether or not the parents are checking on the website updates. For a project that will count for a significant portion of the grade, reaching out with alternate forms of communication to reach every parent is the best approach. (A) is incorrect because there will be some parents who are unable to check the website regularly either because of busy schedules or lack of access to the Internet. (B) is incorrect because one of the characteristics of students with learning disabilities can be forgetfulness and lack of organization skills. Part of teaching the research project is also taking time to teach good planning skills to the students and enlisting parents to help encourage students to stick to the plan at home. (C) is incorrect because students have a tendency to forget oral directions, and many are likely to forget to remind their parents to check the website.

Competency 012

126. **(B)** The correct response is (B). The Reauthorization of 1986 expanded Special Education services to include children from birth to age 5. States had to put Early Childhood Intervention programs in place to locate and provide assistance to children age 0–3 with disabilities. Schools became responsible for the students at age 3. Today, school districts in Texas have Preschool Programs for Children with Disabilities (PPCD) in place for children with disabilities. Children attend PPCD until they are eligible to begin kindergarten. Therefore, (A), (C), and (D) are all incorrect.

Competency 010

127. **(B)** The correct response is (B). Most educators think of writing as a five-step process: prewriting, drafting, revising, editing (proofreading), and publishing. Publishing is the last stage. (A), (C), and (D) are all incorrect answers because they are earlier stages of the writing process.

Competency 008

128. **(D)** The correct response is (D). The more simple the accommodation, the more likely both Special Education and regular education teachers will implement it. When planning accommodations, teachers should start with simple ones and move to more complex accommodations only if the student's performance does not improve. (A) is not correct. Accommodations, particularly simple ones, are implemented with all students on an as-needed basis as part of good teaching. (B) is not the correct answer since the purpose of accommodations is to level the playing field so that all students have an equal opportunity to learn and to showcase their knowledge. (C) is not correct because, while it is appropriate to list accommodations on a student's IEP, it is not required that they be written down in order to be implemented.

Competency 003

129. **(C)** The correct response is (C). Research on effective strategies for teaching math to students with disabilities is clear that a combination of skills (procedural fluency), problem-solving, and conceptual understanding is the best approach. For students with disabilities, an array of manipulatives helps teachers introduce new concepts in concrete ways. (A) is incorrect because skills alone does not help students achieve at the secondary level where math becomes increasingly complex. (B) is incorrect because, while digital programs can be motivating, struggling learners need a balance that includes manipulatives and opportunities for group discussion, not just digital interaction. (D) is incorrect because cooperative learning is a good strategy to employ when appropriate, but students also need opportunities to apply skills independently and in various settings.
   Competency 009

130. **(A)** The correct response is (A). When determining Special Education eligibility, evaluations must be administered in the student's native language, if at all possible. A child's language barrier by itself is not a valid reason to receive Special Education services. Removing that barrier allows educators to see the student's true academic strengths and weaknesses. (B) is incorrect because Special Education eligibility is not based on the level of a student's language acquisition. (C) is not correct because evaluations of the student are generally conducted by a school psychologist or district diagnostician, and parents are generally not present during testing. (D) is incorrect because English language learners can also have special needs alongside their language barrier, and they have the right to be evaluated if a disability is suspected.
   Competency 011

131. **(D)** The correct response is (D). AT evaluations are critically important because some estimates place the percentage of assistive-technology interventions that fail because the student abandons them at 80 percent. Through an AT evaluation, teachers and AT coordinators can test out several AT options with a student and see how the student interacts. An AT evaluation is a worthwhile time investment to help ensure that the intention behind providing the assistive-technology device is actually accomplished. (A) is incorrect because, while a district does try to save money where it can, if an AT device would truly help, there are funds to secure it. (B) is incorrect because IDEA does not require evaluations, although it does state that evaluation is one of the services that a district may need to provide in order to ensure that assistive technology is useful to a student in a school setting. (C) is incorrect because the Special Education teacher's request for an evaluation has nothing to do with her opinion about the math teacher's suggestion. It is all about making sure the assistive technology chosen has a good chance of being successful.
   Competency 004

132. **(C)** The correct response is (C). Reading research has been extremely clear that by teaching skills like phonemic awareness and phonics explicitly, students can improve in both of these foundational skills. Making the concepts as concrete as possible also helps. (A) is not correct because research has shown that when the skills are implicit, the students often don't pick up on them. (B) and (D) are incorrect because phonemic awareness and phonics should be part of a balanced literacy curriculum, not underused or overused.
   Competency 008

133. **(B)** The correct response is (B). When students verbalize the steps they need to take to solve a problem, it helps them slow down and use a logical, sequential approach. For some students, hearing themselves talk through the steps of a problem allows them to confirm their decisions and increases their self-confidence. (A) is incorrect because all students can benefit from verbalization, not just students with learning disabilities. (C) is incorrect because there is no evidence that the teacher tried groups and then moved students to independent work. On the contrary, the evidence points to the teacher deliberately choosing an independent assignment for this lesson so that students could practice their individual problem-solving strategies, such as verbalization. (D) is incorrect because the fact that these students are verbalizing independently is a good sign that they are prepared for a standardized, independent test like STAAR.
   Competency 009

134. **(C)** The correct response is (C). The IQ-Achievement Discrepancy Model has been the traditional method by which learning disabilities are determined. The method assesses whether a substantial difference or discrepancy exists between a student's scores on an individualized test of general intelligence (IQ test) and his or her scores on one or more standardized achievement tests. The accepted criteria to identify a student as having a learning disability is a difference of at least two standard deviations (30 points). (A) is incorrect because the Discrepancy Model requires IQ test results, but those results are only one factor in the determination of disability. (B) is incorrect because the model does not take into account student's grades. It does require achievement scores as one factor in the determination. (D) is incorrect because the Discrepancy Model does not involve an MRI of a the student's brain.
   Competency 011

135. **(B)** The correct response is (B). While the IQ Discrepancy Model is a major factor in determining a learning disability, Special Education professionals are aware of its potential weaknesses. One of those weaknesses is that it can be extremely difficult for young children to show a 30-point discrepancy because they are naturally at the earliest stages of academic skills. For this reason, no one assessment may be used for determining eligibility by itself. ARD committees will take into consideration parent and teacher interviews, checklists, and documented observations along with the IQ Discrepancy. (A) is incorrect because many school districts use the IQ Discrepancy Model at all levels since the model is an established practice and is relatively easy to conduct. (C) is incorrect because the Discrepancy Model is still in use in Texas. (D) is incorrect because diagnostic tests are often administered by a school psychologist or diagnostician. The department head cannot promise to be the one to give the tests.
   Competency 011

ANSWERS SORTED BY DOMAIN AND COMPETENCY

Domain	Competency	Question	Answer	Did You Answer Correctly?
I	1	1	A	
I	1	23	B	
I	1	31	B	
I	1	37	D	
I	1	40	A	
I	1	63	A	
I	1	76	C	
I	1	91	C	
I	1	113	D	
I	2	10	D	
I	2	13	A	
I	2	19	D	
I	2	65	C	
I	2	72	D	
I	2	80	A	
I	2	85	C	
I	2	94	B	
I	2	115	B	
II	3	4	A	
II	3	12	B	
II	3	29	C	
II	3	46	A	
II	3	47	C	
II	3	60	B	
II	3	84	B	
II	3	111	D	
II	3	128	D	
II	4	28	C	
II	4	38	A	
II	4	39	B	
II	4	52	D	
II	4	53	C	

Domain	Competency	Question	Answer	Did You Answer Correctly?
II	4	69	A	
II	4	79	C	
II	4	114	B	
II	4	131	D	
II	5	9	D	
II	5	18	C	
II	5	50	B	
II	5	51	A	
II	5	78	C	
II	5	86	A	
II	5	104	D	
II	5	105	B	
II	5	109	C	
II	6	20	B	
II	6	22	D	
II	6	33	D	
II	6	34	B	
II	6	77	C	
II	6	92	D	
II	6	110	C	
II	6	112	A	
II	6	122	A	
II	7	5	D	
II	7	7	C	
II	7	59	B	
II	7	64	C	
II	7	68	D	
II	7	106	A	
II	7	116	C	
II	7	119	A	
II	7	121	B	
III	8	14	A	

Domain	Competency	Question	Answer	Did You Answer Correctly?
III	8	24	A	
III	8	26	A	
III	8	43	B	
III	8	45	C	
III	8	55	C	
III	8	56	D	
III	8	57	A	
III	8	61	B	
III	8	62	B	
III	8	66	A	
III	8	71	C	
III	8	74	D	
III	8	87	A	
III	8	93	A	
III	8	97	C	
III	8	98	A	
III	8	99	D	
III	8	120	C	
III	8	123	D	
III	8	127	B	
III	8	132	C	
III	9	2	B	
III	9	3	C	
III	9	11	C	
III	9	15	A	
III	9	17	C	
III	9	21	B	
III	9	25	C	
III	9	36	A	
III	9	41	D	
III	9	54	C	
III	9	67	D	
III	9	70	D	
III	9	73	A	
III	9	75	B	
III	9	88	D	

Domain	Competency	Question	Answer	Did You Answer Correctly?
III	9	95	B	
III	9	100	A	
III	9	101	D	
III	9	102	A	
III	9	103	A	
III	9	107	B	
III	9	129	C	
III	9	133	B	
IV	10	6	C	
IV	10	27	D	
IV	10	30	A	
IV	10	32	B	
IV	10	49	C	
IV	10	89	C	
IV	10	117	B	
IV	10	118	A	
IV	10	126	B	
IV	11	8	D	
IV	11	32	D	
IV	11	44	C	
IV	11	58	A	
IV	11	90	B	
IV	11	108	B	
IV	11	130	A	
IV	11	134	C	
IV	11	135	B	
IV	12	16	A	
IV	12	35	C	
IV	12	48	C	
IV	12	81	A	
IV	12	82	B	
IV	12	83	D	
IV	12	96	B	
IV	12	124	D	
IV	12	125	D	

References

Almond, P. J. and B. J. Case. *Alternate Assessments for Students with Significant Cognitive Disabilities*. Pearson Education, 2004. www.pearsonassessments.com/.../AlternateAssessments-Final.pdf

"Alternate Assessments for Students with Disabilities." National Center of Educational Outcomes, 2013.
www.cehd.umn.edu/nceo/topicareas/alternateassessments/altAssessFAQ.htm#looklike

Anghileri, J. *Teaching Number Sense*. New York: Continuum, 2006.

"Attention Deficit Hyperactivity Disorder." *LD Hope*. American Psychiatric Association, 1994.
www.ldhope.com/adhdinfo.htm

"Best Practices in Reading and the RTI Process." *Montana Office of Public Instruction*. 2005.
opi.mt.gov/PDF/SpecED/training/RTl/BestPractices.pdf

"Bloom's Taxonomy of Cognitive Levels." *Teaching Resources*. May 2013.
tep.uoregon.edu/resources/assessment/multiplechoicequestions/blooms.html

Bober, P. A. and S. L. Corbett. *Occupational Therapy and Physical Therapy: A Resource and Planning Guide*. Madison, WI: Wisconsin Dept. of Public Instruction, 2011.

Bresser, R. and C. Holtzman. *Developing Number Sense: Grades 3-6*. Sausalito, CA: Math Solutions Publications, 1999.

Bryant, D. P. *Instructional Strategies for Content-Area Reading Instruction*. 1999.
www.eric.ed.gov/ERICWebPortal/recordDetail?accno=EJ585804

"Building a Legacy IDEA 2004." *U.S. Department of Education*. 2004. idea.ed.gov/

"Categories for Disabilities Under IDEA." National Dissemination Center for Children With Disabilities, March 2012.
nichcy.org/wp-content/uploads/docs/gr3.pdf

Center for Disease Control and Prevention. "CDC Estimates 1 in 88 Children in United States Has Been Identified as Having an Autism Spectrum Disorder." CDC Division of News and Electronic Media. 29 March 2012.
www.cdc.gov/media/releases/2012/p0329_autism_disorder.html

Crawford, E. and J. Torgesen. "Teaching All Students to Read: Practices from Reading First Schools with Strong Intervention Outcomes." Florida Center for Reading Research, 2007.
www.fcrr.org/Interventions/pdf/teachingAllStudentsToReadSummary.pdf

"Data Analysis and Statistics." National Council of Teachers of Mathematics, 2013.
www.nctm.org/standards/content.aspx?id=318

"Early Childhood Intervention Services." Texas Department of Assistive and Rehabilitative Services.
www.dars.state.tx.us/ecis

Flaum, S. "Fostering Visual Literacy in the X-Box Generation." *McGraw-Hill Education PreK-12*, 2012
www.projectedu.com/fostering-visual-literacy-in-the-x-box-generation/

"Formative Assessment Probes: Math Trailblazers 2010-2011." Delaware State Department of

Education, 2011.
www.doe.k12.de.us/infosuites/staff/ci/content_areas/files/math/MTB_Probes.pdf

Giangreco, M. F. et al. "Roles of Related Services Personnel in Inclusion Schools." University of Vermont, 1990.
www.uvm.edu/~cdci/archives/mgiangre/Rolesofrelatedservicespersonnel.pdf

Giangreco, M. F. et al. "Assisting Students Who Use Wheelchairs: Guidelines for School Personnel." Baltimore, P. H. Brookes Publishing Company, 2002.
www.uvm.edu/~cdci/archives/mgiangre/QG3ExtraWC141-154.pdf

"Guidelines for Community-Based Instruction: Draft." Baltimore County Public Schools: Department of Instruction and Learning: Office of Special Education. 2005.
www.bcps.org/offices/special_ed/altmsa_autism/pdf/cbi_handbook.pdf

Griffiths, A. J. et al. "Response to Intervention: Research for Practice." National Association of State Directors of Special Education, 2005.
www.nasdse.org/Portals/0/Documents/RtI_Bibliography2.pdf

Halpern, A. S. and M. J. Fuhrer. *Functional Assessment in Rehabilitation*. Baltimore: P.H. Brookes Publishing Company, 1984.

Harry, B. et al. "Of Rocks and Soft Places: Using Qualitative Methods to Investigate Disproportionality." In D. J. Losen and G. Orfield (Eds.), *Racial Inequity in Special Education:* 71–92. Cambridge, MA: Harvard Education Press, 2002.

Hollingsworth, H. L. "We Need to Talk: Communication Strategies for Effective Communication." *Council for Exceptional Children*. 2001.
familiestogetherinc.com/wp-content/uploads/2011/08/We_Need_to_Talk_Communication_Strategies_of_Effective_Collaboration.pdf

"Istation Reading Curriculum Correlated to Texas Essential Knowledge and Skills" 2010.
www.istation.com/Content/downloads/correlations/tx_k.pdf

Joseph, L. M. "Best Practices in Planning Interventions for Students with Reading Problems." *Reading Rockets*. N.d.
www.nasponline.org/publications/booksproducts/bp5samples/1163_bpv66_72.pdf

Klein, J. L. "Special Education Services as Part of a Unified Delivery System." NYC Department of Education. 2010.
www.uft.org/files/attachments/doe-continuum-of-services.pdf

Kochlar-Bryant, C. A. and R. Lacey. "Alternative Education As A Quality Choice for Youth: Preparing Educators for Effective Programs." Hamilton Fish Institute on School and Community Violence, George Washington University. Washington DC. 2005.
www.nasponline.org/publications/booksproducts/.../1163_bpv66_72.pdf

Lehr, C.A., E.J. Lanners and C.M. Lange. "Alternative Schools: Policy and Legislation Across the U.S. (Research Report 1)." Minneapolis, MN: University of Minnesota, Institute on Community Integration. 2003.
learningalternatives.net/wp-content/uploads/legacy/Legislative_citations_all_states.pdf

Levinson, E. M. and E. J. Palmer. "Preparing Students with Disabilities for School-to-Work Transition and Postschool Life." NASPonline. April 2005.
www.nasponline.org/resources/principals/Transition%20Planning%20WEB.pdf

McCue, M. and M. Pramuka. *Human Brain Function: Rehabilitation* Springer, 1998.

McCue, M. et al. "Functional Assessment of Individuals with Cognitive Disabilities: A Desk Reference for Rehabilitation." Center for Applied Neuropsychology, 1994. patransassessment.pbworks.com/f/Functional+Assessment+of+Individuals+with+Cognitive+Disabili.pdf

Metz, M. L. "Using GAISE and NCTM Standards as Frameworks for Teaching Probability and Statistics to Pre-Service Elementary and Middle School Mathematics Teachers." *Journal of Statistics Education* 18.3 (2010). www.amstat.org/publications/jse/v18n3/metz.pdf.

Minnesota Disability Law Center. *Special Education Transition Planning*. June 2004. mn.gov/mnddc/resources/factsheets/Transition_Planning.htm

"Minorities in Special Education: A Briefing Before the U.S Commission on Civil Rights." U.S. Commission on Civil Rights. 3 December 2007. www.usccr.gov/pubs/MinoritiesinSpecialEducation.pdf

National Assessment of Educational Progress (NAEP). *The Nation's Report Card: Reading and Mathematics 2005*. www.connectlive.com/events/naep/index101905.html

National Association of School Psychologists (NASP). "A National Tragedy: Helping Children Cope." 2002. www.nasponline.org/resources/crisis_safety/terror_general.aspx

National Council of Teachers of English. "21st Century Literacies." Reading Rockets. 2007. http://www.readingrockets.org/article/20832/

Orlich, D. C. et al. *Teaching Strategies: A Guide to Effective Instruction*. Boston, MA: Houghton Mifflin, 2003.

"Practicing Social Skills: How to Teach Your Student Social Interactions ." National Center for Technology Innovation and Center for Implementing Technology in Education, 2007. www.ldonline.org/article/Practicing_Social_Skills%3A_How_to_Teach_Your_Student_Social_Interactions?theme=print

"Principles to Promote Excellence in Learning and Teaching at Griffith University." 2009. www.griffith.edu.au/__data/assets/pdf_file/0006/120201/PrinciplesLandT.pdf

Raywid, M. A. "History and Issues of Alternative Schools." *Education Digest* 64.9 (1999): 47-51.

"Refining Implementation." *RTI Action Network*. 2007. rtinetwork.org/getstarted/evaluate/refiningimplementation

Riccomini, P. J. and B. S. Witzel. *Response to Intervention in Math*. Thousand Oaks, CA: Corwin, 2010.

"Special Education." *National Dissemination Center for Children with Disabilities*. March 2013. / nichcy.org/schoolage/iep/iepcontents/specialeducation

"STAAR® Resources." *Texas Education Agency*. 2013. www.tea.state.tx.us/student.assessment/staar/

Stanberry, K. and L. Swanson. "Effective Reading Interventions for Kids With Learning Disabilities." *Reading Rockets*. 2009. www.readingrockets.org/article/33084/

Stanberry, K. "Transition Planning for Students with IEPs." *GreatSchools*. January 2010.
www.greatschools.org/special-education/health/873-transition-planning-for-students-with-ieps.gs

"State of Learning 2009." National Center for Learning Disabilities, 2009.
www.ncld.org/types-learning-disabilities/what-is-ld/state-of-learning-disabilities

Steedly, K. et al. "Social Skills and Academic Achievement." *Evidence for Education* III.11. 2008.
www.nichcy.org/wp-content/uploads/docs/eesocialskills.pdf

Taylor-Cox, J. "Differentiating Mathematics Instruction So Everyone Learns." McGraw-Hill Education. 2012.
www.mheonline.com/glencoemath/pdf/diffentiating_math.pdf

"Teaching Study Skills, What Works: Evidence-Based Strategies for Youth Practice." S. Kerka (Ed.) Ohio State University, 2007.
cle.osu.edu/lwc-publications/what-works/downloads/WW-Study-Skills.pdf

Texas Department of Assistive and Rehabilitative Services.
www.dars.state.tx.us/

Texas Education Agency. *A Guide to the Admission Review and Dismissal Process*, March 2012.
framework.esc18.net/Documents/ARD%20Guide%20March2012.pdf

Texas Education Agency. "Special Education in Texas A-Z Index." N. d.
www.tea.state.tx.us/index2.aspx?id=2147491399

Tomlinson, C. A. "What Is Differentiated Instruction." *Reading Rockets*. 2000. www.readingrockets.org/article/263/

"Twenty-Eighth Annual Report to Congress on the Implementation of the Individuals with Disabilities Act: Part B and C." *U.S. Department of Education*. 2006.
www2.ed.gov/about/reports/annual/osep/2006/parts-b-c/28th-vol-1.pdf

Vaush, S., J. Wanzek and C. S. Murray. ""Intensive Interventions for Students Struggling in Mathematics." Center on Instruction at RMS Research Corp., 2012.
eric.ed.gov/?id=ED531907

"A Vision of Effective Student Assessment in Mathematics." Microsoft Math Partnership, 2008.
www.microsoftmathpartnership.org/...MMP_Assessment_Vision.final.doc

"What Is the IQ Discrepancy Model." IRIS Center, 2007.
www.rti4success.org/pdf/iq_achievment_discrepancy.pdf

Wren, Carol. *Characteristics of Students with Learning Disabilities*. Pepperdine University, 1985.
www.pepperdine.edu/disabilityservices/students/ldcharacter.htm

Wright, J. "Response To Intervention – RTI Resources." *Teacher Strategies to Promote Learning*. 2001.
www.pasadenaisd.org/curr_instr/intervention/tchrstrategies.pdf

Ziff, B. "Working with the Paraprofessional in Your Classroom: Helpful Hints: Series #10." California State University: Los Angeles. N.d.
www.calstatela.edu/centers/spedintern/hints10theparaprofessional.pdf

Index

Appendix

IDEA's 14 Disability Categories*

Disablility	Definition	Notes
Autism	A developmental disability significantly affecting verbal and nonverbal communication and social interaction, generally evident before age 3, that adversely affects a child's educational performance. Other characteristics often associated with autism are engaging in repetitive activities and stereotyped movements, resistance to environmental change or change in daily routines, and unusual responses to sensory experiences.	The term "autism" does not apply if the child's educational performance is adversely affected primarily because the child has an emotional disturbance, as defined in "Developmental Delay" below. A child who shows the characteristics of autism after age 3 could be diagnosed as having autism if the criteria cited at left are satisfied.
Deaf-Blindness	Concomitant [simultaneous] hearing and visual impairments, the combination of which causes such severe communication and other developmental and educational needs that they cannot be accommodated in special education programs solely for children with deafness or children with blindness.	
Deafness	A hearing impairment so severe that a child is impaired in processing linguistic information through hearing, with or without amplification, that adversely affects a child's educational performance.	

(*continued*)

IDEA's 14 Disability Categories*

Disablility	Definition	Notes
Developmental Delay†	For children from birth to age 3 (under IDEA Part C) and children from ages 3 through 9 (under IDEA Part B), the term "developmental delay," as defined by each state, means a delay in one or more of the following areas: physical development; cognitive development; communication; social or emotional development; or adaptive [behavioral] development.	
Emotional Disturbance	A condition exhibiting one or more of the following characteristics over a long period of time and to a marked degree that adversely affects a child's educational performance: (a) An inability to learn that cannot be explained by intellectual, sensory, or health factors. (b) An inability to build or maintain satisfactory interpersonal relationships with peers and teachers. (c) Inappropriate types of behavior or feelings under normal circumstances. (d) A general pervasive mood of unhappiness or depression. (e) A tendency to develop physical symptoms or fears associated with personal or school problems.	This term includes schizophrenia. The term does not apply to children who are socially maladjusted, unless it is determined that they have an emotional disturbance.
Hearing Impairment	An impairment in hearing, whether permanent or fluctuating, that adversely affects a child's educational performance but is not included under the definition of deafness.	

(continued)

IDEA's 14 Disability Categories*

Disablility	Definition	Notes
Intellectual Disability‡	Significantly subaverage general intellectual functioning, existing concurrently [at the same time] with deficits in adaptive behavior and manifested during the developmental period, that adversely affects a child's educational performance.	
Multiple Disabilities	Concomitant [simultaneous] impairments (such as intellectual disability-blindness, intellectual disability-orthopedic impairment, etc.), the combination of which causes such severe educational needs that they cannot be accommodated in a special education program solely for one of the impairments.	This term does not include deaf-blindness.
Orthopedic Impairment	A severe orthopedic impairment that adversely affects a child's educational performance.	This term includes impairments caused by a congenital anomaly, impairments caused by disease (e.g., poliomyelitis, bone tuberculosis), and impairments from other causes (e.g., cerebral palsy, amputations, and fractures or burns that cause contractures).
Other Health Impairment	Having limited strength, vitality, or alertness, including a heightened alertness to environmental stimuli, that results in limited alertness with respect to the educational environment, that— (a) is due to chronic or acute health problems such as asthma, attention deficit disorder or attention deficit hyperactivity disorder, diabetes, epilepsy, a heart condition, hemophilia, lead poisoning, leukemia, nephritis, rheumatic fever, sickle cell anemia, and Tourette syndrome; and (b) adversely affects a child's educational performance.	

(*continued*)

IDEA's 14 Disability Categories*

Disablility	Definition	Notes
Specific Learning Disability	A disorder in one or more of the basic psychological processes involved in understanding or in using language, spoken or written, that may manifest itself in the imperfect ability to listen, think, speak, read, write, spell, or to do mathematical calculations. The term includes such conditions as perceptual disabilities, brain injury, minimal brain dysfunction, dyslexia, and developmental aphasia.	The term does not include learning problems that are primarily the result of visual, hearing, or motor disabilities; of intellectual disability; of emotional disturbance; or of environmental, cultural, or economic disadvantage.
Speech or Language Impairment	A communication disorder such as stuttering, impaired articulation, a language impairment, or a voice impairment that adversely affects a child's educational performance.	
Traumatic Brain Injury	An acquired injury to the brain caused by an external physical force, resulting in total or partial functional disability or both, that adversely affects a child's educational performance. This term applies psychosocial impairment, to open or closed head injuries resulting in impairments in one or more areas, such as cognition; language; memory; attention; reasoning; abstract thinking; judgment; problem solving; sensory, perceptual, and motor abilities; psychosocial behavior; physical functions; information processing; and speech.	The term does not apply to brain injuries that are congenital or degenerative, or to brain injuries induced by birth trauma.
Visual Impairment Including Blindness	An impairment in vision that, even with correction, adversely affects a child's educational performance.	The term includes both partial sight and blindness.

*IDEA disability definitions reprinted courtesy of the Center for Parent Information and Resources (retrieved May 25, 2016), "Categories of Disability Under IDEA," Newark, N.J., National Dissemination Center for Children with Disabilities.

† Under IDEA, for students aged 3 to 9, the broader disability category termed "Developmental Delay" may be used to determine eligibility for special education and related services. In Texas, this category is known as "Non-Categorical Early Childhood," or NCEC. NCEC is for students aged 3 to 5 who experience delays in their physical, cognitive, communication, social, emotional, or adaptive development.

‡Editor's Note: "Intellectual disability" was added to IDEA after President Obama signed Rosa's Law into law in October 2010. Until then, IDEA had used the term "mental retardation," which had taken on pejorative overtones. The American Psychiatric Association's Diagnostic and Statistical Manual followed suit in May 2013, with the publication of DSM-5. To give publishers time to revise their materials accordingly, Educational Testing Service, the maker of the TExES tests, allowed a grace period before incorporating the new terminology into its tests, including the TExES Special Education EC-12 test covered in this book.

NOTES

NOTES

NOTES

NOTES

NOTES